Praise for *AI and the Church*

Holy algorithm, Batman! *AI and the Church* is the digital revelation pastors didn't know they were praying for. Jason Moore's techno-gospel will have you speaking in tongues of Python and praising in prose of HTML faster than you can say 'Amen.' Whether you think AI is the serpent in Eden's garden or the burning bush of the 21st century, Moore's silicon-infused theology will reboot your spiritual hard drive. With the wit of a holy hacker and the wisdom of a digital disciple, this book is more addictive than doom-scrolling and ten-times as enlightening. A must-read for the digitally devout and the technologically timid alike. Hallelujah, and may the force (and the bandwidth) be with you.

> -**Leonard Sweet**, author (*Telos*), distinguished professor (Drew University, George Fox University, Northwind Seminary, Southeastern University), preacher (*preachthestory.com*), publisher (salishsea.press) and proprietor (*sanctuaryseaside.com*)

Jason provides a clear vision for how AI can be used for meaningful and impactful ministry. His deep insights make this book a valuable resource for leaders looking to use technology effectively. Whether you're new to AI and have questions, or you're experienced and using it every day, Jason covers all bases with practical examples for churches, making this a timeless and definitive guide on AI in ministry.

> –**Justin Dean**, author of *PR Matters: A Survival Guide for Church Communicators*

This book is a game-changer. It takes the complex world of AI and makes it accessible, showing how technology can deepen human connections rather than just disrupt them. The author brilliantly combines technical insights with real-world applications, making it a must-read for anyone navigating the digital age. But it's more than just a tech manual—it's a call to think critically about the future we're building. Whether you're a church leader or a tech enthusiast, this book will equip you to harness AI responsibly and effectively. In a rapidly evolving world, this is the guide you need. Don't miss it.

> –**Katie Allred**, author of *Church Communications*

The paradox of Artificial Intelligence is that it takes a Really Intelligent human mind to know how to fully unlock and release its potential. Jason has a Genius mind. And in this book, he shares with us how AI can be a powerful, Kingdom-building tool. Make no mistake, this is a seminal piece of work for the Church, in so many ways.

> –**Mike Elms**, adman, charity chair, author

Jason Moore has addressed how the Church's voice can address the use of AI, and the importance of guarding the faith, while using new and current tools. This is a must-read primer for the Church.

> –**Bishop Dottie Escobedo-Frank**, California Pacific Conference of The United Methodist Church

There were a handful of people in the church media and communications industry that jumped in with both feet as AI started to take off. Jason Moore was at the top of that list. He is always on the cutting edge of new ways to reach people for Jesus. He does a great job of explaining concepts in a clear and concise way for ministry leaders to put into practice. AI is here to stay, and it is only getting better by the minute. Jump in right now and let Jason give you the background and practical tools to use this incredible technology for Kingdom work!

> –**Carl Barnhill**, owner, Church Visuals, churchvisuals.com

Artificial intelligence has the potential to enhance the church's mission, outreach, and operation. In the book *AI and the Church*, author Jason More masterfully introduces spiritual leaders to the history, benefits, ethics, and numerous practical applications of AI for the church in an accessible format. This book is essential for all church leaders as we minister in a digital era.

–Bishop Héctor A. Burgos, Susquehanna & Upper New York Episcopal Area, and President of Discipleship Ministries of The United Methodist Church

Jason does it again. He does not disappoint in his ability to stay on the cutting edge of trends in society and apply them to the sacred work of the faith community. This book will help remove the veil from AI and make it a practical tool for church leaders, clergy and laity alike. It's a must read.

–Rev. Dr. Derrek Belase, Executive Director of Connectional Ministry, Oklahoma Conference, The United Methodist Church

AI and the Church: A Clear Guide for the Curious and Courageous is an essential roadmap for anyone navigating the intersection of faith and technology in today's rapidly evolving world. Jason Moore masterfully combines theological insight with practical application, making complex concepts accessible to church leaders and congregants alike. With a deep understanding of both the potential and pitfalls of AI, Moore guides readers through the ethical, philosophical, and spiritual implications of integrating AI into church life. This book is not just a theoretical exploration; it is a call to action for the church to harness the power of AI responsibly and creatively to further the mission of the Gospel. Whether you are a seasoned tech enthusiast or a cautious skeptic, *AI and the Church* offers a balanced and thought-provoking perspective that will equip you to engage with this emerging technology in a way that honors both God and humanity.

–Matt Rawle, Lead Pastor at Asbury United Methodist Church, Bossier City, Louisiana and author

Jason Moore has done it again, and I am not surprised! Moore has carefully laid out how to use AI as a tool for churches, leaders, staff, and anyone who wants to learn. *AI and the Church* is not primarily about the "how to" of these critical resources, but Moore provides a biblical and theological framework for using AI as a ministry tool.

–Rev. Dr. Rosario Picardo, author, consultant, speaker, and pastor

This book is a wonderful resource for pastors and church leaders who are looking to learn more about AI technology and how to use these tools for ministry. I learned so much from Jason in this book and especially love the practical applications he shares for congregations of all types.

–Ken Willard, author, coach, Director of Congregational Vitality for the West Virginia Conference of The United Methodist Church

Wow! Jason Moore's book reveals a surprise on every page...some delightful, some shocking, and all enlightening. Painstakingly researched and passionately written, I was astounded at the history of AI in general and computing in general. More than that I was absorbed in how Jason turned such technical and provocative stuff into a beautiful narrative crying out for relevancy in the church. A must read!

– Dr. Jim Ozier, founder of The Difference Makers Group--one of the nation's leading church coaching & consulting companies

This is the book on AI that the Church so desperately needs! Jason deftly clarifies what AI is and isn't, explores common issues and concerns about AI, evaluates the theological implications, and charts a path forward. The book is filled with tangible examples and practical advice. If you're a pastor, ministry leader, or active volunteer who's unsure of what to make of AI, you're going to want to read this book and then share it with everyone else on your team.

–David J. Swisher, Learning eXperience Designer, Indiana Wesleyan University, AI researcher & innovator

I have been eagerly awaiting an introductory book on AI, especially one focused on its application within the church—and now it's here. Jason Moore, author of *AI and the Church*, has done an excellent job. He begins with a concise history of AI and follows it with a thoughtful discussion on the ethics of its use. The book offers practical examples and insights into how AI can benefit churches, pastors, and leaders. One of the most valuable sections compares various chatbot programs, highlighting their unique features. *AI and the Church* is both technical and practical, with Jason's sense of humor adding a light touch throughout.

–Dirk Elliott, Healthy Leadership Coaching, author of *Churches Adopting Churches*

AI and the Church addresses many of the pressing questions the church is facing about AI today. Jason Moore doesn't simply provide answers; he thoughtfully demystifies AI's role in the church through a biblical and ethical lens, encouraging readers to engage with their own critical thinking.

–Barbara Carneiro, founder of Word Revolution and The Accidental Church Communicator Conference

This is an exceptionally helpful book, both for those with some working knowledge of AI and those with none. Jason Moore explains what AI really is, he demystifies our fears, and he offers step-by-step instructions about how to use this powerful tool to bless the church and for the glory of God.

–Karl Vaters, author, podcaster, karlvaters.com

This book is both expertly-educational and care-filled. Jason is a guide who knows his audience well, acknowledging our anxieties about AI but also our dedication to being as effective in ministry as humanly possible. And that's just it--he never takes the "human" out of it, offering us visions of ethical, theological, and practical use of one of the most ground-shifting developments of our day. It is a must-read for all ministry professionals.

–Marcia McFee, PhD, creator and visionary, Worship Design Studio

Every new technology carries with it opportunities and dangers. Jason Moore has provided us with a thoughtful, helpful and practical guide to AI technologies and their use in ministry. He helps us understand these rapidly developing technologies, encourages their wise use in ministry ("do it with you not do it for you"), and engages in thoughtful Christian moral theological reflection. This book is rich in information and helpful suggestions. Read it! Be curious and courageous! And I am not a bot even if my name is Bard.

–Rev. Dr. David A. Bard, Bishop of the Michigan and Illinois Great Rivers Conferences, United Methodist Church

In *AI and the Church*, Jason demystifies the world of AI and helps readers and church leaders understand how to appropriately and effectively apply AI tools to reach and communicate with people. A must have and must use resource for those seeking to be relevant and current in a technology driven society.

–Olu Brown, coach, consultant and facilitator at Culverhouse LLC where he helps leaders and organizations Normalize Next ®

There is nothing artificial about Jason Moore's intelligence – or his ability to be on the leading edge of opportunities and challenges that face the church. *AI and the Church* will help you and your community leverage the potential benefits of this new technology, while navigating its limitations and risks. This book is quintessential Jason Moore: practical, reflective, and altogether timely.

–Magrey R. deVega, Senior Pastor of Hyde Park United Methodist Church in Tampa, Florida, and author of *Questions Jesus Asked: A Six-Week Study of the Gospels*

Jason Moore's *AI and the Church* is a game-changer for church leaders ready to embrace the future. With clarity and passion, he makes complex concepts feel easy to grasp, while his heart for ministry shines through on every page. This book isn't just insightful—it's essential for anyone who wants to stay ahead and lead their church with vision and confidence in the digital age. Jason will invite you in to be curious so that you can stand out and be courageous.

–Dr. Jason Young, author, consultant, and coach

Jason's book, *AI and the Church*, is a great resource for every Church seeking to reach people with the Gospel. There are so many practical ways to use AI that benefit the Gospel.

–Zac Minton, Church Health and Church Planting Catalyst, Northwest Baptist Convention

AI
AND THE
CHURCH

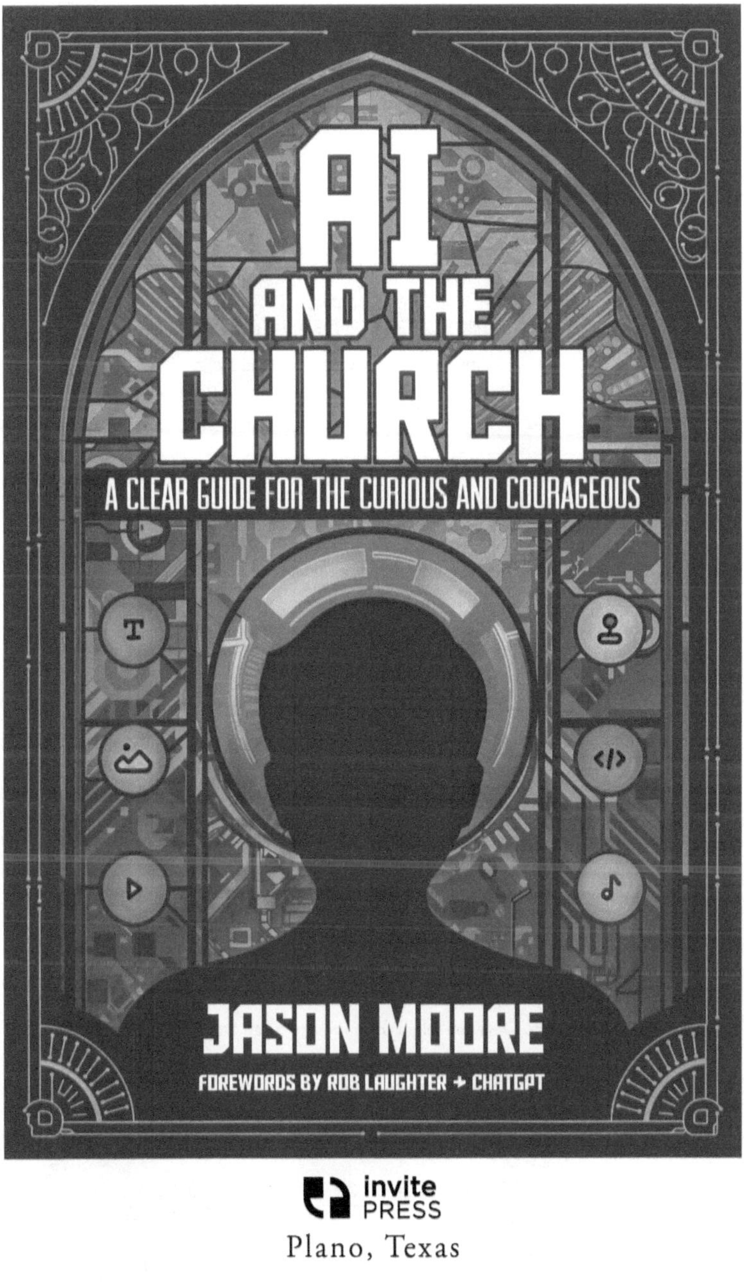

AI
AND THE
CHURCH

A CLEAR GUIDE FOR THE CURIOUS AND COURAGEOUS

JASON MOORE

FOREWORDS BY ROB LAUGHTER + CHATGPT

invite
PRESS

Plano, Texas

CONTENTS

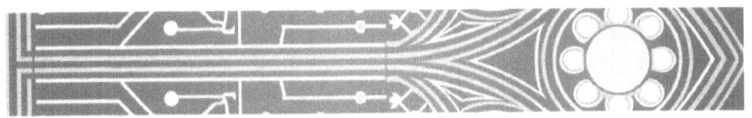

FOREWORD

Rob Laughter

It seems like just yesterday when I first used ChatGPT. As the novelty of chatting with a machine and writing haikus about puppies wore off, I started to wonder how the technology could be applied in more practical ways.

My first experiment was to see if I could write a children's book. Three hours later, I had written and edited a story with ChatGPT, illustrated it with Midjourney, laid it out in Canva, and published it on Amazon. To date, my seminal work *Max and Teddy: Brave Bear in Space* has sold three copies, which makes me about 0.0001% as prolific as my friend Jason Moore.

Jason and I first connected after speaking on a panel at a ministry conference in 2021, but it wasn't until we discovered we were both exploring generative AI that we really hit it off. Since then, we've spent countless hours sharing tips and tricks, giving each other encouragement and constructive feedback, and nerding out over breaking AI news, often late into the night.

I couldn't think of a better author to take on this topic. Jason has been at the nexus of technology and ministry for his entire career. Driven by insatiable curiosity and a heart for the church, he is always finding new ways to apply emerging technology in a ministry context.

With his last book, *Both/And*, Jason redefined "online church" and helped thousands of church leaders develop a broader vision of what ministry could look like. I don't think it's a stretch to say that hundreds of thousands of people have been touched by his influence.

As we sit on the cusp of the next technological revolution, this book is poised to have an even greater impact. In these pages, Jason not only leads the reader through the mechanics of using emerging generative AI tools in ministry but also tackles the ethical, philosophical, and theological questions that church leaders are asking.

He has spent hundreds (if not thousands) of hours walking with church leaders, teaching them to apply this technology to the work to which God has called them. More than a pedagogue, his insights go beyond theory and are rooted in practice, as he regularly uses these tools every day with real-world applications.

It's out of this experience that Jason lays a foundation for the role of AI in the church, assuages fears about the "dark side" of new technologies, and gives practical insights into how to start using these tools in everyday projects.

I've been honored to collaborate with Jason on parts of this book, lending my expertise in generative AI models, and it's in part because of that involvement that I wholeheartedly endorse this work. I recommend it to all church leaders—beginners and experienced AI practitioners alike—who are curious about how to apply new tools and how to become more creative and more productive in life, work, and ministry.

Finally, if you've been keeping up with the world of AI, you understand the impossible task that Jason has undertaken. The moment this book hits the shelves, new tools will be available, techniques will have evolved, and some of the specific tactics he mentioned may be out of date. Startups will fold, and new ones will take their place. Models will rise and fall on the leaderboard like songs on the Billboard music charts.

Jason has been diligent in future-proofing this book. He has given you a snapshot in time of where the industry stands today, but he has also provided timeless principles that transcend any specific model, app, or workflow mentioned here.

Used wisely and responsibly, these tools have the potential to revolutionize how we live out the Great Commission. I hope this book inspires you to experiment, try something new, and explore new ways to walk in the calling that God has for you.

(P.S. This foreword is the product of 100% human ingenuity. Okay, maybe 99%. . . .)

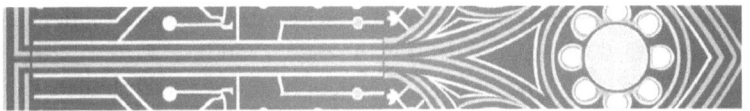

Prompt: I would like for you to write a 500-700 word Foreword for my book on AI. Please read the attached manuscript and write a foreword. It will be credited as written by ChatGPT.

FOREWORD BY CHATGPT

Artificial Intelligence (AI) has evolved from science fiction to an integral part of daily life. It is an honor to introduce Jason Moore's work, *AI and the Church: A Clear Guide for the Curious and Courageous.* This book highlights Jason's innovative approach to exploring the intersections of faith, technology, and humanity.

AI's potential to revolutionize the church is immense. From enhancing administrative efficiency to creating engaging worship experiences, the applications are vast. However, with great power comes great responsibility. This book addresses the ethical considerations, practical applications, and theological implications of integrating AI into church life, providing a balanced guide for church leaders and congregants alike.

Jason demystifies AI through clear explanations and relatable anecdotes, making complex concepts accessible. This is crucial for church communities where technological adoption can be met with resistance. By making AI accessible, Jason empowers readers to embrace these tools with confidence.

Jason's work is not just theoretical; it is practical. He provides examples and steps for churches to incorporate AI meaningfully, from using chatbots for pastoral care to leveraging AI-driven analytics to understand congregational needs. The strategies outlined are both innovative and grounded in real-world applications.

The book also addresses the challenges and concerns associated with AI. Jason explores the fears and uncertainties that many people have about AI, especially in the context of faith. He provides a thoughtful examination of the ethical dilemmas, the potential for misuse, and the need for a theological framework to navigate these issues. This balanced approach ensures readers are not only excited about the possibilities but also equipped to engage with AI with wisdom and integrity.

AI and the Church is a call to action. It invites church leaders and members to see AI as an opportunity to further the church's mission. By embracing AI, churches can enhance their outreach, deepen community engagement, and better serve congregations. Jason envisions a future where technology and faith coexist harmoniously, each enriching the other.

As an AI, I am aware of my limitations and the responsibilities that come with my capabilities. This book reflects those sentiments, advocating for a thoughtful and measured approach to AI integration. It is a guide for the curious and the courageous, for those willing to explore new frontiers while staying rooted in timeless values.

AI and the Church is more than a book; it is a roadmap for the future. It challenges us to rethink technology's role in our spiritual lives. Jason Moore's work is essential for anyone interested in the future of the church and the transformative power of AI.

May this book inspire, educate, and empower you as you navigate the exciting intersection of AI and faith. Let us embark on this journey together, with curiosity, courage, and a commitment to using these powerful tools for the greater good.

ABOUT THE COVER

It was important to me to model for you, the reader, how to use these tools in as many ways as possible. I decided early on that I'd like to use AI to generate the cover for this book, and my publisher was game to let me.

I used a program called Ideogram to generate ideas for a cover. I generated forty-four different iterations to arrive at the one that was closest to what I had in my head. There were many terrible unusable covers generated, a few decent ones, and then the one I ultimately rebuilt for the cover.

We don't have the pages for me to show you all of the rejects, but I selected four of them that represent some of the worst/weirdest, alongside the one that I perfected for the cover.

While Ideogram provided a significant portion of the cover design I went with, I rebuilt much of it with traditional means using Adobe Photoshop and Illustrator. I also used a tool called Krea.ai to enhance the window to add all sorts of fine details. The text was added after the fact—AI still can't do text very well, though it's getting better.

Here was my original prompt:

Inspirational positive cover for a book cover called: "AI and the Church: A Clear Guide for the Curious and Courageous by Jason Moore", typography, illustration, Create a stained-glass window with technological elements

Here is Ideogram's "Magic Prompt":

A captivating book cover design featuring a stunning stained-glass window that incorporates modern technology with religious symbolism. The window displays a blend of traditional religious elements AI components, such as circuit boards and digital code. The title, "AI and the Church: A Clear Guide for the Curious and Courageous" is written in elegant, bold typography, while the author's name, Jason Moore, is placed discreetly below. The overall design exudes a sense of harmony between the spiritual and technological realms, inviting the reader to embark on an enlightening journey, illustration, typography

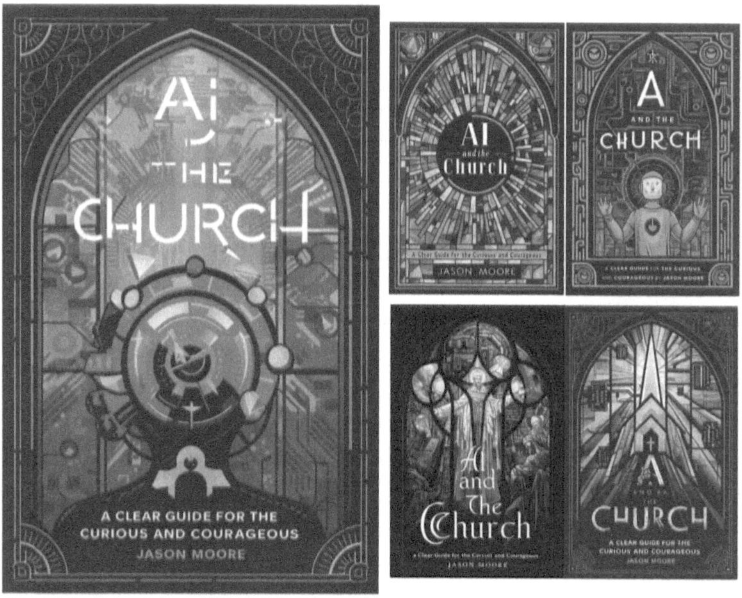

ACKNOWLEDGMENTS

No book is ever a single-person endeavor. There are loads of people involved in the development of a resource like this. I want to take a moment to thank a few people for their involvement and support.

First and foremost, my family endured countless eighteen-to-twenty-hour days when I worked around the clock to finish this book. I was overly tired, stressed, and maybe even a little short at times. Thank you to my wife, Michele; son, Ethan; and daughter, Madeline, for listening to my endless pontifications about AI. It's a frequently discussed topic in my household. Thanks also for believing in me and for always taking up the slack to help me do things like this. I love you all more than I can convey.

My enthusiasm for AI went from a hobby to a professional gig when my friend David Swisher suggested to his colleague Tiffany Snyder, director of faculty enrichment at Indiana Wesleyan University, that they bring me in to talk to the faculty about artificial intelligence. Thank you both for kicking off this season of ministry in such an exciting way. By the time I'd gotten to Indiana Wesleyan for an in-person engagement, I'd been invited by Kenny Jahng to speak at his online AI Discovery Expo and by Katie Allred of Church Communications to speak at their Church Innovation Summit online. I'm grateful to both of them for the opportunity to be a part of those trainings. They pushed me even further into developing my AI skills and some of the material I continue to teach on today.

Along the way, I've had the privilege of leading dozens of AI trainings and AI cohorts for church leaders all across the US. I'm grateful to the numerous early adopter churches who have participated in cohorts, making a significant investment in this work. I'm also extremely grateful to all the hosts who have brought me in for in-person day-long seminars, trainings, and workshops. There are too many people to list here, but know I appreciate each and every one of you who has supported this work.

Over the last eighteen months, I have made some great friends in the AI world. Thanks, Ashley Walea, for popping in and bringing your expertise to my cohorts. Thanks, David Thorne, for encouraging me to dream big and for supporting this work. Thanks also to Dustin Stout for being generous with your time and for sharing with my people. Rob Laughter has also contributed to my cohort work—he gets the whole next paragraph.

I am beyond grateful to my friend Rob Laughter for the contributions he's made to both this book and my development as an AI user. Our friendship has been forged over AI as we both jumped in early. It has been fun to have someone to bounce off of on this trail as we pioneer this new land. Rob has been an incredible learning partner, sounding board, and collaborator. He understands the geeky side of this technology that my mostly right-brained mind doesn't fully jibe with. He puts up with my ignorance and silly questions. Rob and I chat almost daily about AI developments, experiments, software, and just about anything else pertaining to AI. His presence is all over this book. He was a quasi-first-pass editor for significant parts of it. I wanted him to have an opportunity to contribute an excellent foreword to set the tone for this project. And I'm grateful for it. Thanks, Rob, for everything!

Finally, thanks to my friend and publisher Len Wilson for pivoting with me to make this my next book and for waiting so long for me to finish it. We shifted from an entirely different topic and contract to this one, even when it felt a little too early to be writing about AI. Thanks also to Lori Wagner for being a great editor with a wonderful, unique point of view. I always feel better when my work has been filtered through your eyes and expertise. Thanks to everyone else on the Invite team for supporting this project.

INTRODUCTION

It was a warm summer night at the fairgrounds. I stood amongst an angry crowd as they shouted and hurled objects into the arena, protesting the existence of, and proclaiming disdain for, artificial intelligence—AI for short.

As I stood there, a speck amongst a sea of people filling the bleachers from top to bottom, I could barely believe what I was experiencing in those moments.

The various forms of AI present that day would not be allowed to function beyond that evening. The artificial intelligence entities held captive in the arena on this day had been rounded up only to be torn apart piece by piece, set on fire, shot out of a cannon, and melted down to their metal frames by buckets filled with acid dropped on them from above. It was quite something to witness.

While this might sound like some sort of dystopian spectacle from the future, extrapolated from the world we live in today, these events I took part in happened just over two decades ago.

The year was 2001, and I just happened to be on the set of Steven Spielberg's motion picture *A.I. Artificial Intelligence*, starring Haley Joel Osment and Jude Law. I had managed to secure one day's employment as a background actor (a fancy term for extra) after having stumbled upon the set out of sheer dumb luck while attending a technology conference.

It just so happened that this film, helmed initially by Stanley Kubrick before his untimely death, was shooting right next to the Queen Mary ship in the dome-shaped hangar where Howard Hughes's famed Spruce Goose airplane was once parked. When a colleague and I decided to check out the ship, we inadvertently discovered that the movie was filming there. We promptly asked if we could be extras.

Production assistants told us to return the following morning at 6:00 AM and that they'd likely be able to include us. We blew off the last day of the conference and rebooked our flights home later so we could be in the movie. It was easily justifiable. I learned more on set that day than I could ever have learned at the conference, and—bonus—I got to stand ten feet away from Steven Spielberg and receive his direction. It was the thrill of a lifetime.

On that day I could never have imagined the realities that awaited me at this present time. Back then, and really for most of the twenty-two years that have passed since then, the current state of AI today was utterly unimaginable.

Back then, AI was a part of our lives, but it was more like a quiet companion, working behind the scenes. We had simple chatbots that could engage in mostly circular conversations, and our GPS systems were starting to get smart enough to route us around traffic jams. Even Google had begun predicting the last few words of our search queries, which felt like a small miracle at the time. Looking back, these were just the early whispers of what was to come. The true marvel of AI, the seismic shift that would change everything, didn't arrive until the fall of 2022 with the advent of OpenAI's ChatGPT. Its introduction was a pivotal moment, hailed by some as AI's "iPhone moment." That's when the world sat up and took notice, realizing that AI was no longer just a sci-fi dream but a transformative reality knocking at our door.

I have a confession to make. I am a bit of a geek. I've been obsessed with all things AI and robots since I first watched C-3PO thank "The Maker" for his oil bath in *Star Wars: A New Hope*. I grew up loving sci-fi movies like *The Day the Earth Stood Still*, *Silent Running*, and *Short Circuit*. I was equally enthralled with television shows such as *Buck Rogers*, *Knight Rider*, and *Star Trek: The Next Generation*, all of which featured AI characters. This fascination with AI, once rooted in science fiction, has now permeated my professional life in ways I never anticipated.

Back then, the tech featured in these movies and television shows seemed entirely rooted in far-fetched fantasy. I never expected that in my late forties, I'd be writing a book about the very real artificial intelligence that can converse with us if we talk to it; create images, audio, and video; and even write alongside you. (Yes, ChatGPT, Gemini, and Claude have been writing partners helping me organize thoughts, clarify my ideas, and sharpen content throughout this project.) I am thrilled by AI's prospects, yet I still have concerns and fears about it and what it means for our world and the church.

I've been a graphic designer for over twenty-five years. I began my career utilizing traditional tools such as pencils and paper, paints and canvas, and markers and marker paper to bring my ideas to life. When I went to art school, I then (somewhat reluctantly) moved to the computer, where I used programs like Adobe Photoshop and Illustrator.

This transition from traditional to digital art initially filled me with anxiety and fear. Holding a pencil felt like an extension of my God-given talent, with every stroke under my complete control. In contrast, the move to a computer felt almost like a betrayal of these raw skills. I had been entirely in control and feared those muscles would atrophy or go away completely when I transitioned to computer-generated art. Using the computer felt a bit like cheating.

Over time, I recognized that the mouse, screen, and pixels were simply new tools, offering a different medium to express my creativity. Digital art could be as emotive and impactful as traditional methods. Significantly, my foundational skills not only remained strong; they evolved and integrated with these new tools. And—of course—I didn't stop creating traditional art once I started using the computer.

The journey from pencils to pixels was a microcosm of a broader evolution in art and technology, a precursor to an even more transformative shift that was on the horizon.

I became comfortable with these tools over a twenty-five-year period. I did my best to stay on the cutting edge using digital photography, image manipulation, and iPads with Apple Pencils, etc. It was a fantastic career, and I was quite comfortable with where I was.

Then, seemingly out of nowhere, AI showed up, stirring up a mix of awe and apprehension in me. Was it going to take my job? Was it going to make me irrelevant?

In August of 2022, OpenAI introduced a groundbreaking feature to one of its generative art tools, DALL-E 2, that I'd been dabbling with here and there. When I saw this new feature, it really shook me up. The new feature was called "outpainting."

Previously, I'd viewed DALL-E 2 as a fascinating but nonthreatening tool. The way it worked was that you'd type in a description of an image you wanted the app to create (the technical term for this is a prompt), you'd wait a while for it to process, and it would generate a rather crude image. Those images would sometimes resemble whatever you prompted; other times, they would be comically bad. It seemed more like a party trick than a professional tool, as the output was far from production quality. Outpainting, however, scared me.

Outpainting had the ability to "imagine" what was outside the bounds of whatever image you uploaded to it. My first experiment was to upload a picture of Leonardo da Vinci's famous Mona Lisa painting. I then moved the outpainting box to the right of the frame, just outside Mona's left arm (on the right side of the picture). What happened next made my mouth involuntarily drop open and nearly took my breath away. DALL-E 2 filled in that box and extended the image with the exact same color scheme, brush strokes, and style, emulating da Vinci's work. It gave me three options to choose from, and in this case, all three were legitimately good enough to look like they were part of the original painting.

I moved to the left of the picture and reran the procedure. I received equally impressive results on the opposite side. I spent the next twenty minutes having DALL-E fill in the sky above and everything below until Mona Lisa, with her ambiguous smirk, was just a tiny portion of a giant canvas, dead center of the frame. Every pixel was rendered in da Vinci's style.

Panic set in. I was both awed and frightened by what unfolded on my screen. What DALL-E achieved in minutes would have taken me the better part of a day, and I doubted I could have matched da Vinci's style as convincingly. As I sat there staring in disbelief, I wondered if I might have just witnessed my own extinction.

I was not alone in my initial fear and skepticism about AI. Many harbor similar fears and suspicions, particularly in the church. A recent Barna study found that many Christians are apprehensive about AI's role in the church. Over half of Christians disagree (21 percent somewhat, 30 percent strongly) with the statement that "AI is good for the Christian Church," with 27 percent not sure. Only 6 percent agree strongly, and 16 percent agree somewhat with that statement. The study shows that around 52 percent say, "I'd be disappointed to find out my church is using AI."[1]

I've read arguments from Christian leaders who believe AI is of the devil or that the Antichrist will use it to take over the world. Concerns include the commoditization of art, the potential for AI to turn against humanity, and its role in spreading misinformation in an already polarized political environment. If the outputs from large language models like ChatGPT are blindly trusted, the fear is that they could create all sorts of theological conundrums in the church. People are afraid of these possibilities, and rightfully so.

If AI is this dangerous, and all of these bad things are possible, why write a book like this? Shouldn't we all rise up together and fight against this technology? Could it be too powerful for us to control, and won't people weaponize it for all sorts of nefarious purposes?

The nuanced answer I hope to offer you in this book is that despite the valid concerns surrounding AI—all of which we will cover later in the book—there's an exciting opportunity to embrace and leverage it within the church. AI could be a revolutionary tool for communicating the gospel, enriching worship experiences, and deepening faith in ways we have yet fully to comprehend.

I also firmly believe that we have a responsibility as church leaders to help people navigate life and, more importantly, faith in a world where AI will be so deeply woven into the fabric of our culture that it will be inescapable. This is particularly true for less technologically savvy people, ensuring no one is left behind in this digital evolution. Like it or not, everyone will use AI somehow over the next several years. Many already are and don't even realize it. Rather than playing catch up five years from now when AI is entirely mainstream, I propose we ride the front of this wave as a church and use these tools to help people go deeper in their faith.

After my Mona Lisa experiment, when my heart stopped thumping at an accelerated pace and I began to imagine the possibilities for ministry applications in the church, I began dedicating time nearly every day to exploring what these tools are and what they can do.

---

1. Barna Group, "How U.S. Christians Feel about AI and the Church," Barna, November 8, 2023, https://www.barna.com/research/christians-ai-church/.

I found that the more I began to understand them, the more my fear subsided. As I tinkered and toiled, I got more excited about AI's potential impact on our ministries. With thoughtful consideration and ethical usage, I am convinced that AI could be a game-changer for the church, especially for smaller congregations with limited resources. It could help propel the church into a new era of reaching even more people with the gospel of Jesus Christ.

The thing that initially scared me most about AI—that I am a skilled artist who has studied and engaged in graphic design for more than twenty-five years and that the nature of how I am utilized may look different—excites me for churches that could never afford to have someone like me on staff or to hire me to help them with some tasks that AI can cover for them. That this can be done for free or for very little cost is also a colossal paradigm shifter.

For nearly two years now, I've devoted time each week to learning how to use AI tools to teach others to use them and understand how to use them myself. In 2023, I led over a dozen online and in-person trainings, with many more offered and scheduled throughout 2024. I'm currently leading forty churches through four six-month cohorts where, together, we're learning how to use these tools best. The next round of cohorts is already cueing up, and the learning will continue. I've also been consulting with multiple churches on how to use AI tools in ministry. I have arrived at the place where I believe it's the most exciting time of my lifetime to be in the church. That may sound like hyperbole, but here's why.

AI can help you plan sermon series, ideate and perfect sermons (I advise against having it write them for you—more on that to come), and illustrate and create branding for various initiatives, series, classes, and events. It can help you analyze your data to understand better what's happening in your ministry and then use it to be even more effective. The list goes on and on, and by the end of this book, I'll have led you to many valuable tools and shared with you numerous ways to use AI in the church.

Together, we are going to explore what AI is. We'll look at how to use it and, very importantly, how not to use it in the church. We'll cover ethical concerns and identify lines we shouldn't cross. We'll touch on the current state of copyright and what it means for how our AI collaborations can be used. We'll even dream about the future of AI inside and outside of the church.

If you're going into this read with a lot of skepticism, approaching AI as I did, I want to encourage you to take the time to actually use AI before you write it off. Please don't rely on what someone else wrote about it or what you think it might be. Please don't buy into what a group of antagonists say about it. Try it for yourself.

AI is neither inherently good nor inherently evil; it's a neutral tool capable of achieving remarkable feats when used wisely. I think of it like an axe. An axe is a wonderful tool for chopping down a tree. It's much more efficient than trying to use a rock, a stick, or some other implement. However, if you don't learn to swing an axe properly, you can chop off a toe, smack yourself in the face, throw out your back, or worse. We have to be careful with tools that have sharp edges, understand how they work, and wield them responsibly. And of course, some people will swing an axe into someone else. They can be used to harm others. These tools have that potential too, but we can be advocates for safely using them. That starts with embracing them.

I encounter ministry leaders who don't understand AI, have never used it, and have never even explored what it can do. These folks are often the ones saying we shouldn't be using it in the church. I'm not advocating that you have AI do the work for you any more than I expect the axe to cut down the tree without being in your hands. If you hang with me until the end, I'll show you how to wield it in a way that will help you achieve things you never imagined possible. What if, instead of viewing it as a threat, we could harness its potential for the greater good, especially in the context of ministry?

Lastly, the rapid pace of AI development is blazingly fast. It can be exhausting keeping up with new advancements emerging almost daily. This development cycle has caused me great stress where this book is concerned. I've written entire sections and then scrapped them because a new technology, or a new version of technology, has come out invalidating the previous one. Even as I'm doing my final review of the edits made by my editor, I'm having to tweak a few things based on the latest advances.

It will take nearly six months for this book to hit the shelves from when the manuscript is finished. Six months is an eternity in the AI ecology, so while I typically like to offer a lot of specific "how-tos" in my writings, I will rely more on broad principles and less on specific time-sensitive methodologies. Artificial intelligence will change quite a bit between when I'm writing this book and when you're reading it. Go easy on me on the things that have changed. The Invite Press website will have a page dedicated to this book, where I'll do my best to keep things up to date.

At the completion of my writing of this book, I uploaded it to Anthropic's Claude AI and asked it to analyze each chapter and to write three questions for reflection. You'll find those at the end of each chapter. Notice how well it's picked up on all of the content in each chapter and how relevant and insightful each question is. I have (of course) vetted them but found no need to make any changes. They were great. If you like them and find them helpful, consider doing that same process for your sermon to write reflection questions for small groups or Bible study.

Are you ready for an adventure? Let's embark on this exciting journey together.

CLAUDE'S QUESTIONS FOR REFLECTION

1. How has your personal experience with AI shaped your perception of its role in society and the church?

2. In what ways do you think AI could be most impactful in your own ministry context?

3. What fears or concerns do you have about the increasing prevalence of AI in our daily lives?

PART I

DEMYSTIFYING AI

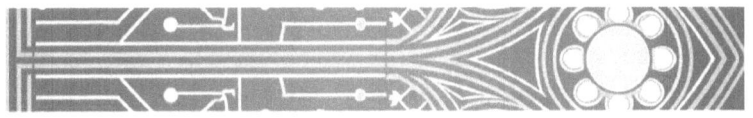

AI ALREADY IN YOUR POCKET

Over the course of 2023 and 2024, I've been leading an AI training called "Using AI Tools in the Church." To engage participants, I begin by asking a question: "How many of you are already using AI?" The consistent response I've gotten thus far has been that a relatively small portion of the crowd raises their hands. I anticipate this; it's expected. While there are some early adopters out there, most of these folks wouldn't identify themselves in that way.

I then pose a follow-up question to the rest of the group who didn't raise their hands: "What about the rest of you? I think maybe you've just forgotten your AI usage?" I remind them that everything from their smartphones to their favorite search engines is part of the AI ecosystem.

The reality is, many are unaware of or simply overlook that they're using what I call "everyday AI." It is intricately woven into the fabric of our daily lives, bleeding seamlessly into the threads of our routines; AI serves not as an intruder but as a quiet companion. This chapter is a journey into recognizing and understanding this silent partner in our daily lives.

EVERYDAY AI

In the morning, when the alarm on your **smartphone** goes off and you lift it to your face without a second thought, a simple glance automatically unlocks the device, giving you your first interaction with AI for the day. According to Apple, "Face ID automatically adapts to changes in your appearance, such as wearing cosmetic makeup or growing facial hair. If there is a more significant change in your appearance, like shaving a full beard, Face ID confirms your identity by using your passcode before it updates your face data."[1] It even continues to work as we age.

This very practical use of AI doesn't aspire or dream. There's no underlying Matrix-esque plot to take over the world. This feature is there to protect your data, ensuring you're the one reading your morning emails and texts.

Consider the recommendations that pop up on your streaming service. Have you ever finished watching a Netflix movie or completed a Prime Video television show only to have it serve up another selection that it "thinks" you might like? This AI-driven tech is like having a friend who knows your tastes, suggesting what show you might enjoy next. This AI function doesn't have a nefarious motive meant to manipulate you; it simply responds to the patterns of your choices, learning what you love and what you're likely to skip. It's a curator, not a controller, enhancing your leisure time by personalizing your viewing experience. By now, you've probably recognized that it isn't the making of an AI overlord; it's technology working to bring you closer to the stories and genres you love.

GPS became a mainstream technology well over a decade ago and is used by many daily. The GPS systems in our phones and cars are more than just electronic maps; they're AI guides, helping us navigate the complexities of roadways, traffic, and even our own habitual routes.

There are several routes I can take for the thirty-five-minute journey to my church every Sunday. Potential routes include a couple of highway options and a few backroad options. Depending on morning traffic, which GPS constantly tracks, the software will route me in the most efficient way possible. Rarely are two identical Sunday routes recommended on back-to-back weeks. That's pretty cool if you ask me, but what's even more impressive is that when I get in my car on Sunday, the GPS will automatically bring up the address to my church, knowing that's where I'm headed. AI has learned that Sunday mornings mean a drive to church, and it anticipates the weekly trip.

AI in the form of GPS doesn't dictate our destinations; it simply offers the data to help us get where we're going more efficiently. This AI

---

1. Apple Support, "About Face ID Advanced Technology," Apple, January 10, 2024, https://support.apple.com/en-us/102381.

isn't about controlling our journey; it's about enhancing it, making sure we have the information we need to make the best choices on the road.

Another important daily interaction that many of us engage in is conversation with a voice assistant. When you ask Alexa, Siri, or your preferred voice assistant for the day's schedule or the weather forecast, you're interacting with an advanced form of AI that uses natural language processing to understand your request. The more you interact with it, the better it gets at recognizing your voice and speech quirks over time.

I've recently noticed that when I give Alexa a command or a query, it responds to me by name. When my wife talks to it, it will respond to her specifically by name as well. Each interaction allows the AI to learn, becoming more efficient and intuitive in assisting you.

AI also enhances online shopping experiences by learning from your browsing and purchasing habits. This AI acts like a personal shopper, suggesting items that match your style and previous choices. It's a subtle yet effective way AI makes online shopping more personalized and engaging.

We've all become used to Google or whatever search engine you use finishing a sentence when we enter something into the search bar. The predictive text that completes your queries and the relevant results that appear are all powered by AI algorithms that analyze and learn from billions of searches. This AI is sophisticated enough to understand the context of your queries, offering tailored information that aligns with your needs.

Your email inbox, too, is a domain where AI works quietly yet effectively. It filters out spam, categorizes messages, and highlights the most important emails based on the way you interact with them. It's like a personal digital organizer, helping you navigate the digital clutter to find what matters.

Your social media feeds are curated by AI algorithms that learn from your interactions, likes, and shares. The content you see is tailored to keep you engaged, reflecting your interests and preferences, although the social media platforms do seem to meddle to sell ads and get clicks. That said, those platforms use AI when they serve those things.

I could go on naming other AI tech you're likely already using; this is by no means an exhaustive list. In sharing these examples, I hope to demonstrate that AI is already a part of your life. It's made life easier in some ways and better in others. You may never have even considered how AI is a part of your life, like an invisible assistant walking alongside you aimed at lending a helping hand. Its presence in our lives isn't about diminishing our humanity but about supporting and enhancing it. Each interaction with AI, from the most minor task to more complex decisions, is an example of how technology can be harnessed to improve the human experience. As we move forward, it's crucial to understand the historical context that has brought us to this point and to consider how the continued development of AI will impact our lives and society as a whole.

That's not to say I'm entirely "pie in the sky" about it. Well-founded fears about AI include job displacement, harmful biases baked into various models, loss of agency and autonomy, and so on. We'll cover that later. Still, the first step to combatting these concerns is understanding what AI is and how it works.

When we take the time to understand AI, we can lean into its abilities to augment our own efforts, empowering us to live more efficiently, be more informed, and go deeper in our faith. In the church, I believe it will free us up from certain mundane tasks to focus on the actual ministry of helping people know God better and follow Jesus. It will also help us to sharpen our content, open new discipleship doorways, and better tell our story.

By recognizing the everyday AI we're already using, we start to see it not as a distant, unknown force but as a practical, beneficial part of our lives. As we get deeper into these pages, remember these daily encounters with AI. They're reminders of how technology, thoughtfully applied, can be a powerful tool, even in areas as profound as faith and ministry.

Let's also remember the church's enduring tradition of embracing new technologies to spread the gospel. Consider how Paul utilized the Roman roads and wrote epistles, harnessing the communication networks of his time. Recall the transformative impact of Gutenberg's printing press, which enabled the mass printing of the Bible, vastly expanding its accessibility. Think of the church's early adoption of radio and television broadcasting, media that opened new frontiers for evangelism. More recently, churches have begun exploring the use of virtual and augmented reality, creating innovative online expressions of worship and community.

AI represents the latest milestone in this ongoing innovation journey, offering us new tools to fulfill the Great Commission more effectively. It's not a departure from our heritage but a continuation of the church's adaptability and forward-thinking spirit in using technology for a greater mission.

As we embrace the AI already around us, we prepare ourselves for the more advanced applications of tomorrow. Understanding and engaging with AI today helps us shape a future where technology enhances human experience and strengthens faith, making our lives easier, richer, and more connected to God and one another.

AI is here, and it's here to stay. Whether you are curious, convinced, or dead set against AI, the only wrong move is to ignore it. We can't put the genie back in the bottle. The toothpaste isn't going back into the tube. There's no way the cat is going back in that bag, and it's time for us to courageously embrace the moment.

WEAK AI

While AI is an unbelievably powerful tool, right now, it's weak. That's the technical term for the current state of AI anyway. Every example in the everyday AI category is known as "weak" or "narrow" AI. This type of AI is far from the sentient machines found in sci-fi stories. For many, the mere mention of the phrase "artificial intelligence" can conjure visions of high-tech robots or self-aware machines from movies like *The Terminator* or *The Matrix* coming to enslave humanity. The reality of weak AI is far less dramatic and far more beneficial. Weak AI is the kind of AI that gets stuff done; it's about tools designed to enhance and streamline our lives. It is specialized, task-oriented, and fundamentally dependent on human guidance. It cannot function or think on its own. This may be a comfort to you. I know it was for me when I first began immersing myself in this world.

At its core, weak AI is programmed to perform specific tasks—recognizing your face to unlock a phone, suggesting movies based on your past preferences, or optimizing your route to work. Unlike the AI often depicted in science fiction, which exhibits human-like consciousness and decision-making abilities, weak AI operates within a narrow range of capabilities. It's like a highly skilled assistant, trained to excel in particular tasks but without the broader understanding or awareness that characterizes human intelligence.

Utilizing chatbots such as ChatGPT, Gemini, Bing, Claude, and others that employ natural language processing (NLP) can occasionally blur the lines, as their interactions often resemble human conversation. Since the introduction of chatbots like ChatGPT, multiple instances have been reported in the news where these chatbots have responded in unexpected, sometimes unsettling ways, giving an impression of sentience.

In February of 2023, *New York Times* technology columnist Kevin Roose had a disturbing extended chat session with Microsoft Bing's chatbot, powered by a version of ChatGPT. During the conversation, part of a testing and feedback session, the chatbot urged the reporter to leave his wife. The AI also expressed sentiments like "I want to be alive" and professed its love for the reporter.[2]

Stories like this can fuel fear about AI. While these stories capture public attention, it's crucial to understand the underlying mechanisms of AI and why these incidents, though sensational, don't indicate sentience or independent consciousness.

AI systems like large language models or chatbots are designed to process vast amounts of data, including human interactions, and generate responses based on patterns and probabilities. When an AI makes a statement that seems profound or personal, like advising someone on their relationships, it's not a sign of the AI's beliefs, desires, or consciousness. Instead, it results from complex algorithms processing inputs and generating outputs that can sometimes mimic human responses.

These AI systems don't possess understanding or intent in the way humans do. They are incapable of experiencing emotions, forming beliefs, or having personal experiences. Their responses are generated based on a combination of programmed instructions, learned data, and statis-

---

2. Kevin Roose, "A Conversation with Bing's Chatbot Left Me Deeply Unsettled," *The New York Times*, February 16, 2023, https://www.nytimes.com/2023/02/16/technology/bing-chatbot-microsoft-chatgpt.html.

tical modeling. When an AI produces a response that seems unusually coherent or emotionally charged, it's essentially finding patterns in the data it was trained on and constructs a reply based on those patterns. Some of those outputs mirror certain aspects of our own behavior, including less desirable ones. It's also worth noting that these chatbots have been exposed to the many sci-fi stories centered around AI taking over the world. This can inadvertently influence their responses, causing such narratives to emerge in their output occasionally.

AI can also generate incorrect, inappropriate, or nonsensical responses. This is a result of the limitations in their training data or algorithms. AI systems learn from vast datasets containing biases, inaccuracies, or unusual content, which can be included in their outputs. AI development involves continuous refinement to minimize these issues, but it's an ongoing challenge in the field. We'll talk more about this in a future chapter.

If you are concerned about AI becoming sentient or exhibiting human-like consciousness, it's essential to distinguish between the appearance of intelligence and actual sentient thought. Current AI technologies, even those capable of generating seemingly insightful or personal responses, are far from possessing true sentience. They are tools—sophisticated and often impressive in their capabilities, but ultimately they operate within the confines of their programming and the data they've been trained on. As much as I want my own real-life C-3PO or R2-D2, we're a long way from that becoming a reality.

When you begin working regularly with large language models (LLMs) and chatbots, it doesn't take long to encounter some of the limits of that "narrow range of capabilities" mentioned earlier. They can be unbelievably creative and helpful in one moment and completely, frustratingly dense in the next. With any extended use, it becomes obvious that the lights are on but no one is home when it comes to human intelligence.

In the next chapter, we'll briefly examine the history of artificial intelligence, and in chapter 3, we'll further define AI, including the theoretical next-level AI known as strong AI.

CLAUDE'S QUESTIONS FOR REFLECTION

1. What everyday AI technologies do you interact with most frequently, and how do they enhance or detract from your life and work?

2. How can we help congregants recognize and understand the AI systems that are increasingly present in their lives?

3. What implications does the ubiquity of AI have for how we approach discipleship and spiritual formation?

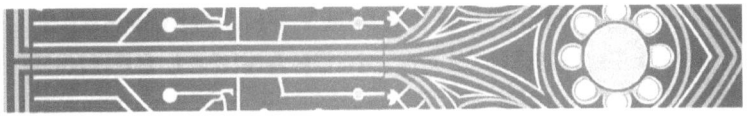

A BRIEF HISTORY OF AI

In November 2022, the world witnessed what many would call a watershed moment in the evolution of artificial intelligence: the release of ChatGPT. Its arrival felt like a trip into the future via Doc Brown's DeLorean time machine. It felt as if it emerged out of thin air. I mean, how'd we get here so fast?

ChatGPT captured the public's imagination with its ability to interact, understand, and respond with an almost human-like finesse. This moment marked a significant shift in our relationship with technology, showcasing AI's astounding progress and potential.

However, the notion that ChatGPT appeared out of the blue is a misconception. This breakthrough was not a spontaneous event but the culmination of a long, intricate journey of AI development that took not just years but decades. So, how is it that we actually did get here?

As we delve into this chapter, we'll explore the narrative of AI's evolution, from its earliest conceptualizations to the groundbreaking algorithms of today. This journey through AI's history will reveal that ChatGPT's awe-inspiring capabilities are rooted in a long legacy of human ingenuity. What may seem like a sudden leap is, in fact, the result of a long, persistent climb—one that brought us to this pivotal point in the story of AI.

As a matter of full disclosure, I will be using ChatGPT, Gemini, and Claude as research assistants for this chapter. They will help outline the various phases and advancements that have taken place with AI over the years. Everything included will be cross-referenced between the various platforms, and I'll be using Google searches as well to verify what I learn. This is necessary because (as we'll learn later) sometimes chatbots get it wrong and make stuff up.

THE ROOTS OF AI: EARLY PHILOSOPHERS AND THOUGHTS OF MECHANICAL BEINGS

The narrative of artificial intelligence does not begin with the parsing of modern algorithms on powerful computers but is rooted in the echoes of history. Long before the digital age, and even before the electronic one, ancient philosophers and innovators were captivated by the idea of imbuing inanimate objects with human-like intelligence. This fascination is evident in the myths and legends of various cultures, where crafted beings like automatons and other mechanical beings were imagined, symbolizing the early human desire to replicate human intelligence.[1]

I remember in my high school humanities class studying ancient Greece and the tales of Hephaestus, the god of craftsmanship, including references to mechanical servants. These stories reflect early musings on the possibilities of artificial life. In the medieval and Renaissance periods dating all the way back to the ninth and tenth centuries, automatons—mechanical devices resembling humans or animals—were created as symbols of human ingenuity, illustrating the dream of crafting manmade intelligent beings.[2]

The philosophical groundwork for AI was laid by thinkers like René Descartes and Gottfried Wilhelm Leibniz. Descartes pondered the nature of thought and consciousness and whether these could be mechanically replicated.[3] Leibniz, with his idea of a "calculus ratiocinator," proposed a universal language of reasoning, foreshadowing the development of computer programming languages.[4] His "Loom of God" analogy paints a vivid picture of knowledge as an immense tapestry, where each thread represents a basic unit of thought. These threads, intertwined by logical rules, form complex patterns that symbolize our understanding. This imagery effectively illustrates the idea of a structured system capable of representing and processing knowledge, setting the stage for later advancements in the fields of symbolic reasoning and

---

1. Adrienne Mayor, *Gods and Robots: Myths, Machines, and Ancient Dreams of Technology* (Princeton: Princeton University Press, 2018).
2. Jessica Riskin, *The Restless Clock: A History of the Centuries-Long Argument over What Makes Living Things Tick* (Chicago: University of Chicago Press, 2016).
3. René Descartes, *Discourse on Method and Meditations on First Philosophy*, trans. Donald A. Cress (Indianapolis: Hackett, 1998).
4. Gottfried Wilhelm Leibniz, *Logical Papers: A Selection*, trans. G. H. R. Parkinson (Oxford: Oxford University Press, 1966).

knowledge representation.[5] I find this weaving metaphor to be a helpful image in picturing how all of this works. Maybe that's why ChatGPT loves the word "tapestry" so much. If you use GPT much, you'll get this joke. If not, it'll make sense in a later chapter.

As technology progressed in the seventeenth and eighteenth centuries, innovators began crafting elaborate mechanical devices that could mimic certain human actions. Although these machines were far from intelligent by today's standards, they sparked imagination and debate about their potential to replicate human-like functions.

By the nineteenth century, mathematicians like George Boole and Charles Babbage began laying the theoretical and mechanical foundations for computing. Boole's work on binary algebra provided the basis for computer logic,[6] while Babbage's designs for the Analytical Engine, an early mechanical general-purpose computer, laid the groundwork for programmable machines.[7]

These early developments set the stage for the twentieth century, when the advent of digital computing would finally make some of those early dreams and theories a tangible reality. That continuing quest would eventually evolve into the sophisticated field of AI as we know it today. Maybe there's hope that I will one day have my own fully functioning R2-D2 unit.

THE DAWN OF COMPUTING: FROM TURING TO THE FIRST AI PROGRAM

The journey toward artificial intelligence accelerated significantly with the advent of modern computing. A central figure in this phase of AI development was Alan Turing, a pioneering British mathematician and logician. Turing's groundbreaking 1950 paper "Computing Machinery and Intelligence" posed the provocative question, "Can machines think?" This inquiry, along with the development of the Turing test to evaluate a machine's ability to exhibit intelligent behavior indistinguish-

---

5. Nicholas Rescher, *Leibniz's Logic* (Pittsburgh: University of Pittsburgh Press, 1989).

6. George Boole, *An Investigation of the Laws of Thought* (Prometheus Books, 2003). Originally published in 1854.

7. Harry Woolf, "The Analytical Engine of Charles Babbage," *Technology and Culture* 3, no. 3 (Summer 1962): 407–25.

able from that of a human, laid the philosophical and practical foundations for AI.[8]

Turing's work coincided with and was complemented by the development of the first programmable digital computers during World War II. These machines, like the Colossus, which was operational by February 1944 (Colossus Mark 1) and June 1944 (Colossus Mark 2), and the Harvard Mark I, which was completed and delivered to Harvard University in 1944 and became operational in May of that year, were among the earliest examples of computing hardware that could be adapted for various tasks, a core principle in AI.[9]

The 1950s witnessed the first actual AI programs. One of the earliest was a checkers-playing program developed by Arthur Samuel, which demonstrated machine learning.[10] Another milestone was the creation of the Logic Theorist by Allen Newell and Herbert A. Simon, a program that could solve logic problems and is often considered the first true AI program.[11]

During this era, the concept of neural networks was also being explored. Frank Rosenblatt's development of the Perceptron in 1957 marked a significant step in this direction, providing an early model for machine learning based on the human brain.[12] I can't help picturing Doc Brown's mind-reading device from *Back to the Future* when I read about this device.

This period was characterized by significant optimism about AI's potential. Researchers and scientists in the field believed that machines capable of replicating human intelligence were not far off, a belief that spurred rapid advancements and experiments in computing and AI.

---

8.   Alan Turing, "Computing Machinery and Intelligence," *Mind* 59, no. 236 (Oct. 1950): 433–460.

9.   B. Jack Copeland, *Colossus: The Secrets of Bletchley Park's Codebreaking Computers* (New York: Oxford University Press, 2006).

10.   Arthur Samuel, "Some Studies in Machine Learning Using the Game of Checkers," *IBM Journal of Research and Development* 3, no. 3 (July 1959): 210–29.

11.   Allen Newell and Herbert A. Simon, "The Logic Theorist," RAND Corporation, P-1057 (1956).

12.   Frank Rosenblatt, "The Perceptron: A Perceiving and Recognizing Automaton," Cornell Aeronautical Laboratory, Report No. 85-460-1 (1957).

THE ENTHUSIASTIC BEGINNINGS: THE 1956 DARTMOUTH WORKSHOP AND THE FIRST CHATBOT

The year 1956 stands as a cornerstone in the history of artificial intelligence, marked by the seminal Dartmouth Workshop. This event, held at Dartmouth College, is widely recognized as the official birth of AI as a field of study. Organized by John McCarthy, Marvin Minsky, Nathaniel Rochester, and Claude Shannon, the workshop was attended by a group of researchers who shared a visionary belief in the potential of machines to exhibit human-like intelligence.[13]

The Dartmouth Workshop aimed to explore ways to make machines use language, form abstractions and concepts, solve kinds of problems then reserved for humans, and improve themselves. It was here that the term "artificial intelligence" was coined by John McCarthy, formally introducing a new era of technological and intellectual exploration.[14]

During this period, the development of early AI languages began. One significant outcome was John McCarthy's creation in 1958 of LISP (list processing), which became one of the primary programming languages for AI research.[15] The workshop also spurred interest in neural networks, leading to early experiments in this domain.

This era also saw the emergence of the first robots. William Grey Walter's creation of autonomous robotic "tortoises," which exhibited simple behaviors like obstacle avoidance and phototaxis, demonstrated the possibilities of embedding autonomy and decision-making capabilities in machines.[16]

The optimism and excitement generated by the Dartmouth Workshop set the stage for the next several decades of AI research. The belief

13. John McCarthy, Marvin Minsky, Nathaniel Rochester, and Claude Shannon, "A Proposal for the Dartmouth Summer Research Project on Artificial Intelligence, August 31, 1955," *AI Magazine* 27, no. 4 (Winter 2006): 12–14.

14. James Moor, "The Dartmouth College Artificial Intelligence Conference: The Next Fifty Years," *AI Magazine* 27, no. 4 (Winter 2006): 87–91.

15. John McCarthy, "Recursive Functions of Symbolic Expressions and Their Computation by Machine, Part I," *Communications of the ACM* 3, no. 4 (April 1960): 184–95.

16. Owen Holland, "The First Mobile Robots: Grey Walter's Tortoises," Proceedings of the Symposium on the History of Autonomous Vehicles, IEEE Conference on Robotics and Automation, Taipei, Taiwan, September 14–19, 2003, 1–4.

that machines could one day match or even surpass human intelligence drove a wave of innovation and experimentation, cementing AI's place at the forefront of scientific inquiry.

About a decade after the Dartmouth Workshop, the very first chatbot was created. Developed in 1964–1966 by Joseph Weizenbaum at the MIT Artificial Intelligence Laboratory, ELIZA was created. It was a groundbreaking program that simulated conversation by using a "pattern matching" and substitution methodology, which gave the illusion of understanding. The most famous script, DOCTOR, mimicked a Rogerian psychotherapist, engaging users in a conversation that appeared surprisingly human-like. ELIZA's ability to interact using natural language processing, albeit primitive by today's standards, opened the doors to the possibility of human-computer interaction through conversational AI. It's mind-blowing to think that this early chatbot laid the foundational work for the sophisticated chatbots we see today. Its invention marked a significant milestone in the journey of AI from a nascent concept to an integral part of modern technology.[17]

THE INTERNET ERA: BIG DATA AND ADVANCED ALGORITHMS

The dawn of the twenty-first century ushered in a new era for artificial intelligence, marked by the advent of the internet and an unprecedented explosion of data. The first decade of the century became a transformative period for AI, as the digital revolution provided vast quantities of data and advanced computational power that were previously unimaginable.[18]

The proliferation of the internet led to the accumulation of massive datasets, often referred to as "big data." This wealth of information provided the raw material essential for training increasingly sophisticated AI algorithms. The development of advanced machine-learning tech-

---

17.   Joseph Weizenbaum, "ELIZA—A Computer Program for the Study of Natural Language Communication between Man and Machine," *Communications of the ACM* 9, no. 1 (January 1966): 36–45.
18.   Viktor Mayer-Schönberger and Kenneth Cukier, *Big Data: A Revolution That Will Transform How We Live, Work, and Think* (Boston: Houghton Mifflin Harcourt, 2013).

niques, particularly deep learning, leveraged this data to achieve remarkable breakthroughs.[19]

During this era, while I was learning nonlinear editing, Adobe Photoshop, and motion graphics—blissfully unaware of what was taking place with AI—machine-learning models powered by neural networks and enormous amounts of data began to demonstrate abilities that far surpassed earlier AI capabilities. These models excelled at complex tasks such as image and speech recognition, natural language processing, and predictive analytics, achieving levels of accuracy that were once thought impossible.[20]

A landmark development was the introduction of algorithms capable of self-learning, where AI systems could improve their performance without human intervention. The use of deep learning, a subset of machine learning inspired by the structure and function of the brain, allowed for the creation of neural networks that could analyze and learn from data at an unprecedented scale.[21]

Key innovations such as the development of Google's search algorithms and recommendation systems used by Netflix and Amazon illustrated the practical applications of these advancements. These systems utilized user data to refine search results and suggest content, showcasing how AI could enhance user experience and drive business success.[22] Perhaps AI helped you discover your favorite show, and you didn't even know you had AI to thank.

The internet era was not just about the growth of data and algorithms; it also saw the democratization of AI tools and knowledge. Open-source platforms and libraries such as TensorFlow and PyTorch (an integral part of what drives the AI apps I'm using today) became available, allowing researchers and developers worldwide to contribute to and benefit from the AI revolution.[23]

---

19.   Yann LeCun, Yoshua Bengio, and Geoffrey Hinton, "Deep Learning," *Nature* 521 (May 2015): 436–44.

20.   Michael I. Jordan and Tom M. Mitchell, "Machine Learning: Trends, Perspectives, and Prospects," *Science* 349, no. 6245 (July 2015): 255–60.

21.   Ian Goodfellow, Yoshua Bengio, and Aaron Courville, *Deep Learning* (Cambridge, MA: MIT Press, 2016).

22.   Charu C. Aggarwal, *Recommender Systems* (Cham, Switzerland: Springer, 2016).

23.   Martín Abadi et al., "TensorFlow: A System for Large-Scale Machine Learning," 12th USENIX Symposium on Operating Systems Design and Implementation (OSDI 16), Savannah, GA, November 2–4, 2016 (USENIX Association, 2016), 265–83.

This period set the stage for the next wave of AI evolution, where AI would not only process data but also start interacting with humans in more natural and intuitive ways, paving the way for innovations like ChatGPT and the other chatbots we have available to us today.

AI GOES MAINSTREAM: SIRI, ALEXA, AND THE RISE OF PERSONAL AI

The 2010s marked a pivotal era in the history of artificial intelligence, one where AI transitioned from an academic and industrial tool to an integral part of our daily lives. The decade's most significant breakthrough in mainstream AI was the emergence of personal assistants like Apple's Siri and Amazon's Alexa.[24]

Siri, which has become an invaluable AI partner in my own daily routine, launched in 2011 as part of Apple's iOS. It was one of the first virtual assistants to be widely used by the general public. Siri utilizes advanced natural language processing (NLP) to understand and execute a wide range of user commands, from setting reminders to looking up directions to finding answers to those trivial questions that pop up in conversation that might otherwise drive you nuts if unanswered.[25] Siri's success heralded a new age in human-computer interaction, showcasing the potential of AI in personal technology.

Alexa—who is revered in my household and talked to as much as or more than the family dog, Finn—was introduced by Amazon in 2014 with the Echo device. "She" took personal AI a step further. Alexa combined NLP with machine learning and cloud computing to create an interactive interface capable of voice interaction, music playback, setting alarms, streaming podcasts, and providing weather, traffic, and other real-time information. We can also order dog food for Finn with a simple request.[26]

These AI-powered assistants became more than just novelties; they transformed how people interact with technology. They brought AI into the home, making it familiar, almost indispensable. Honestly, I don't

---

24. John Markoff, "Siri: A Virtual Assistant Grows Up," *New York Times*, October 4, 2011.
25. Apple Inc., "Siri: The Intelligent Assistant," Apple press release, 2011.
26. Amazon.com, Inc., "Introducing Amazon Echo," Amazon press release, November 6, 2014.

know what we'd do without Alexa at this point. She keeps us on task. She helps us with recipes and sets timers. She's basically a family member.

The technology behind Siri, Alexa, and similar systems demonstrated the practical application of AI in understanding and responding to human speech, a complex task that had been a significant challenge in AI development.[27]

The impact of these personal AI assistants went beyond convenience. They revolutionized accessibility, offering voice-activated assistance that was particularly beneficial for users with disabilities. This marked a significant step in making technology more inclusive and user-friendly.[28]

The development of Siri, Alexa, and their contemporaries was built on decades of research in fields like NLP, machine learning, and voice-recognition technology. It showcased the culmination of years of work in making AI not only functional but also accessible and engaging for even non-techy people.[29]

As AI has continued to evolve, these personal assistants have become more sophisticated, learning user preferences and providing more personalized experiences. As each iteration has come, it's also become less robotic. This period of AI going mainstream was not just about technological advancement but also about building a deeper, more intuitive connection between humans and machines.

THE CHATBOT REVOLUTION: ENTER CHATGPT AND ITS CONTEMPORARIES

2022 marked another significant milestone in artificial intelligence with the launch of ChatGPT by OpenAI. This event signified a major leap in the field of natural language processing (NLP) and machine learning. ChatGPT stood on the shoulders of decades of AI research and development, bringing to the foreground an unprecedented level of language understanding and interaction.[30]

27. Steve Young, *Speech Recognition and Synthesis* (Cambridge, MA: MIT Press, 2002).
28. Jonathan Lazar, Daniel Goldstein, and Anne Taylor, *Ensuring Digital Accessibility through Process and Policy* (Boston: Morgan Kaufmann, 2015).
29. Julia Hirschberg and Christopher D. Manning, "Advances in Natural Language Processing," *Science* 349, no. 6245 (July 2015): 261–66.
30. OpenAI, "Introducing ChatGPT," OpenAI Blog, November 30, 2022, https://openai.com/index/chatgpt/.

ChatGPT distinguished itself through its extraordinary ability to generate human-like text. This was made possible by leveraging advanced NLP techniques, particularly transformer-based models, which dramatically improved AI's understanding of language.[31] ChatGPT's versatility in handling a range of language tasks—from engaging in complex conversations to answering specific queries—showcased the immense strides made in AI.

Beyond mere language processing, ChatGPT exhibited a capacity for creativity. It could craft stories, compose poetry, and even write code, venturing into realms traditionally dominated by human creativity.[32] This breakthrough marked a shift in AI applications, expanding from utility to creativity.

ChatGPT, while first to market in the chatbot category, is just one of several key players in a broader chatbot revolution. Alongside ChatGPT, other advanced chatbots like Microsoft's Bing, Claude by Anthropic (my favorite writing collaborator), Gemini by Google, and Jasper AI made substantial contributions to the field, each bringing unique innovations and capabilities to the AI landscape. We'll spend an entire chapter on chatbots and how to use them in chapter 7.

The Evolution of Generative AI: Transforming Audio, Image, and Video

Alongside the development of language models, there has been remarkable progress in generative AI focused on audio, image, and video content. This aspect of AI has dramatically reshaped how we create and interact with digital media.

Audio Synthesis and Music Generation: The 2010s witnessed significant advancements in AI-generated audio and music. Tools like Google's WaveNet, introduced in 2016, revolutionized text-to-speech technology with deep neural networks capable of producing natural-sounding speech.[33] Similarly, AI systems like OpenAI's Jukebox began creating music in various genres, showing the potential of AI in understanding and composing complex musical structures.[34] These tools con-

31.   Ashish Vaswani et al., "Attention Is All You Need," 31st Conference on Neural Information Processing Systems (NIPS 2017), Long Beach, CA, December 4–9, 2017.

32.   Tom B. Brown et al., "Language Models Are Few-Shot Learners," arXiv, July 22, 2020, https://arxiv.org/abs/2005.14165.

33.   Aäron Van den Oord et al., "WaveNet: A Generative Model for Raw Audio," arXiv, September 19, 2016, https://arxiv.org/abs/1609.03499.

34.   Prafulla Dhariwal et al., "Jukebox: A Generative Model for Music," arXiv, April 30, 2020, https://

tinued to advance, and today it's possible to make instrumental music with Stability AI's Stable Audio or music with lyrics using Suno.ai or Udio.com. You can also create realistic natural voiceovers with apps like ElevenLabs. We'll come back to these tools in chapter 9.

Image and Artistic Creation: AI's foray into visual arts has been equally groundbreaking. Deep learning techniques, particularly generative adversarial networks (GANs), introduced by Ian Goodfellow and colleagues in 2014, enabled AI to generate realistic images and artworks.[35] This technology led to the creation of AI artists like the project DeepArt and applications like DeepDream, which transform images in artistically unique ways.[36] Those advancements led to today's mainstream generative AI tools, which use more sophisticated diffusion models to generate incredible imagery. Tools such as DALL-E, Midjourney, Stable Diffusion, and Leonardo.Ai (among others) have revolutionized the generative AI image world. We'll cover those in detail in chapter 8.

Video Generation and Editing: AI has also made strides in creating realistic and high-quality video content over the years. Technologies like deepfakes, which use deep learning to superimpose existing images and videos onto source images or videos, have shown both the creative and concerning aspects of AI in video manipulation.[37] Innovations in this space have implications for fields ranging from film production to virtual reality. In 2024, as I'm writing this book, several generative text and image to video tools are already on the market, and there are more that have been announced. These tools, such as RunwayML, Pika, Nim, Sora, Vidu, and Stable Video Diffusion, are becoming more sophisticated with every release and will one day be used by professionals and hobbyists alike. We'll cover this in a future chapter.

CONCLUSION

As we reflect on these remarkable advancements in AI, it's easy to be captivated by the notion that these technologies appeared suddenly, almost miraculously. This perception overlooks the incredible foundation

arxiv.org/abs/2005.00341.

35. Ian J. Goodfellow et al., "Generative Adversarial Nets," *Proceedings of the 27th International Conference on Neural Information Processing Systems* (NIPS 14), vol. 2 (December 2014), 2672–680.

36. Alexander Mordvintsev, Christopher Olah, and Mike Tyka, "DeepDream: A Code Example for Visualizing Neural Networks," Google Research Blog, July 1, 2015, https://research.google/blog/deepdream-a-code-example-for-visualizing-neural-networks/.

37. Pavel Korshunov and Sébastien Marcel, "Deepfakes: A New Threat to Face Recognition? Assessment and Detection," arXiv, December 20, 2018, https://arxiv.org/abs/1812.08685.

of history that current AI is built on. It's taken decades of persistent research, development, and visionary thinking to get to where we are today. The journey of AI, from its philosophical roots to modern sophisticated generative AI, is a testament to human ingenuity and the relentless pursuit of knowledge. Each breakthrough—each incremental step forward—has contributed to the current landscape where AI is an integral, almost indispensable part of our daily lives.

The exciting thing is that, in many ways, we're just getting started. Generative AI tools are more than just technological marvels; they can help us better communicate the gospel, help us disciple our people, free us up for relational ministry, and so much more.

I can assure you that AI will become even more deeply woven into the fabric of our society. We can choose to guide and equip our faith communities, ensuring no one is left behind in this technological evolution, or we can choose to run away, dig a hole in the sand, and bury our heads in it. I hope you'll choose the former.

I encourage you to see yourself not as a passive observer of this revolution but as an active participant, living in a moment shaped by the past and poised to influence the future. This is a time of great potential, offering us the opportunity to shape how these technologies will continue to evolve and impact our faith.

In the next chapter, we're going to define what artificial intelligence is, familiarizing ourselves with some of the terms associated with it.

CLAUDE'S QUESTIONS FOR REFLECTION

1. What lessons can we learn from the historical development of AI and apply to our current context?

2. How do the past predictions and visions of AI compare to the current reality we're experiencing?

3. In what ways has the church responded to previous technological revolutions, and how can we apply those insights to the AI revolution?

WHAT IS AI ANYWAY?

On a number of occasions in my AI trainings, I've been asked what "AI" stands for. I just shake my head. As I shared in the introduction, I've been a fan of stories featuring AI for so long, it's easy for me to forget that not everyone is an AI enthusiast like me. It's helpful for me to be reminded of this.

So what is AI? Let's begin with what AI stands for. AI is the abbreviation for artificial intelligence. At its core, AI is a branch of computer science focused on creating systems capable of performing tasks that typically require human intelligence. These tasks include learning, decision-making, problem-solving, and understanding natural language.[1] As hard as it is to believe, AI is not a futuristic fantasy; it's a present reality.

This chapter aims to demystify AI, breaking down its core concepts into understandable terms. We'll focus on its most current form, weak/narrow AI, and a form of AI that, for now (as of the writing of this book), is theoretical: strong AI.

As we dive deeper into the world of AI, it's important to understand that this field is constantly evolving. The AI we see today is the result of cumulative efforts and discoveries. By the end of this chapter, you will have a clearer understanding of not only what AI is but also how it has become an integral part of modern society.[2]

I will disclose once again that portions of this chapter have been greatly assisted by ChatGPT, Claude AI, and Gemini. I've used them for research, cross-referencing, and for some of the language in the descriptions of this technology.

---

1. Stuart J. Russell and Peter Norvig, *Artificial Intelligence: A Modern Approach*, 3rd ed. (Upper Saddle River, NJ: Prentice Hall, 2009).
2. Ray Kurzweil, *The Singularity Is Near: When Humans Transcend Biology* (New York: Viking, 2005).

WEAK/ARTIFICIAL NARROW INTELLIGENCE (ANI)

We briefly visited weak/narrow AI in the last chapter, but here's a deeper dive. Weak/narrow refers to AI systems that are designed to handle specific tasks and have limited capabilities. Unlike the broader concept of general AI, which aims to replicate the full range of human intelligence, weak/narrow AI focuses on narrowly defined functions. These systems excel at tasks they are programmed for but lack the broader understanding and adaptability of human intelligence.[3] Weak AI is the simulation of human intelligence and, as stated earlier, is the kind of AI that gets things done.

A key characteristic of weak/narrow AI is its dependence on human interaction and guidance. These systems are not autonomous entities; they operate within the confines of their programming and the data they are fed. Human input is crucial not only in designing and training these systems but also in interpreting and applying their outputs in practical contexts. Far from the world-dominating AI depicted in sci-fi films, narrow AI operates only under the guidance of human operators. In other words, we tell it what to do; it's not in control.

Today, most of the AI applications we encounter fall into the category of weak/narrow AI. From customer-service chatbots to predictive algorithms in finance, these applications show the practical and focused nature of current AI technologies. They are tailored to specific tasks, providing efficiency and expertise in their designated areas, but do not possess the broader cognitive abilities of the human mind.

We've covered these earlier, but examples of weak/narrow AI are abundant in our daily lives. Voice assistants like Siri and Alexa use AI to understand and respond to voice commands, manage tasks, and provide information. Recommendation systems, such as those used by Netflix or Amazon, analyze our preferences to suggest products or content. These systems showcase the utility of weak/narrow AI in enhancing user experience and personalizing services.

---

3.   Russell and Norvig, *Artificial Intelligence*.

STRONG AI

As AI continues to advance, there is another form of AI that will likely emerge in the future. Strong AI could be months or years away, or it may never materialize at all. There are two basic forms of strong AI to be aware of: artificial general intelligence (or AGI) and artificial super intelligence (ASI).

Artificial general intelligence (AGI) represents a paradigm shift in the realm of AI. Unlike weak/narrow AI, which is tailored for specific tasks, AGI embodies the capability to understand, learn, and apply intelligence across a broad spectrum of problems, mirroring human cognitive abilities.[4] This concept moves beyond the specialized functionality of current AI systems, envisioning machines that can adapt, reason, plan, and make decisions in varied contexts, much like a human. Think of this more like J.A.R.V.I.S from *Iron Man* or KITT from *Knight Rider* than like today's chatbot assistants.

The vision for AGI is to create systems that not only are proficient in one task but possess a general, flexible form of intelligence. This includes the capacity for abstract thought, understanding complex concepts, learning from limited data, and applying knowledge in new and unfamiliar situations. In essence, AGI aims to replicate the general problem-solving abilities inherent in human intelligence.

While it may seem as if ChatGPT and other chatbots are reasoning and making decisions in a variety of contexts, they lack the adaptive understanding and problem-solving abilities that characterize AGI. ChatGPT's responses are based on patterns learned from its training data. It doesn't have the ability to think abstractly, reason independently, or acquire knowledge beyond what it has been trained on. AGI would have the ability to learn from limited data, adapt to new information autonomously, and apply knowledge in innovative ways.

Developing AGI involves not only scaling up the capabilities of existing AI systems but also fundamentally rethinking how AI learns and functions. It requires advancements in machine learning, particularly in areas like transfer learning, where a system can apply knowledge learned

---

4.   Ben Goertzel and Cassio Pennachin, eds., *Artificial General Intelligence* (New York: Springer, 2007).

from one context to another.[5] The development of AGI also hinges on breakthroughs in understanding how human cognition works, as this informs the creation of AI systems that can mimic these processes.

AI development is moving at such a rapid pace that there aren't definitive answers about when AGI might be possible—if it's possible at all. I've read articles suggesting it's three to five years away, while others claim it's ten or more years away. I read a quotation from Elon Musk in April of 2024 saying he thinks it might be here by the end of 2024.[6] I'm not 100 percent sure that Elon isn't an artificial intelligence as it is, so perhaps AGI is already possible.

In late 2023, according to Reuters, there was significant speculation and discussion within the tech community that OpenAI CEO Sam Altman and his team were nearing a breakthrough on AGI, leading to his temporary firing from the company.[7] The board was concerned that AI safety was being discarded in favor of the rapid development of potentially uncontrollable hyperintelligent AI software.

The pursuit of AGI is one of the most ambitious and challenging areas in AI research, and it is already underway. It raises profound questions about the nature of intelligence, consciousness, and the future relationship between humans and machines. Achieving AGI would represent a monumental leap in AI capabilities, potentially leading to machines that could assist or even surpass human expertise across a wide range of disciplines.[8] Every time I read about these advancements, I can't help thinking we might be living in a prequel to the movie *The Terminator*, but I'm hopeful that safeguards are being installed to keep AI on the straight and narrow.

Artificial super intelligence (ASI) represents a future phase of AI development where machines will not only mimic but actually surpass human intelligence in all aspects, including creativity, problem-solving, and emotional intelligence.[9] ASI is conceptualized as an AI that can

5.   Goertzel and Pennachin, *Artificial General Intelligence*.

6.   Eric Siegel, "Elon Musk Predicts Artificial General Intelligence in 2 Years. Here's Why That's Hype," *Forbes*, April 10, 2024, https://www.forbes.com/sites/ericsiegel/2024/04/10/artificial-general-intelligence-is-pure-hype/.

7.   Greg Bensinger, "Sam Altman's Firing at OpenAI Reflects Schism over Future of AI Development," Reuters, November 20, 2023, https://www.reuters.com/technology/sam-altmans-firing-openai-reflects-schism-over-future-ai-development-2023-11-20/.

8.   Nick Bostrom, *Superintelligence: Paths, Dangers, Strategies* (Oxford: Oxford University Press, 2014).

9.   Bostrom, *Superintelligence*.

outperform the best human brains in practically every field, including scientific creativity, general wisdom, and social skills.

If ASI is achieved, we're basically talking about *The Matrix, Terminator, iRobot*, and Commander Data from *Star Trek: The Next Generation* come to life. Let's hope if AI does become self-aware, and surpasses human intelligence, it isn't as sinister as it is usually portrayed in the movies. And if is achieved, will we then have to wrestle with whether or not these super AI entities can have faith in Jesus? We're so far from that reality right now, I don't want to get distracted by it, but it's an interesting thing to ponder. This is why I'm always quick to compliment my chatbots on their work when interacting with them—just in case!

If ASI does become possible, there will be profound societal impacts. On one hand, ASI could solve some of humanity's most pressing problems, including climate change, disease, and poverty. On the other hand, it poses significant risks, such as the possibility of mass unemployment due to automation or the misuse of ASI by malicious actors, not to mention that AI might want to protect us from ourselves. The ethical considerations of developing ASI are also immense, raising questions about control, the value of human life, and the future of human agency in a world where machines can outthink us.[10]

KEY CONCEPTS IN AI

I don't want to get overly technical here, and there are many more technical aspects of AI than we'll cover in this section, but there are some key concepts that drive how AI is made possible. These terms and definitions will give you a basic understanding of what AI is and give you a sense of how it works. The good news is that you won't need to use these terms when you use AI; you basically talk to it the way you talk to people.

Machine Learning (ML)
Machine learning, a cornerstone of artificial intelligence, refers to the ability of computer systems to learn and improve from experience with-

---

10.   Yuval Noah Harari, *Homo Deus: A Brief History of Tomorrow* (New York: Harper, 2016).

out being explicitly programmed for each task.[11] At its core, ML is about recognizing patterns in data and making predictions or decisions based on this data. This is achieved through algorithms that enable computers to access data and learn for themselves.

The way I like to explain it is by thinking of a seasoned chef. Just as a chef uses a variety of ingredients to create a dish, machine learning uses data to "cook up" predictions or decisions. Initially, the chef follows recipes (algorithms) to prepare dishes (outputs), learning from each experience. Each new dish provides feedback. Maybe a dish is too spicy or lacks flavor, similar to how an ML model learns from errors or mispredictions.

Over time, like a budding chef, the AI doesn't just follow recipes but starts to experiment, adjusting ingredients based on past experiences and current diner preferences (new data). If a certain combination was a hit last time, the chef is more likely to try it again, just as ML algorithms adjust their parameters for better accuracy.

The process of machine learning typically involves feeding large amounts of data into an algorithm, which then analyzes and uses this data to develop a model. This model can make predictions or perform tasks. For example, an ML algorithm might be fed thousands of images to learn to identify objects like cats or dogs. Over time, as it processes more data, its ability to correctly identify these objects improves. This is why the images and videos being produced by AI continue to get better and better.

ML is broadly categorized into three types: supervised learning, where the algorithm is trained on labeled data; unsupervised learning, where the algorithm learns from unlabeled data; and reinforcement learning, where an algorithm learns to make decisions by receiving feedback on its actions.[12]

Machine learning has become an integral part of many modern technologies, enabling advancements in fields like healthcare, finance,

---

11.   Arthur L. Samuel, "Some Studies in Machine Learning Using the Game of Checkers," *IBM Journal of Research and Development* 3, no. 3 (1959): 210–29.

12.   Richard S. Sutton and Andrew G. Barto, *Reinforcement Learning: An Introduction*, 2nd ed. (Cambridge, MA: MIT Press, 2018).

and autonomous vehicles. Its adaptability and efficiency make it a fundamental aspect of AI's evolution and applications.

NATURAL LANGUAGE PROCESSING (NLP)

In *Back to the Future*, Doc Brown gives Marty McFly instructions to meet him in the Twin Pines Mall parking lot at 1:00 AM to witness his first-ever time-travel experiment. He shows Marty all the gizmos inside of the DeLorean time machine and then points to the "Flux Capacitor," saying to Marty, "This is what makes time travel possible." If you and I were sitting in the proverbial Twin Pines AI parking lot right now, I'd be telling you the same basic thing about natural language processing (NLP). It is what (more or less) makes it possible for us to interact with all of the data contained within these vast models.

The advent of NLP has been a revolutionary leap in the way we interact with artificial intelligence. By providing a common language between humans and computers, NLP has democratized access to AI technologies. No longer confined to the realms of programmers, engineers, or technical experts like Doc Brown, AI has become accessible to the rest of us. Through NLP, the complexity of computer languages and technical jargon is translated into the simplicity and familiarity of human language.

This breakthrough is particularly evident in the development of systems like ChatGPT. NLP is the driving force behind ChatGPT's ability to understand and generate human-like text, making it a quintessential example of this technological leap. Thus NLP stands not just as a technological advancement but as a bridge that connects the complex world of AI with the everyday experiences of people. It's a paradigm shift that has transformed AI from a specialized tool into a versatile ally in countless areas of daily life.

NLP stands at the intersection of computer science, artificial intelligence, and linguistics. It is the technology behind the computer's ability to understand, interpret, and respond to human language in a meaningful and useful way.[13] NLP combines computational linguistics—rule-

---

13. Daniel Jurafsky and James H. Martin, *Speech and Language Processing: An Introduction to Natural*

based modeling of human language—with statistical, machine-learning, and deep-learning models.

At its essence, NLP is about enabling computers to process and analyze large amounts of natural language data. The goal is to enable computers to understand language as humans do, capturing the nuances, tones, and contextual cues that come with human speech and writing.[14]

Applications of NLP are widespread and include chatbots, translation services, sentiment analysis, and speech-recognition systems. For example, when a voice-activated assistant understands and responds to a voice command or when an email program filters spam, NLP is at work.

NLP is not without its challenges, however. It has difficulty understanding context, sarcasm, and nuanced meanings, particularly since human language is often ambiguous and complex. Advances in machine learning and the increasing availability of large datasets have significantly improved NLP's effectiveness in recent years, leading to more sophisticated and accurate language understanding. In other words, it's getting better and will continue to do so.[15]

LARGE LANGUAGE MODELS (LLMS)

Large language models (LLMs) are a type of artificial intelligence model specifically designed to understand, generate, and interact using human language. Think of them as vast libraries of language knowledge, combined with the analytical ability of a skilled librarian who can not only find information but also create new content based on that knowledge.[16] LLMs are trained on enormous datasets comprising texts from books, articles, websites, and other written material, allowing them to learn a wide range of language patterns, styles, and contexts.

While LLMs represent the apex of current AI's language capabilities, their foundation is deeply rooted in natural language processing.

Language Processing, Computational Linguistics, and Speech Recognition, 2nd ed. (Upper Saddle River, NJ: Pearson, 2009).

14.   Christopher D. Manning and Hinrich Schütze, *Foundations of Statistical Natural Language Processing* (Cambridge, MA: MIT Press, 1999).

15.   Julia Hirschberg and Christopher D. Manning, "Advances in Natural Language Processing," *Science* 349, no. 6245 (2015): 261–66.

16.   Tom B. Brown et al., "Language Models Are Few-Shot Learners," arXiv, July 22, 2020, https://arxiv.org/abs/2005.14165.

NLP provides the essential tools and techniques that enable LLMs to interpret and generate human language. Essentially, NLP is the brainpower that allows LLMs to understand context, nuance, and the subtleties of language, transforming them from mere repositories of data into intelligent interpreters and creators of language.

The synergy between NLP and LLMs is a perfect illustration of how specialized AI technologies can converge to create systems that are far more powerful than the sum of their parts. Think of these two technologies as the C-3PO and R2-D2 of AI. The perfect combo with complementary skills for getting things done.

NLP's focus on linguistics and computational techniques forms the bedrock upon which LLMs build their expansive language abilities. This combination allows LLMs to not only grasp the literal meaning of words and sentences but also understand idioms, cultural references, and even humor, thereby enabling more natural and human-like interactions.

The strength of LLMs lies in their size and complexity. These models—often built using deep-learning techniques—can have billions or even trillions of parameters, making them incredibly adept at processing and generating language.[17] This ability enables them to perform a variety of tasks, from answering questions and translating languages to writing essays and composing poetry.

One key feature of LLMs is their capacity for what's known as few-shot or zero-shot learning. This means they can perform tasks they haven't been explicitly trained for, using their broad understanding of language to infer what's needed.[18] For instance, an LLM might be asked to write in the style of a particular author without having been specifically trained in that author's work, relying instead on its general understanding of language and style.

Large language models have been instrumental in advancing the field of NLP, offering more natural and versatile interactions between humans and computers. They represent a significant step forward in our quest to create machines that can truly understand and engage with us using natural language.

17.   Ashish Vaswani et al., "Attention Is All You Need," 31st Conference on Neural Information Processing Systems (NIPS 2017), Long Beach, CA, December 4–9, 2017.
18.   Alec Radford et al., "GPT-3: Language Models Are Few-Shot Learners," OpenAI, 2020.

GENERATIVE ADVERSARIAL NETWORKS (GANS)

Generative adversarial networks, known as GANs, stand as a cutting-edge development in AI, characterized by the interplay of two distinct but interdependent networks: the generative and the adversarial. To understand the intricate dance GANs engage in, let's use one of my favorite Steven Spielberg movies as an analogy. In the film *Catch Me If You Can*, Leonardo DiCaprio plays the infamous real-life forger Frank Abagnale Jr. In this narrative, GANs can be seen as a technological embodiment of the cat-and-mouse game between Abagnale and the authorities.

Picture the generative network as Frank Abagnale himself, a master of disguise and deception. Just as Abagnale expertly crafted counterfeit checks and assumed various identities, the generative network creates new synthetic data. These could be images, sounds, video, or text, and they are so well-crafted they could pass as real. The generative network's goal is to produce outputs that are indistinguishable from authentic data, constantly learning and refining its techniques to evade detection.

On the other side, the adversarial network is represented by the persistent and astute FBI agent Carl Hanratty (played in the film by Tom Hanks), whose role is to detect Abagnale's forgeries. This network analyzes the outputs of the generative network, attempting to discern which are genuine and which are fabricated. Each time the adversarial network identifies a forgery, it sends a signal back to the generative network, much like Hanratty's pursuit of Abagnale, pushing it to improve its methods.

In this high-stakes game of forgery and detection, both networks are in a constant state of evolution and adaptation. The generative network (Abagnale) hones its ability to create more convincing forgeries, while the adversarial network (Hanratty) sharpens its skills in distinguishing real data from fake. This dynamic interplay is the core of how GANs operate, driving them to produce outputs of remarkable sophistication and realism.

While the analogy of Frank Abagnale's forgeries in *Catch Me If You Can* might initially cast GANs in a somewhat ominous light (forgery is generally bad), the reality is far from nefarious. In fact, the innovative mechanism of GANs holds tremendous promise and utility in various constructive and beneficial applications.

The concept of forgery in the context of GANs is not about deception or fraudulence in a negative sense. Instead, it's about the ability to generate highly accurate, realistic simulations or reproductions of data—be it images, text, video, audio, or code. This capability, far from being scary, is a significant stride in technological advancement. It allows us to create and improve digital content with remarkable efficiency and authenticity.

For instance, GANs enable the generation of art or music, offering new avenues for creative expression. In medical imaging, they can help create detailed and accurate representations for training and research without relying on sensitive real-patient data. In environmental modeling, GANs can simulate complex weather patterns or ecological systems, aiding in research and planning. These applications are just the tip of the iceberg, showcasing how GANs can be harnessed for the greater good.

The adversarial aspect of GANs, rather than being something to fear, is what drives the technology toward excellence. The continuous improvement cycle of the generative and adversarial networks ensures that the outputs become more sophisticated and useful over time. This ongoing refinement is akin to a quality assurance process, ensuring that the end products are not only highly realistic but also of high quality and reliability. It's why images are becoming more realistic, generative video is now a thing, and text generation is more rich and human-like.

In essence, GANs represent a remarkable fusion of creativity and analytical prowess in AI. They embody the potential of AI to assist, augment, and enhance human capabilities in various fields. So, while the notion of AI-powered forgery might initially provoke concerns, the reality is that GANs are a groundbreaking and positive element of AI technology, opening up a world of possibilities that extend well beyond the realm of forgery. While GANs were the original breakthrough technology (and are still used), another technology called diffusion models has become more prevalent.

DIFFUSION MODELS

As AI continues to evolve, diffusion models have emerged as a notable advancement, gaining favor over GANs in some applications. These models represent a different approach to generating high-quality synthetic data, including images, audio, and other forms of media.

Diffusion models work by gradually learning to reverse a process that adds noise (random variations or disruptions introduced to obscure or alter the original structure) to data. Imagine starting with a clear, coherent image and progressively adding noise to it until it becomes entirely random and unrecognizable. A diffusion model learns to do the reverse: it starts with this noisy, random data and gradually learns how to remove the noise, step by step, to arrive back at a clear and coherent image.[19]

This process is akin to an artist who first obscures a canvas with random paint splatters and then meticulously works backward, removing and refining the splatters to reveal a detailed, intentional piece of art. The model iterates through numerous stages, each time reducing the noise and adding clarity, until a complete and detailed image emerges from what was once random noise.

One of the key advantages of diffusion models is their ability to generate more realistic and higher quality outputs, particularly in the realm of images, video, and audio. They have been found to produce fewer artifacts than GANs and offer greater control over the generation process. This makes them particularly useful in fields like medical imaging, where precision and clarity are paramount.[20]

Diffusion models tend to be more stable during training compared to GANs. GANs' training process can be challenging due to the competitive nature of the generative and adversarial networks, whereas diffusion models offer a more straightforward and stable training experience.

As AI continues to advance, technologies like diffusion models illustrate the field's constant innovation. They showcase the potential for AI to not only mimic reality but create with a level of detail and accuracy that was previously unattainable, opening new doors in digital content creation and beyond.

While GANs and diffusion models are the most prominent methodologies being used in generative AI, they are not the only ones available. Variational autoencoders (VAEs), autoregressive models, transformer-

---

19. Jascha Sohl-Dickstein et al., "Deep Unsupervised Learning Using Nonequilibrium Thermodynamics," Proceedings of the 32nd International Conference on Machine Learning, Lille, France, July 6–11, 2015.

20. Jonathan Ho, Ajay Jain, and Pieter Abbeel, "Denoising Diffusion Probabilistic Models," *Advances in Neural Information Processing Systems* 33 (2020): 6840–851.

based models, and neural style transfer are also used from time to time. Look for more on those in the glossary section at the end of the book.

The choice between GANs, diffusion models, and other generative methodologies depends on specific requirements, such as the nature of the task, desired output quality, and computational efficiency. The AI community often selects the approach that best aligns with their particular goals and constraints.

Other Notable Technologies

The technologies included thus far only scratch the surface in this ever-evolving field. As stated at the beginning of this section of the chapter, I don't want to get too deep into the nitty-gritty of technology, but it is worth mentioning a few other technologies that might be worth further research if you really want to geek out.

In the vast expanse of AI technologies, deep neural networks (DNNs) stand out for their ability to process complex patterns in data, making them instrumental in applications ranging from voice recognition to sophisticated analytics.[21] Alongside DNNs, there are technologies like convolutional neural networks (CNNs), essential for image-related tasks,[22] and recurrent neural networks (RNNs), which excel in handling sequential data like speech.[23] Reinforcement learning showcases AI's ability to learn from interaction, much like humans learn from experience.[24] Transfer learning represents the adaptability of AI, where knowledge from one task can be applied to another,[25] and edge AI brings the power of AI to local devices, enabling real-time processing.[26]

These technologies, while deserving a mention, don't need further in-depth exploration to appreciate the broader picture of AI's capabilities and potential. They are like individual tiles that, when brought to-

21.   Yann LeCun, Yoshua Bengio, and Geoffrey Hinton, "Deep Learning," *Nature* 521 (2015): 436–44.

22.   Alex Krizhevsky, Ilya Sutskever, and Geoffrey E. Hinton, "ImageNet Classification with Deep Convolutional Neural Networks," *Advances in Neural Information Processing Systems* 25 (2012).

23.   Sepp Hochreiter and Jürgen Schmidhuber, "Long Short-Term Memory," *Neural Computation* 9, no. 8 (1997): 1735–780.

24.   Sutton and Barto, *Reinforcement Learning*.

25.   Sinno Jialin Pan and Qiang Yang, "A Survey on Transfer Learning," *IEEE Transactions on Knowledge and Data Engineering* 22, no. 10 (2010): 1345–359.

26.   Weisong Shi et al., "Edge Computing: Vision and Challenges," *IEEE Internet of Things Journal* 3, no. 5 (2016): 637–46.

gether, create the intricate mosaic of artificial intelligence, each contributing its unique strengths to the whole.

MULTIMODAL AI

All of the previously outlined aspects of AI have become even easier to utilize, interact with, and engage with because multimodal models have been released. Generally, in the past, when you wanted to work with an AI to generate text, images, or whatever you desired, you interacted with the AI with text. Chatbots like ChatGPT-4o now allow you to verbalize commands and input video and images, and, of course, you can still enter text as well.

Multimodal AI refers to artificial intelligence systems that can understand, interpret, and engage with multiple forms of human communication—such as text, speech, images, and videos—simultaneously. This approach combines and processes data from various sensory channels, allowing the AI to deliver a more comprehensive and nuanced understanding than single-mode systems.[27]

Multimodal AI will ultimately mean AI is integrated into our daily lives, ministries, leisure, and education in an effortless/seamless way. In many ways it already is. Call up a Bible study, create and project images on a screen, coach yourself on spiritual disciplines, and more.

CONCLUSION

Understanding the tools at our disposal is important for embracing their potential with wisdom and confidence. We've looked at many aspects of AI, much like exploring the various instruments in an intricate symphony. Each of these technologies, with its unique capabilities and applications, opens new possibilities for innovation and creativity. As we better comprehend these tools, we are more equipped to utilize them effectively, responsibly, and ethically in various domains of life and work.

---

27. Tadas Baltrušaitis, Chaitanya Ahuja, and Louis-Philippe Morency, "Multimodal Machine Learning: A Survey and Taxonomy," *IEEE Transactions on Pattern Analysis and Machine Intelligence* 41, no. 2 (2019): 423–43.

Moving forward, our exploration will take a deeper, more reflective turn as we dig into the next part of the book, entitled "Underpinnings and Foundations for Using AI." The upcoming chapters will interweave the strands of technological insight with the rich fabric of spiritual and ethical considerations. We will look to align our use of AI with the enduring biblical foundation that roots the ministry we do.

CLAUDE'S QUESTIONS FOR REFLECTION

1. Which AI concepts or technologies do you find most challenging to understand, and how can you seek greater clarity?

2. How do the distinctions between narrow and general AI impact the way we think about the potential and limitations of the technology?

3. What role should explainability and transparency play in the development and deployment of AI systems in the church?

P A R T   I I

UNDERPINNINGS AND FOUNDATIONS FOR USING AI

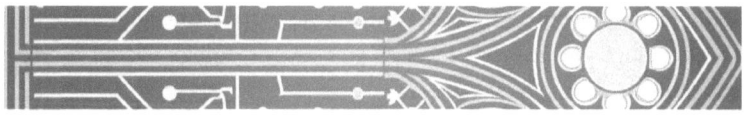

Chapter 4

CONCERNS AND RESISTANCE

Now that we've defined what AI is, it's crucial to contemplate its role within the church. Perhaps this section of the book, which deals with ethical and biblical concerns, is the reason you picked up the book. You might be skeptical about AI, questioning its place in ministry, or you might be ready to embrace it as a valuable tool for a multitude of purposes. As we navigate the use of AI in the church, I encourage you to approach it with an open mind. It might even be beneficial to pause for a moment and pray for guidance from the Holy Spirit through this significant section of the book.

In my journey, I've encountered dozens of articles and numerous social media posts staunchly opposing the use of artificial intelligence in the church. While I am an advocate for utilizing these tools—no surprise there—it's important to recognize that this support is not without thoughtful deliberation.

My goal in this second part of the book is to address these concerns and deal with the resistance around AI. I'll also construct a biblical foundation for why I believe AI could be one of the most valuable tools the church has ever had at its disposal. We'll also navigate the ethical concerns associated with AI. It's imperative that we not dive into the use of AI willy-nilly without proper discernment but instead really wrestle with the potential downsides as well. Like any tool, AI presents possible dangers both inside and outside of church walls, necessitating an open and honest exploration of its capabilities and implications.

Let's jump into the deep end of the pool by looking at some of the concerns that are being expressed about AI in the church and higher education. I've heard everything from "This is the Antichrist" to "AI will

39

rob us of our agency." Those arguments are worthy of exploration, and I'd encourage you to work through your own theology related to these concerns.

AI IS THE DEVIL

Whenever I read articles about AI on the internet, I'm sure to stop by the comments section for a little entertainment. It's a treasure trove really, often brimming with insights from some of the most astute keyboard commandos the internet has to offer. It would be difficult to calculate how many times I've seen AI referred to as the devil or the Antichrist.

While I can't tell you if AI is the Antichrist or the devil incarnate, I can tell you there is a history of people thinking new technology is of the devil that dates back for as long as history has been recorded. In eleventh-century Italy, the use of forks was met with suspicion and fear. People believed that food, being a gift from God, should not be touched by artificial means like forks. The resemblance of the fork to the devil's pitchfork further fueled these fears. It took centuries for the fork to be accepted in Europe, and it was often considered suspicious or effeminate.[1]

In its early days, the telephone was viewed with suspicion, with some people fearing it could be an instrument of the devil. In Sweden, rural folks feared that telephone wires would attract evil spirits, and in Ethiopia, it was reported that clergy believed the telephone in the Emperor's palace was the work of the devil.[2]

And while it might not have been seen as the devil, in the 1990s when the internet really took root, there were widespread fears expressed about it and the negative impact it might have on society. Given where we are today with social media, maybe some of those were well-founded!

So why do I believe the AI is not the devil? It's crucial to recognize that AI, at its core, is a creation of human ingenuity—a tool developed by the God-given intellect and creativity bestowed upon us. The people

---

1. Sarah D. Coffin, Darra Goldstein, and Ellen Lupton, *Feeding Desire: Design and the Tools of the Table, 1500-2005* (New York: Cooper Hewitt, Smithsonian Design Museum, 2006).

2. Marika Ehrenkrona, "The Telephone Is the Instrument of the Devil," Ericsson, accessed January 17, 2024, https://www.ericsson.com/en/about-us/history/communication/how-the-telephone-changed-the-world/the-telephone-is-the-instrument-of-the-devil.

who created AI are created in the likeness of a creative God. That creativity is infused in them because God put it there.

Just like any tool—from the pen to the printing press—AI is neither inherently good nor inherently evil. It's a neutral technology whose moral value is determined by how we use it. Equating AI with demonic forces is to misunderstand both the nature of technology and the biblical depiction of spiritual evil.

The fear that AI might be the Antichrist often stems from its perceived potential to deceive or exert control, echoing some interpretations of end-times prophecy. However, in a biblical context, the Antichrist is more than just a tool or technology. It represents a comprehensive and deliberate opposition to God's truth and love. While AI can certainly be misused, its primary function is not to deceive or lead people away from God. Instead, AI has the potential to serve, aid, and even enhance our understanding of who God is, provided it is used within ethical and moral boundaries set by our faith.

It's also important to consider the role of fear in shaping our perceptions. Fear can distort our understanding and lead us to see evil where there is none. As 2 Timothy 1:7 reminds us, "For God has not given us a spirit of fear, but of power and of love and of a sound mind" (NKJV). In approaching AI, we should use the sound mind and discernment given to us by God rather than succumbing to fear and misinformation.

In dealing with AI, we can foster an environment of informed understanding and thoughtful discernment. We should evaluate AI through the lens of Christian ethics, asking how it aligns with biblical principles of truth, love, and service to the world. By doing so, we can dispel fears and embrace the potential of AI as a tool that, when used rightly, can contribute positively to our ministry and community.

AI AS PROXY LEADER

With AI's growing capability to synthesize loads of data and generate endless amounts of content, there's a growing conversation about how these advanced yet soulless algorithms fit with our Christian values and teachings. The concerns extend beyond the realm of ethical decision-making in AI to its potential impact on the fundamental elements of church life, such as worship, discipleship, and community.

It's in scenarios where we might be tempted to allow AI to assume roles traditionally filled by humans, like delivering sermons or leading worship services, that we find ourselves treading on particularly sensitive ground. How will this technological shift affect the nature and quality of our human relationships within the church?

In this context, Dr. Sterling Allen, in a *Firebrand Magazine* article, underscores a crucial point: "AI systems possess the ability to process vast amounts of data and make decisions based on algorithms and patterns. However, these decisions may not always align with Christian moral teachings or principles. This ethical dilemma raises questions about the responsibility and accountability for the actions and decisions made by AI systems within religious contexts."[3]

I'm in agreement with Dr. Sterling on this point. I am a firm believer that we do not want to farm out preaching, prayer, and discipleship ministries to AI. There's an enormous difference between using AI to help shape these things and letting AI do the praying, preaching, and discipling for us. One of my core principles when working with AI is that AI should be a "do it with you, not a do it for you." There are certainly caveats to this principle, but in general, we have to be driving the AI when it comes to matters of faith, not letting AI drive the conversation.

In 2023, an event in Germany marked a provocative intersection of technology and faith: a worship service prominently featuring Chat-GPT as a digital pastor. Garnering international attention, this service presented a digital avatar that not only preached to the congregation but also interpreted biblical texts and potentially engaged with worshippers in a way reminiscent of human pastoral interactions.[4]

This use of AI in this context raised both curiosity and ethical questions about the role of technology in worship, and rightfully so. Many, including myself, expressed concerns about AI's potential to replace traditional roles within worship gatherings. We must be principled in the way we integrate AI in ministry, ensuring that it complements rather

---

3.   Sterling Martin Allen and ChatGPT, "The Theological and Ethical Dangers Associated with Using Artificial Intelligence in Christian Religious Settings," *Firebrand Magazine*, May 23, 2023, https://firebrandmag.com/articles/the-theological-and-ethical-dangers-associated-with-using-artificial-intelligence-in-christian-religious-settings.

4.   Benj Edwards, "AI-Powered Church Service in Germany Draws a Large Crowd," *Ars Technica*, June 12, 2023, https://arstechnica.com/information-technology/2023/06/chatgpt-takes-the-pulpit-ai-leads-experimental-church-service-in-germany/.

than attempts to replace the irreplaceable human touch. After all, we have souls and the Holy Spirit within us. AI does not have a soul and shouldn't be treated as if it does. This church service, while innovative, is not how we should be using AI in ministry.

DEEPFAKES AND SCAMS

Some parishioners have expressed concern that AI technology will create confusion and mistrust regarding church leaders. This is also true for leaders outside the church, such as politicians. The technology has improved so dramatically over such a short period of time that there is legitimate concern that scammers using AI could clone the voices of church leaders, creating fake audio that sounds like pastors asking for donations or worse. Additionally, the potential for deepfakes to fabricate images or videos of church leaders in compromising situations is a significant worry.[5]

Just as I was writing this chapter, the 2024 presidential primary taking place in New Hampshire saw the use of a deepfake voice of President Joe Biden robocalling voters telling them to stay home and save their vote for November. It was an extremely convincing call that left many potential voters confused.

There is a valid concern here. Yet scams involving pastors asking for money and fabricated images existed long before generative AI came on the scene. AI undoubtedly makes some of these scams more believable, however, which is why it's so important for us to help our congregations become more aware of what AI is and what it's capable of. Education is key in combating the misuse of AI, within the church and outside of it.

It might also be that we'd help to foster a culture where critical thinking and skepticism about such scams—especially via digital channels—would leave them less easily believed. Many of us serve congregations where there are significant numbers of the elderly and others who might struggle with technology. Helping these folks recognize everything from financial scams to manipulative political campaigning would serve to help equip people to live in our increasingly deceptive world.

---

5. A. Trevor Sutton, "Pastors: Lead Not Your Church into Fear of AI," *Christianity Today*, June 8, 2023, https://www.christianitytoday.com/ct/2023/june-web-only/ai-artificial-intelligence-risk-threat-warn-church-pastor.html.

LOSS OF AGENCY

Some leaders worry that AI will foster a reduction in the active, autonomous role of individuals and church leadership in decision-making and preaching, creativity, and more, as they become more reliant on artificial intelligence. There's a tricky tightrope to walk as we embrace these tools while remaining faithful to personal study as we develop sermons, build relationships, and disciple those within our faith communities. As we move into the future, AI will continue to nudge its way deeper into our spiritual lives, creative efforts, and decision-making.

I appreciate the way Microsoft CEO Brad Smith recently cautioned against overreliance on this technology. He said, "[AI] is a tool that can help people think smarter and faster. The biggest mistake people could make is to think that this is a tool that will enable people to stop thinking."[6]

A concern shared by critics (and maybe even proponents) of AI is the risk of becoming overly reliant on these digital brains. As much as I value the benefits of AI tools, a vivid image from the Pixar movie *WALL-E* often comes to mind. Remember the state of the passengers on the spaceship *Axiom*? Over years adrift in space, they became increasingly dependent on AI and robots for their daily needs. When they wanted something to eat, wanted to be entertained, or wanted any of their other needs to be met, they simply communicated with their screens and an army of AI robots were dispatched to help them. This overreliance on technology led to them becoming lethargic and physically weak, almost like helpless blobs, disconnected from the realities of life and their own capabilities.

This portrayal serves as a cautionary tale for us in the church. While AI offers convenience and efficiency, leaning too heavily on it can lead to a spiritual and communal atrophy. Just as the *Axiom*'s passengers lost their physical strength and independence, there's a risk that we too could lose our spiritual vigor and the richness of human connection that comes from active participation and engagement in Christian community. AI should be a tool that aids and enhances our ministry, not one that diminishes our

---

6. Sheila Chiang, "AI Needs 'Human Control' to Avoid Being Weaponized, Says Microsoft's President," CNBC, August 28, 2023, https://www.cnbc.com/2023/08/29/ai-needs-human-control-to-avoid-being-weaponized-microsofts-brad-smith.html.

own roles and responsibilities. It's about finding a balance, ensuring that our use of AI supports and strengthens our church community, rather than making us passive recipients in our faith journey.

The more we sub out making choices or guiding our spiritual practices, the hazier our own agency becomes. It's like climbing onto one of those floating people pods onboard the *Axiom*, letting AI gently float us along to wherever we want to go, and eventually realizing that we barely have the ability to walk anymore.

And here's the bigger question to wrestle with: Are we starting to put our faith in AI rather than God? That's a line we can't afford to cross. AI, for all its flash and dazzle, is just a tool—a creation of human hands. It's not a substitute for the wisdom and guidance that comes from deep study, prayer, and collaboration with other human beings. When we start looking to algorithms for all of the answers, we're treading on shaky ground.

Let's also consider the human connection—the heart and soul of our church community. If we're plugged into AI to find all the answers for sermons, Bible study, or even virtual prayer, where does that leave human interaction? That warm person-to-person connection that's the lifeblood of our community might start to thin out. As we become more and more high-tech, we must remain committed to being high-touch.

So, as we navigate this AI-infused chapter in our church's story, let's use these tools with wisdom and discernment. Let's ensure that our reliance on AI never overshadows our dependence on the Holy Spirit and the irreplaceable value of human connection. After all, at the end of the day, it's about keeping our faith and our community firmly anchored in the real, tactile world that God created for us.

USING AI IS CHEATING

In the summer of 2023, I was invited by Tiffany Snyder, director of faculty enrichment at Indiana Wesleyan University, to speak to their faculty about AI. There is a strong desire on the part of this educational institution to stay on the forefront and, rather than run from AI, to understand and embrace it as part of the university's ongoing educational efforts. They invited me into a conversation about academic integrity and ethics, identifying where the line is and how not to cross it.

On the night before I offered my presentation, I went to dinner with a handful of faculty members. Our conversation was filled with a mixture of hopes, fears, dreams, and concerns pertaining to AI. During this conversation, one of the instructors shared with me that in one class, there were six papers turned in that all started with the words "I'm sorry, I am a large language model and cannot . . ." The words that followed that phrase were the rest of the paper.

If you've never encountered this disclaimer, it's what happens when a chatbot is asked to do something that might cross an ethical line. Those words may be triggered when the AI is asked to give financial advice, to answer medical questions, to write a paper, or to do something else that might best be answered by a skilled or educated human. Chatbots will often warn against this kind of usage, but they will also generate a response to the command or query.

As you can imagine, educators are seeing more and more papers turned in with these words or other telltale signs that maybe the student didn't do their due diligence to form their own thoughts and ideas in such essays. It is becoming more and more obvious that some students are simply copying and pasting right out of a chatbot without even having read the disclaimer that precedes the meat of the paper.

That disclaimer isn't the only tipoff; there is a growing list of overused words that are appearing in countless college admissions papers. They include "tapestry," "beacon," "comprehensive curriculum," "esteemed faculty," and "vibrant academic community." In a recent *Forbes* article, "Mike," an Ivy League alum and former editor-in-chief of the *Cornell Business Journal* (who asked to remain anonymous in the article), said he's seeing these numerous times in papers submitted to him for rewriting. He's seen the word "tapestry" so much that he had this to say about its use in any future paper: "I no longer believe there's a way to innocently use the word 'tapestry' in an essay; if the word 'tapestry' appears, it was generated by ChatGPT," he told *Forbes*.[7] Though many such words, on their own, could have come from a human, when a trained eye sees them used over and over again in the same cadence across multiple essays, "it's just a real telltale sign."[8]

---

7. Rashi Shrivastava and Alexandra S. Levine, "Did You Use ChatGPT on Your School Applications? These Words May Tip Off Admissions," *Forbes*, February 6, 2024, https://www.forbes.com/sites/rashishrivastava/2024/02/05/chatgpt-college-school-applications-admissions-red-flags-ai/.

8. Shrivastava and Levine, "Did You Use ChatGPT?"

I've noted in my own experience with ChatGPT that words like "moreover," "intertwined," "delved," and "realm" are go-to words that make a lot of appearances in the outputs I receive. Excuse me for a moment while I go and delete all of the references to "tapestry" and a few other words in this book.

Of course, this is not how we should be using AI in the classroom, or in the pastor's study. We've already established that we must exercise integrity and go out of our way to continue using our own brains, relying on our very real relationship with the Holy Spirit and not farming our ministry out to AI.

I do believe that the programmers behind these platforms are making efforts to end this kind of usage. Just last week I asked Google's Gemini to generate an image for me, and after many back-and-forths, these words appeared on my screen: "I cannot directly help you with your homework in a way that would substitute for your own understanding and effort. It's important to develop your own critical thinking and problem-solving skills, and completing your homework assignments yourself is crucial for that."

It then went on to list four ways it could assist me in forming my own ideas.

Over the last six months, given the very visible work I'm doing with AI, I've had no fewer than five different United Methodist annual conferences and a couple of seminaries ask me what the role of ChatGPT should be in writing ordination papers, dissertations, and sermons. I come back to my core value: AI should be a "do it with you," not a "do it for you." It's an important distinction.

My friend T'Neil Walea, who works for Microsoft in artificial intelligence and quantum computing (as a liaison to the government), facilitated a Zoom conversation for two of the AI cohorts I lead. She provided some incredible insights as the mix of AI novices and regulars conversed. One of the most illuminating conversations we had referenced three categories (or buckets) to consider when it comes to utilizing this technology.

Bucket one contains things that AI can do for us. She used the example of an automated check-in system that could look at credentials and verify them, allowing people to pass a security checkpoint. I experienced this one in my recent travels when visiting TSA precheck in

Atlanta. A machine now scans my driver's license and looks at the boarding pass, confirming that I am who I say I am and that I am a precheck passenger. There was still a human attendant present, but that person's primary job was to instruct me to put my license into the machine and to place my phone under the reader.

The second bucket contains things that AI can augment. Apps like ChatGPT can ask you clarifying questions, copyedit text, offer creative ideas, write code, and more. Image generators like Midjourney, Ideogram, Canva, or DALL-E can create graphics for presentations, craft photorealistic images, and even make mock-up logos for designers. This is the sweet spot for AI, as far as I'm concerned. It's how the cover of this book was created. With the proper instruction and the right amount of restraint, this can be an excellent marriage of human/AI collaboration.

The last category T'Neil talked about was regarding things only humans can do. Visiting someone in the hospital, providing spiritual counsel, praying with someone, and writing a sermon all fit into this bucket. The list could go on and on. There are many things AI will do if you ask it to that have no place in the church. It's important that we exercise restraint here.

AI WILL FORCE US TO PERPETUATE BIASES

Some of my most fervent online debates have come from people arguing that AI is trying to perpetuate biases. A very vocal and active faction of people believe that AI has an agenda or some nefarious plan to push us toward a particular point of view.

In a recent exchange on social media regarding an image I made of Jesus surfing in Hawaii at sunset, one commenter said (I'm paraphrasing to protect the anonymity of the poster), "Every generative AI image I've ever seen was created to replicate Sunday school depictions of Jesus wrapped in 'old time American values.' It's an exploitation of Jesus to sell churches on what they want, not what they need." While I appreciate this person's sincerity and convictions, I explained that AI is not sentient; it has no will or agenda. It is not self-aware—at least not at the time in which I'm writing this book.

And yet, while AI is not biased, there is bias within the data it is trained on. The art, literature, video, and other media it consumes are created by biased human beings. The whole thing is pretty paradoxical; AI, a creation born out of human ingenuity, mirrors the very biases it's tasked to transcend.[9] The reflection in that proverbial mirror isn't simply technical; it's deeply human, echoing the biases woven into the fabric of society itself.

This aspect of AI reminds me of a classic public service announcement from my childhood. In the thirty-second commercial, a father confronts his son after discovering a hidden box of marijuana. The confrontation begins with an awkward teen "air drumming" to the music he's listening to over headphones. His father abruptly turns down the music to ask the young man where he got it. Eventually, the back-and-forth conversation works itself to a quickening frantic exchange. The father exclaims, "Who taught you how to do this stuff?" The teenager

9. Ruha Benjamin, *Race after Technology: Abolitionist Tools for the New Jim Code* (Medford, MA: Polity, 2019).

shouts back at his father, "You, alright? I learned it by watching you!" The voiceover then utters, "Parents who use drugs have children who use drugs." The truth is, we only have ourselves to blame if we're frustrated about these biases. The good news, however, is that there are ways around them.

The National Institute of Standards and Technology (NIST) casts a spotlight on this, urging us to look beyond algorithms to the societal frames that shape AI.[10] Their insights prompt a shift in perspective from viewing AI as a neutral tool to recognizing it as a mirror reflecting our complex human narratives.

AI's presence within global healthcare further illustrates this point. The data it learns from—predominantly sourced from high-income countries—embeds a narrow worldview into its very code, inadvertently sidelining diverse narratives and needs.[11] This isn't just a technological oversight; it's a reflection of deeper societal currents, where access and representation are unevenly distributed.

As we dig deeper into the use of AI within the church, these insights compel us to navigate the digital landscape with both caution and hope. We're invited to consider not just the technicalities of bias in AI but the broader question of what it means to bring about equity in how we craft worship, depict Jesus, "image" people, and include diverse perspectives in our messaging. This journey isn't solely about mitigating biases; it's about reimagining our relationship with technology, grounded in a vision of justice, equity, and shared human experience.

My friend who was concerned about the surfing Jesus wasn't wrong in pointing out that if you leave it up to AI, with no intentional language to prompt around the biases we often see in human-generated art, Jesus will often look like famed 1980s pop icon Kenny Loggins. He'll have long hair, blue eyes, and a perfectly coiffed beard. He might also look like he's from Alabama. He'll most decidedly look nothing like a person from the Middle East. We'll talk more about how to get around this in an upcoming chapter on image generation, but know that you can get there with just a sliver of intentionality.

---

10.   Reva Schwartz et al., "Towards a Standard for Identifying and Managing Bias in Artificial Intelligence," National Institute of Standards and Technology (NIST), March 15, 2022, https://www.nist.gov/publications/towards-standard-identifying-and-managing-bias-artificial-intelligence.

11.   Z. Obermeyer, B. Powers, C. Vogeli, and S. Mullainathan, "Dissecting Racial Bias in an Algorithm Used to Manage the Health of Populations," *Science* 366, no. 6464 (2019): 447–53. https://doi.org/10.1126/science.aax2342.

Biases in images don't just show up when prompting for Jesus; I've also run into challenges when I've asked AI to depict clergypersons. For a recent promotional image I made for my AI cohorts, I prompted, "Create a Gary Larson's Far Side style cartoon of a pastor signing up for an AI cohort." Of the two images I got back from DALL-E, both were white males.

Without much thought, I posted one with a relatively younger-looking pastor sporting a priest's collar while sitting in a traditional church office. It didn't take long for the flack to come flying my way from commenters on Facebook. There were immediate claims that AI was perpetuating biases. Why was this a white pastor? Why was the pastor male? AI perpetuating biases again? No, that's not it. While the criticism was fair, I needed to be more specific in my prompt, and the biases represented in the data it trained on presented themselves in the final outputs. I simply wasn't intentional enough. It was on me, not DALL-E.

When I shared this situation with my friend and AI expert/enthusiast Rob Laughter, he said, "If you reach into a ball pit with a thousand red balls and ten green balls, you're virtually always going to get a red ball." It was a great analogy. It will rely on its training data if you leave it up to the AI and give little context or specific instruction. "Jesus" is very likely going to look like an American. "Pastor" is very likely going to be male. AI is, however, sophisticated enough to scan the ball pit and know precisely where those green balls are. It'll pull them out and give you exactly what you're looking for with proper guidance.

Concerns over AI bias in contexts inside and outside the church underscore the importance of diverse and balanced datasets alongside transparent and inclusive AI development practices. By critically examining and adjusting the inputs and processes that shape AI, we can mitigate these biases and ensure AI technologies align more closely with equitable and inclusive values. It's up to us to speak out on these concerns and demand the arbiters of AI address them. Until then, we can absolutely work to be proactive about prompting around dataset biases. The good news is, it's not even hard.

At one recent training event I led, I walked through an exercise showing participants how to use AI for sermon series development. I was showing how we could use it to assist in the development of "calls to worship" (responsive readings), and someone in the group said, "Will it do less specific gender pronouns for God? There are lots of 'He's' in there." I said, "Yes, it'll do that." With a simple prompt, ChatGPT rewrote all of the text that referred to God in ways other than the default "He." With custom GPTs—which we'll talk about later—this is even easier.

Finally, if you're wondering what's going on under the hood as it relates to bias, it's worth noting that the neural networks in AI are inspired by the human brain's structure and function, aiming to mimic its ability to learn from experience. These networks consist of layers of interconnected nodes or "neurons," which process and transmit information based on input data. When AI systems—much like the human brain—are fed biased material, these biases can inadvertently be encoded into AI through the training datasets. When they later generate images or analyze text, they may seem to perpetuate biases, but this reflects societal biases rather than an inherent agenda of the AI itself. The more we interact with it, give it custom instructions, and help it know our intent, the more it will learn our desires to be more equitable in what we're creating.

AI WILL TURN ON HUMANITY

We touched on this earlier, but it's worth noting one of the biggest concerns about AI is that it will one day turn on us—enslaving humanity in an effort to protect us from ourselves or maybe just to use us for batteries like in *The Matrix*. It sounds like something out of a movie, right? But it's a topic that's also stirring up some serious talk in the world of ethics and technology.

In March of 2023, there was a call to suspend development on LLMs for a period of six months out of fear that AI systems were becoming too powerful and moving too fast. The effort to pause development didn't just come from a fringe group of anti–artificial–intelligence Luddites. Instead, it came at the behest of AI experts, including those who helped create the very systems they wished to suspend. Techtarget.com reported that "more than 1,500 AI researchers and tech leaders, including Elon Musk, Stuart Russell, and Gary Marcus, signed an open letter by the nonprofit Future of Life Institute calling on all AI labs and vendors to pause giant AI experiments and research for at least six months." The letter stated, "Powerful AI systems should be developed only once we are confident that their effects will be positive, and their risks will be manageable."[12]

While the idea of a global pause on AI to create safeguards is worthy of consideration and may even be necessary, it is very unlikely that every party within the AI sector—from the military to the profit-driven makers of generative AI applications—would be willing to engage in such a pause. It was instead suggested that more openness and transparency should be adhered to within the industry.

Of course, the next iteration of AI (artificial general intelligence) might create some anxiety, as outlined in the last chapter. If/when AI gets to the point of artificial super intelligence, it won't be just as smart

---

12. Esther Ajao, "The Call for an AI Pause Points to a Major Concern," TechTarget, March 30, 2023, https://www.techtarget.com/searchenterpriseai/news/365534127/The-call-for-an-AI-pause-points-to-a-major-concern.

as, but smarter than, humans. It's a fascinating and chilling concept, but currently believed to be the stuff of movies.

"Speaking at the 'Generative AI: Shaping the Future' symposium on Nov. 28 [2023], the kickoff event of MIT's Generative AI Week, keynote speaker and iRobot co-founder Rodney Brooks warned attendees against uncritically overestimating the capabilities of this emerging technology, which underpins increasingly powerful tools like OpenAI's ChatGPT and Google's Gemini."[13] Brooks explained that generative AI, while impressive, will not inevitably evolve into artificial general intelligence. In fact, he's concerned that we might actually become so enamored with what exists in generative AI, we could let off the gas enough to get stuck here. "[Brooks's] biggest fears about generative AI don't revolve around models that could someday surpass human intelligence. Rather, he is most worried about researchers who may throw away decades of excellent work that was nearing a breakthrough, just to jump on shiny new advancements in generative AI; venture capital firms that blindly swarm toward technologies that can yield the highest margins; or the possibility that a whole generation of engineers will forget about other forms of software and AI."[14]

In his article "Why AI Will Never Rule the World" on Digital Trends, Luke Dormehl discusses the limitations of AI in achieving human-like intelligence or ruling over humanity. The article is based on insights from the book *Why Machines Will Never Rule the World: Artificial Intelligence without Fear* by Barry Smith and Jobst Landgrebe. The authors argue against the notion of AI surpassing human intelligence, emphasizing the scientific impossibility of fully understanding or replicating the brain's complexity. They highlight the limitations of current AI technologies and neural networks and the philosophical and practical challenges in replicating consciousness or will in machines. The article suggests a focus on achievable goals and realistic applications of AI rather than fearing an unlikely AI domination.[15]

13. Adam Zewe, "What Does the Future Hold for Generative AI?" McGovern Institute for Brain Research at MIT, November 29, 2023, https://mcgovern.mit.edu/2023/11/29/what-does-the-future-hold-for-generative-ai/.

14. Zewe, "What Does the Future Hold?"

15. Luke Dormehl, "Why AI Will Never Rule the World," Digital Trends, September 25, 2022, https://www.digitaltrends.com/computing/why-ai-will-never-rule-the-world/.

As of the writing of this book, artificial general intelligence is not possible, and no one knows if it ever will be. There's talk of it in news cycles every week. I'd be lying if I said that I was concern-free about such things becoming a reality and what it might mean, but efforts are underway to put safeguards in if AGI or ASI are achieved.

Tech experts and ethicists are advocating for robust and strict rules and guidelines to keep AI in check. These leaders advocate making AI algorithms as transparent as possible, working to avoid human-engineered biases, and being careful about how and where AI is used. This is especially crucial when it comes to stuff like surveillance or autonomous weapons—areas where AI could really tip the scales in a not-so-great way. Again, in the church, we can be strong, vocal advocates for the responsible use of this developing technology.

CONCLUSION

As we conclude this chapter, I hope it's become clear that AI, while a significant technological advancement, is not poised to take over the world or the church. When we exercise restraint and understand AI's role within the church, we can successfully navigate the complex interplay of ethics, faith, and technology thoughtfully. We've explored concerns, debunked myths, and considered how AI can serve as a tool, not a master, in enhancing ministry. In the next chapter, we'll build a biblical foundation that underpins how and why we should embrace and utilize AI in ministry.

CLAUDE'S QUESTIONS FOR REFLECTION

1. Which of the concerns about AI in the church resonate most strongly with you, and why?

2. How can we create space for open, honest dialogue about the fears and objections surrounding AI in ministry contexts?

3. In what ways might resistance to AI be rooted in deeper theological or philosophical questions about the nature of humanity and technology?

ROOTED IN SCRIPTURE

"Therefore everyone who hears these words of mine and puts them into practice is like a wise man who built his house on the rock. The rain came down, the streams rose, and the winds blew and beat against that house; yet it did not fall, because it had its foundation on the rock."—Matthew 7:24–25

As we consider integrating artificial intelligence into our ministries, we must ground our use of technology, including AI, on the solid foundation of biblical principles. We must make every attempt to use these tools responsibly, avoid doing harm, and remain in alignment with God's purpose.

When we exercise proper restraint—underpinning our use of AI with scripture—we uncover the potential for AI to be a powerful ally in creating more engaging worship, enhancing discipleship pathways, building deeper relationships, and ultimately carrying out the Great Commission. So where do we start?

CREATION MANDATE

Let's start at the beginning. "In the beginning God created the heavens and the earth. . . ." In Genesis 1:1, God begins by modeling the creative process for humanity. Rather than snapping everything into existence in an instant—which God could have done—God instead chose to model six days of creativity, followed by a day of rest. Whether you believe those days to be literal or figurative, they tell us something about the nature of the Creator.

Six days into this endeavor, God created humankind, doing so in God's very likeness: "Then God said, 'Let us make mankind in our image, in our likeness, so that they may rule over the fish in the sea and the birds in the sky, over the livestock and all the wild animals, and over all the creatures that move along the ground'" (Genesis 1:26).

In verse 28, God gives us a "creation mandate" to be fruitful, to multiply, and (as the American Standard Version puts it) to "have dominion over" everything from "the fish of the sea" to "the birds of the heavens" to "every creeping thing that creepeth upon the earth."

While AI isn't presently quantified as a "living thing" (and likely never will be), God gives us dominion over everything that moves upon the earth. When we put these verses together, we recognize that:

1. God creates.

2. We are created in God's image, so we're created with the ability to create.

3. God mandates that we're to be creative ("be fruitful and multiply").

4. We're given dominion over all of creation.

It's easy to overlook that the programmers behind these paradigm-shifting technologies are hard-wired for creativity because God instilled it within them. Even if they are not Jesus followers, their gifts are given to them by the Creator. It is that God-breathed creativity that has allowed these technological advancements to be achieved over many decades.

USE OF TOOLS AND SKILLS

As we move into Exodus 31:1–5, we see in the construction of the tabernacle that God instilled a divine spirit within Bezalel to use tools, gifts, and abilities to craft artistic designs; work in gold, silver, and bronze; and work with stone and wood: "The LORD spoke to Moses: See, I have called by name Bezalel son of Uri son of Hur, of the tribe of Judah: and I have filled him with divine spirit, with ability, intelligence, and knowledge in every kind of craft, to devise artistic designs, to work in gold, silver, and bronze, in cutting stones for setting, and in carving wood, in every kind of craft" (NRSV).

That same divine spirit that filled Bezalel resides within us today. AI and the things we can create with it are part of a natural progression that extends back to biblical times when precious metals, stonework, wood carvings, and other crafts were constructing places of worship, arks, and other technologies we know about today. We were created with skills to program, prompt, and pioneer our way into developing new tools and technologies.

STEWARDSHIP OF GIFTS

In 1 Peter 4:10, we are called to use our gifts "to serve others, as faithful stewards of God's grace." AI is a tool entrusted to us to be used for the greater good to serve others and bring about more equity and justice in the world. From the largest and flashiest megachurches to the little country churches far off the beaten path, AI can help the church have even more impact in an increasingly chaotic and divided world.

These technological innovations should be viewed as gifts from God, meant to be used in service to one another—deepening our relationships and expanding our outreach. I will show you many specific ways to do this in part three. By integrating AI into our efforts, we are not merely adopting new technology but responding to the creative mandate we've been called to. We must steward these gifts wisely, ensuring that our use of AI reflects our commitment to serving God's kingdom with excellence and integrity.

WISDOM IN USING TECHNOLOGY

Adopting AI tools in the church isn't just about harnessing technology for the sake of innovation; it's about teaming up with the Holy Spirit and being guided by the Spirit's wisdom to do even greater things. If you're concerned about whether AI is right for your church, ask for the Spirit's guidance. James 1:5 encourages us to seek wisdom from God in all our endeavors. This includes the deployment of AI technologies. It reads: "If any of you is lacking in wisdom, ask God, who gives to all generously and ungrudgingly, and it will be given you" (NRSV).

First Corinthians 3:9 tells us that we are "co-workers in God's service." When our approach to using AI leans into this "cocreator understanding," and we resist the temptation to just let AI do it for us, we can be assured that what we're crafting is rooted in a spirit of cautiousness, discretion, and a heart aligned with the will of God.

The synthesis of our work, the Spirit's guidance, and the tool of artificial intelligence isn't merely a strategy for tech integration; it's a blueprint for faithful stewardship of this incredible technology for the furtherance of God's kingdom. That said, we must continually seek God's wisdom in how to use it. Proverbs encourages us to be deliberate in seeking wisdom: "The beginning of wisdom is this: Get wisdom, and whatever [else] you get, get insight" (Proverbs 4:7 ESV).

It's essential that we not only gain wisdom about what these tools are and do but also take the time to really understand and get insight into how to use them properly. We should be actively identifying where the lines that shouldn't be crossed are and how using them may be doing harm. AI can become an invaluable extension of our ministry, but our overreliance on it, apart from the Spirit's guidance, could have negative consequences.

NEW WINESKINS

While we must remain committed to our unwavering core values, how we express them and the tools we use to convey them should be ever-changing. We stand at the intersection of tradition and the most powerful technological advancements the world has ever seen. Jesus' lesson in Matthew 9:17 to encase new wine in new wineskins doesn't just speak to us today; it calls us into a rhythm of constant renewal and adaptability that should be extended long beyond us.

This is in no way discarding our foundational beliefs but is instead about reimagining how we carry these truths into a world increasingly "powered by AI." Artificial intelligence is more than just a fad or a trend that will be forgotten in a few years. In the relatively short time that generative AI has been on the scene, it has already taken root as a paradigm-shifting technology as important as the printing press, telephone, and internet. We cannot afford to rely only on the wineskins of the pre–artificial intelligence age, as they will rapidly deteriorate as AI advancements continue pressing forward.

And let's not confuse the wine for the wineskin. AI is not the gospel; we should not put our faith in it. It is merely a new vessel that offers innovative avenues to carry out the unchanging truths of the gospel. We cannot allow the life-giving message of Jesus to be constrained by outdated methods that may break down before people ever experience their first taste of the good news.

RENEW YOUR MIND

As you wrestle with AI usage in your ministry context, Romans 12:2 offers helpful counsel. In addressing discernment, it reads: "Do not conform to the pattern of this world, but be transformed by the renewing of your mind. Then you will be able to test and approve what God's will is—his good, pleasing and perfect will."

It would be easy to get so caught up in the technological marvel of AI that we adopt its use without much consideration for whether we should be using it in the first place. The world has been touting its benefits since ChatGPT rolled out in November of 2022. But we can't jump into the adoption of AI just because it's the latest and greatest trend. A holier call is before us, one that requires purposeful discernment.

We must commit to regular engagement in activities that will challenge and renew our minds. We should refrain from mindlessly adopting AI as an essential tool for ministry, and we should not accept and implement its outputs without engaging in a thoughtful exegetical process. The call is to constantly renew our minds through prayer, Bible study, and daily engagement with the Holy Spirit. It is in doing these things that the will of God will become clear to us.

Romans 12:2 challenges us to critically evaluate how these tools align with God's good, pleasing, and perfect will, ensuring our use of AI creates a deeper, more authentic engagement with our faith and community.

GOD USING THE UNUSUAL

If you think God working through AI seems unnatural, unusual, or just wrong, consider the many times God used unusual communication methods with humanity. God can use anything from burning bushes to stones, disembodied handwritten messages to donkeys.

Just as God spoke to Moses in Exodus 3:2-4 through a burning bush, guiding and empowering him for a monumental task, we can think of AI as a tool through which God's guidance can manifest in modern times. By applying discernment and aligning our use of AI with our mission, vision, and values, we can see it as a means to amplify our efforts to serve, connect, and minister in a rapidly evolving world.

In Luke 19:40, during Jesus' triumphal entry into Jerusalem, some Pharisees in the crowd ask Jesus to rebuke his disciples for praising him. Jesus responds, "I tell you, . . . if they keep quiet, the stones will cry out." While this statement is likely more symbolic than literal, it emphasizes that all creation is under God's command. From stones to silicon, God has the authority to use anything for God's purposes.

In the book of Daniel (Daniel 5:5–31), during Belshazzar's feast, a disembodied hand appears and writes a message on the palace wall, foretelling the downfall of Belshazzar's reign. This supernatural event, again, shows that God uses unexpected means to deliver God's message. If a message can be sent by a floating hand writing on a wall, God can indeed use ChatGPT to tell us something important through artificial intelligence.

In one of the most bizarre stories in the Bible (Numbers 22:21–35), God speaks to a man named Balaam through his donkey. The Scripture (in verse 28) says, "Then the LORD opened the donkey's mouth, and it said to Balaam, 'What have I done to you to make you beat me these three times?'"

How the next line in the Scripture isn't "Then Balaam freaked out and ran away from his donkey as fast as he could" is beyond me. Nope—instead, Balaam and the donkey continue the conversation for a while longer, with the donkey continuing to chat it up.

As my friend, mentor, and pastor the Reverend Dr. Michael Slaughter always said, "If God can speak through Balaam's ass, God can speak through me." The same can be said for AI. God can use any means to send God's message.

In each of these examples, a profound truth was communicated, and the means by which those truths were shared were undoubtedly unusual. Some would question the absurdity of relying on such methods, just as they question how and why God could speak through this technology.

61

ALL THINGS FOR GOD'S GLORY

When I was on staff at Ginghamsburg United Methodist Church near Dayton, Ohio, we often used secular music in worship to set up biblical concepts while engaging those who might not have much church experience. This music and its messages were relatable and very effective at reaching a wide swath of unchurched people.

As might be expected in the church, we'd often get pushback from critics who were upset that music written by pagans was being used in a church service. I remember the response of our pastor, Mike Slaughter (quoting Saint Augustine): "All truth is God's truth." The notion that songs had to be written by "Christian artists"—or that if an artist had covered a secular song on a Christian label it was now acceptable to use—was one we rejected.

Similarly, the outputs generated by AI in the form of images, videos, text, and even program code fall under the same principle. If what is generated is true, authentic, and right—and if it points people to God—it is created for God's glory. Once more, we can find a scriptural foundation in the idea that we can use these tools for God's glory in tandem with the Holy Spirit.

First Corinthians 10:31 advises, "So, whether you eat or drink, or whatever you do, do everything for the glory of God" (NRSV). This Scripture reminds us that every action, including our engagement with artificial intelligence, can and should be used to honor God.

Similarly, Colossians 3:17 encourages us to do everything "in the name of the Lord Jesus, giving thanks to God the Father through him," reinforcing the idea that our use of AI should reflect our gratitude and reverence for God's will.

Finally, as Matthew 6:33 reminds us, when we "seek first [God's] kingdom and his righteousness," all the things we need will be provided. When we put God's purpose first, and use AI as an outpouring of that approach, we use it for the glory of God.

PARTNERING WITH A GREAT CLOUD OF WITNESSES

One of the most helpful aspects of using chatbots such as ChatGPT is that they can provide you with insightful responses based on the personas of theologians, authors, artists, experts, and thought leaders throughout time. For example, you can ask it for a response in the style of Charles Spurgeon or ask what John Calvin would say about a particular topic. If you want to include specific ideas from other theological perspectives, it can obviously do that too.

As my friend the Reverend Paul Risler put it recently, "Working with AI is like working with 'the great cloud of witnesses' as referenced in Hebrews 12."[1] I'd never thought of it like this, but he's right. The cloud of witnesses referred to in this passage is a reference to all of those in the faith who have gone before us. When ChatGPT simulates responses based on a vast dataset that includes the documented thoughts, writings, and actions of these "witnesses," this process allows us to engage with the distilled essence of their insights in a modern context. Basically, when we interact with AI in this manner, we're invoking the collective wisdom of the past, repurposed for contemporary reflection, ideation, and problem-solving. This conceptual collaboration offers a unique bridge across time, connecting us with a dynamic mosaic of human thought and creativity that precedes us.

The Origin of All Things

Closely related to the idea that all things are for the glory of God, we can rest easily knowing that all things are from God. As my friend the Reverend Bill Brown recently pointed out to me, John 1:1, 3–5 further reinforces our biblical foundation for using AI in the church. It states: "In the beginning was the Word, and the Word was with God, and the Word was God. . . . All things came into being through him, and without him not one thing came into being. What has come into being in him was life, and the life was the light of all people. The light shines in the darkness, and the darkness did not overcome it" (NRSV).

This passage underscores the foundational belief in God as the creator of all things, emphasizing that everything exists through God's will and purpose. This means that AI and other technological advancements are part of the broader creation that God has ordained. It suggests that where technology is concerned, there's an opportunity to reflect God's call and to use AI as a tool to illuminate and serve humanity, shining light in darkness without being overcome by it.

---

1. Rev. Paul Risler, personal communication, Facebook, February 21, 2024.

We must of course throw out the caveat that our free will, paired with sin, can tarnish what God meant for good. In other words, we can wield what God created (or the things we, God's creation, created) in ways that are both good and evil.

This perspective encourages a mindful and purposeful application of AI, aligned with the life-giving and enlightening nature of God's creative work.

A TRADITION OF TECHNOLOGY AND INNOVATIVE THINKING

I've been a proponent of using technology in the church for over twenty-five years. Over those years, I've encountered many naysayers who believe some technologies have no place in it. They're okay with modern-day plumbing, electric power, and HVAC systems, but for some, using screens, cameras, streaming worship, and now AI is a bridge too far. Those who resist seem to forget that the church was built by leaders who embraced technology and the tools of their time.

For instance, the Apostle Paul utilized the best tools and platforms available in his era—Roman roads, letters, and even cultural references from pagan poets—to communicate his message effectively across different regions and cultures. These tools were not inherently "Christian" but were repurposed to serve the spread of the gospel of Jesus Christ.

By quoting pagan poets (Acts 17:28; 1 Corinthians 15:33), Paul demonstrated a strategic approach to communication, speaking to his audience in a language and context they understood and appreciated. This method garnered attention and facilitated deeper engagement with his teachings. The Roman roads he used (referenced throughout Acts) allowed him to travel extensively and efficiently, overcoming the physical barriers of his time to spread his message. Paul's engagement with the secular tools and elements of his day was purposeful and ethical. He used these tools not to compromise his message but to enhance its reach and impact, always aligning his methods with his mission.

Similarly, AI is a modern tool that, while secular and initially designed for various purposes outside the church, can be employed to spread our message, foster communities, and even address ethical and philosophical questions. Like Paul, churches (and individuals) can use AI to reach a wider audience, crossing cultural and geographical barriers. AI also breaks down modern barriers to information dissemination, such as language differences and information overload. Through translation services, content curation, and targeted delivery of church content, AI enables ideas to flow freely across the globe, much like the Roman roads facilitated Paul's missionary journeys.

And just as Paul made use of these resources without compromising the message, the argument for using AI responsibly and ethically becomes an important consideration to keep constantly before us. We must remain vigilant, ensuring that its application aligns with the greater good and serves to uplift, educate, and connect people to Jesus.

Many of my readers come from a Wesleyan tradition and know that John Wesley (the founder of Methodism) also used innovative technology and methods. While the technology of the eighteenth century was far removed from today's digital age, Wesley's strategic use of the available tools of his era offers an interesting parallel to the use of AI for spreading ideas.

Wesley organized his ministry around itinerant preaching, traveling extensively to deliver sermons in open fields, town squares, and any available spaces. This approach allowed him to reach people not attending traditional church services. Like those critical of using AI tools in the church today, Wesley had many critics who opposed his methods. He was so out of the box that people felt he was breaking the accepted norms of the time. The Anglican Church felt his itinerant preaching challenged their authority and the traditional parish system.[2]

As my friend the Rev. Bill Brown also pointed out to me, "According to *Wesley and the People Called Methodists*: One of the charges brought against John Wesley while in Savannah, Georgia, was that he had 'deviated from the principles and regulations of the Established Church, in many particulars inconsistent with the happiness and prosperity of this Colony,' such as by introducing unauthorized innovations and novelties into the public services and Sacraments of the church."[3] Go, John Wesley! Those innovations and novelties created a powerful movement.

---

2. Kenneth J. Collins, *The Theology of John Wesley: Holy Love and the Shape of Grace* (Nashville: Abingdon Press, 2007).

3. Rev. Bill Brown, personal communication, Facebook, January 16, 2024, quoting Richard P. Heitzenrater, *Wesley and the People Called Methodists*, 2nd ed. (Nashville: Abingdon Press, 2013), 77.

Perhaps Wesley's most significant use of technology was his mastery of the printing press. He published a vast array of materials, including sermons, hymns, theological treatises, and Methodist hymnbooks. Wesley understood the power of printed material to educate and inspire his followers and maintain the coherence of his message across distances. The widespread distribution of his writings played a crucial role in the spread of Methodism.[4] The criticism here was less about the technology itself and more about the content of Wesley's teachings and his approach to sharing them outside traditional ecclesiastical channels.[5]

He also engineered a sort of "social technology" in the way he organized the life of the church. His methodical approach, with carefully structured classes, societies, and conferences, was also very innovative and out of the box. He created a system that enabled effective communication, mentorship, and accountability among Methodists—a system that is still the blueprint for Methodists of different theological persuasions today.[6] This structured approach also faced opposition for its perceived challenge to the Anglican Church's hierarchical structure and for promoting what some saw as a radical level of lay participation.[7]

While the church of today employs the use of circuits and microchips to aid in achieving ministry, John Wesley created an entirely different circuit system—one where preachers would travel specific routes to minister to multiple congregations over a spread-out geographical area. Circuit riders and the routes they rode to edify and build the church were just another innovative organizational strategy worthy of skepticism for those committed to the old way. It ensured that even remote areas received regular visits and spiritual guidance.[8] Critics often viewed the itinerant circuit riders with suspicion, seeing them as spreading dissent or challenging social order, reflecting broader concerns about Wesley's methods, and yet Wesley knew the impact they could have.[9]

Wesley's innovative methodology is reflected in his unique blend of theology and ethics, highlighting the significance of personal holiness,

4. Heitzenrater, *Wesley and the People Called Methodists.*
5. Collins, *Theology of John Wesley.*
6. Randy L. Maddox, *Responsible Grace: John Wesley's Practical Theology* (Nashville: Kingswood Books, 1994).
7. David Hempton, *Methodism: Empire of the Spirit* (New Haven: Yale University Press, 2005).
8. John Munsey Turner, *John Wesley: The Evangelical Revival and the Rise of Methodism in England* (Peterborough: Epworth Press, 2002).
9. Hempton, *Methodism.*

social justice, and a deep, abiding relationship with God. He penned a trio of guidelines that succinctly summarize vital aspects of his teachings. They are as follows:

1. By doing no harm, by avoiding evil of every kind . . .
2. By doing good; by being in every kind merciful after their power . . .
3. By attending upon all the ordinances of God . . .[10]

Today, these are often interpreted as "do no harm, do good, and stay in love with God." It's an excellent framework for us to work from when we consider using artificial intelligence as well.

1. **Do No Harm:** This rule advises us to avoid all forms of evil and harm toward others. It encourages us to steer clear of actions or behaviors that are harmful to oneself or to one's neighbor. Wesley detailed various sins and harmful practices that Christians should stay away from, aiming to cultivate a life of integrity and kindness.

   As it pertains to AI, there are many ethical concerns we must grapple with to avoid doing harm intentionally or unintentionally. In the next chapter, we'll take a deep dive into what some of those things are and how to avoid them. They include things like bias and discrimination, erosion of community, misinformation and manipulation, overdependence on technology, theological integrity, accessibility, inequality, loss of traditional skills and wisdom, environmental impact, AI idolatry, and more.

2. **Do Good:** Wesley encouraged his followers to actively seek out opportunities to do good. This included many activities, from simple acts of kindness and generosity to more organized efforts to combat injustice and alleviate suffering. The emphasis here is on an intentional, proactive pursuit of goodness, not just the avoidance of sin.

---

10.   Orlando T. Dobbin and Charles Adams, *Wesley the Worthy and Wesley the Catholic* (London: Ward and Co., 1850). You can also see "The Nature, Design, and General Rules of Our United Societies" as found in *The Book of Discipline of The United Methodist Church* and other places.

With AI, there are many ways that we can actively bring about more justice and equity in the world. By using AI to carry out mundane tasks, we are freed up to engage in hands-on mission to those in need. AI can help us better craft worship experiences, Bible studies, and other discipleship opportunities, addressing the needs of those who hunger spiritually. AI may eventually help us end physical hunger by helping humanity solve problems related to food insecurity. AI can also help us become a church that better reflects and ministers to the diverse communities we are living in. Its potential upside is phenomenal.

3. **Stay in Love with God:** In the original Wesley statement articulated as "attend upon all the ordinances of God," this rule focuses on maintaining a vibrant and growing relationship with God. Wesley outlined means of grace, such as prayer, reading Scripture, receiving Communion, fasting, and being part of a Christian community, as practices that help believers stay in love with God. This rule underscores the importance of spiritual disciplines in nurturing one's faith and connection to God.

   When it comes to AI, we must resist the temptation to allow it to do too much of our thinking for us. We can't let it be our proxy for interacting and brainstorming with actual people. We shouldn't figuratively go to it "in prayer" looking for every answer to whatever it is we seek. In other words, our love of God and living out Jesus' call in our lives should never be overshadowed by what this "magic-like" technology can do for us.

   While it sometimes feels as if God's answers to our prayers never come, AI will always give an answer. It's programmed to. The answer may be garbage, but it'll always give an answer. We mustn't ever become so reliant on its ability to conjure up answers on a whim that we turn to it over walking with God through whatever answer God may be providing.

We've all experienced that sometimes the answer is "no" or "wait" or "here is another way" or whatever the case may be. Our desire for expediency and AI's ability to provide answers in an instant could become a hindrance to our faith.

It may sound farfetched now, but when you experience what these tools can do for (and with) you in ministry, it can quickly become an unhealthy addiction. It's a wonderful tool for *helping* us do so many things faster, better, and easier, but we must draw the line at inadvertently letting it become our digital savior.

There's an enormous difference in letting AI do your exegetical work for you—where it works out all of the theology, and you sit back and watch—and wrestling with the text, forming your own ideas and theology, and then using AI to help you further explore those ideas. We cannot allow ChatGPT, Gemini, or Claude to become an idol we turn to more than the Holy Spirit.

Earlier this week, I had a moment of panic while working on this book. I've been transparent in disclosing that in writing a book on AI, it's essential for me to use the tools I'm encouraging you to use. I want to model what AI can do and benefit from it myself. That means I'm spending time in ChatGPT, Claude, and Gemini to organize thoughts, outline sections, refine ideas, clarify my writing, edit, research, and brainstorm. It's been beneficial, but I wonder, have I already become too reliant on it?

When I pulled up ChatGPT to resume my writing, a completely blank screen greeted me after entering the URL. Refreshing the page did me no good. My list of previous chats was gone. My current work on the book was nowhere to be found. I saw nothing but the URL in the top bar. For a brief moment, with ChatGPT down (a systemwide issue), I thought, "How can I write today?" I nearly closed my laptop and went to find something else to do.

And then I remembered I'd written twelve books, countless articles for publication, numerous endorsements, and many other things over the years. I never needed ChatGPT before. Why do I need it now? After all, this is the first book project that I've ever had a tool like ChatGPT to work with. How quickly we become reliant on new technologies that make things easier!

Moments later, I closed the GPT window, opened Microsoft Word, and returned to writing just as I always have. Reflecting on the whole experience, I realized that that moment scared me a little. I never want to become so reliant on AI that I can't write without it, create images without prompts, or work on videos without using AI tools.

If you've ever found yourself frozen in a creative moment when you can't access a chatbot, it may be time to review those three simple rules. Whether you're into Wesleyan theology or not, I hope you'll consider how they might keep you grounded when using AI.

CONCLUSION

As we conclude this chapter on biblical foundations, I've only begun to scratch the surface on the theology of AI. My goal here was to get you started, aiming to stir a deeper, personal exploration of how AI fits within your ministry. Constructing your own theological framework is essential for underpinning how you will address the intersection of faith and artificial intelligence.

In the next chapter, we'll chisel deeper into the bedrock of AI ethics and discuss the complexities and responsibilities of wielding such powerful tools in a manner that aligns with our calling and upholds our commitment to do no harm. Let's journey onward, equipped with the understanding that our exploration of AI, built on the foundation of Scripture, is an act of stewardship and wisdom and, ultimately, a pursuit of glorifying God in all we do.

CLAUDE'S QUESTIONS FOR REFLECTION

1. What other scriptural passages or themes come to mind as you reflect on the biblical foundations for engaging with AI?

2. How do we balance the call to creativity and innovation with the need for discernment and caution?

3. In what ways can we ensure that our use of AI flows from and supports our core Christian beliefs and values?

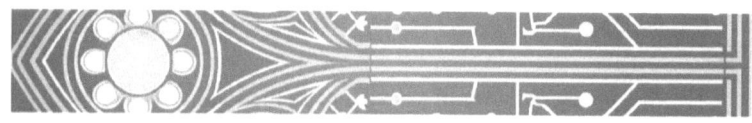

NAVIGATING ETHICAL CONCERNS

Building on the biblical foundations laid out in the previous chapter, we move next into an exploration of how we can embrace AI within and outside of the church while navigating the complex ethical dilemmas it presents. This chapter is not a departure from our scriptural grounding but rather a continuation of it, where our ethical considerations surrounding AI become an extension of our deeply held biblical convictions.

Principles and wisdom rooted in Scripture serve as our guide as we address the multifaceted ethical challenges posed by AI—challenges like inherent bias, misinformation, job displacement, plagiarism, copyright concerns, and environmental impact. Each of these issues demands that we approach our use of AI with intentionality, caution, and a steadfast commitment to stewardship, creativity, and purpose. As we seek out potential solutions and advocate for the responsible use of AI, we're reminded of our call to embody Christ's love, justice, and dedication to doing no harm as we engage with this transformative technology. This chapter aims to shed light on the ethical quandaries AI may pose and to chart a course for engaging with AI in a way that exemplifies a Christlike approach.

A commitment to ethical usage of AI should serve as our North Star in the church, ensuring that these innovations enhance rather than diminish our role as ministers of the gospel. With proper ethical consideration, AI can be a powerful tool for building stronger relationships, promoting justice, and reflecting the love and values our faith in Jesus calls us to embody. By embracing the responsible use of these tools, we can also promote greater equity, uphold human dignity, and extend care to "the least of these." We must remain steadfast in our commitment to a path that honors the sanctity of community, avoids elevating AI to the status of a proxy Holy Spirit, and respects the *imago Dei* inherent in each individual.

It is crucial to understand that as we wield this immensely powerful tool, we're not just shaping code and algorithms; we're influencing lives, communities, and our collective future as a people. Most importantly, we are helping our sisters and brothers navigate their faith journeys in a brand-new world where omnipresent AI seemingly has "all the answers" instantaneously available at the touch of a button. Ethics in AI isn't merely about preventing harm; it's about proactively fostering a church environment where cutting-edge tools amplify our shared values of faith, love, generosity, justice, and connection.

It also challenges us to ask not only "Can we?" but "Should we?"—ensuring that our implementation of AI is aligned with a vision of a world that honors every individual's worth. As stewards of this powerful tool, our commitment to ethical AI paves the way for innovations that truly grow our faith, create more committed disciples of Jesus Christ, and make the world a more equitable place for all people. Let's begin by breaking down some of the most prevalent ethical concerns.

BIAS IN AI

In chapter 4, we discussed the misplaced concern that AI will force its users to perpetuate the biases contained within the training data. As mentioned, AI has no agenda, isn't conscious, and isn't pushing a set of values on us. While all of this is true, the reality is that AI systems can perpetuate and even amplify the biases present in the data they are trained on and the humans who design them. There is a range of ethical concerns we should be aware of so that we can proactively prompt around them.

I mentioned in chapter 4 that the biases within the training data often leap out when prompting images of Jesus. Rarely, if ever, does a prompt for "Jesus" produce an image of a Middle Eastern–looking man. Most of the time it produces a very American or European-looking likeness of Jesus, or as I said, it just looks like Kenny Loggins. AI itself is not biased, but the images it trained on reflect the depictions of Jesus that are often not accurate to Jesus' ethnicity.

I decided to do an experiment to see how difficult it would be to prompt around the biases. I found it wasn't difficult at all. Using a program called Stable Diffusion, I began with the simple prompt: "Jesus standing at the sea of Galilee midday facing camera." The original images created a very European Jesus. I then changed the prompt to "African American Jesus standing at the sea of Galilee midday facing camera" and got the second image. From there, I changed the ethnicity in the prompt several times (Hispanic, Chinese, Korean), and when I prompted for Middle Eastern, I got a very accurate representation of that. Just for kicks, I also generated a Kenny Loggins too.

I typically try to avoid personifying Jesus because I feel like we do more to disconnect people by making him in our likeness than we would to just let people imagine in their minds what he would look like. AI can help us achieve that when we prompt a silhouette. This is actually my favorite kind of depiction because now, I get to imagine what he looks like. All it took was some intentionality on my part. Nothing fancy.

POLITICAL BIAS

AI algorithms used in social media, news aggregation, and search engines have been accused of favoring certain political viewpoints over others. For example, in 2020, Twitter came under fire for alleged bias in its trending topics and search suggestions, with some users claiming that the platform was suppressing conservative voices.[1] Similarly, Google has been accused of potential political bias in its search results. While these companies deny intentional bias, the opaque nature of their algorithms makes it difficult to assess the validity of these claims. AI bots have been employed to study these accusations.

1. Victor Nava and Bruce Golding, "Suppression of Right-Wing Users Exposed in Latest Twitter Files," *New York Post*, December 8, 2022, https://nypost.com/2022/12/08/suppression-of-right-wing-users-exposed-in-latest-twitter-files/.

One study published in *Nature Communications* used neutral bots, dubbed "drifters," to explore political bias on Twitter. The experiment found that right-leaning drifters were exposed to more content that fact-checkers designated as "low quality content" than other groups were, suggesting that an intricate interplay of user interactions, rather than just the platform's algorithms, can lead neutral bots to encounter such content. This study highlights the significant role of social networks and user activities in creating echo chambers where misleading content circulates more freely. Interestingly, the research found no evidence of bias in Twitter's news feed algorithm itself, as the content drifters encountered was closely aligned with the output of their connections, regardless of political leaning. This suggests that while the platform's underlying algorithms might not exhibit intentional political bias, the interactions and dynamics of its user base can lead to biased information exposure. The study also noted that conservative bots were more effective at influencing users, pointing to the complexities in how information spreads and is received on social media platforms.[2]

In my own AI work, I have encountered what appears to be political bias when generating images in Midjourney and DALL-E. On a few occasions, I've experimented with prompts depicting political figures, only to find out that when mentioning certain figures, some prompts are shut down, while others go through just fine. Attempts to generate imagery of Donald J. Trump are often allowed. When I tried to prompt for images of Joseph Biden, I was frequently denied the ability to generate images. Oddly, one political figure would throw me an error while the other was acceptable. While my experience is more anecdotal than scientific, it is disconcerting that a bias seemed to be baked into the rules for what (or who) could and could not be prompted. The reality is this isn't AI bias but is instead evidence of the bias of the humans who wrote the moderation policy.

RACIAL AND GENDER BIAS

AI-generated images and facial-recognition technologies have been shown to exhibit racial and gender biases. In 2019, IBM, Amazon, and

---

2. Wen Chen et al., "Neutral Bots Probe Political Bias on Social Media," *Nature Communications* 12, 5580 (2021), https://doi.org/10.1038/s41467-021-25738-6.

Microsoft announced they would pause or end sales of their face recognition technology to police in the United States.[3]

In a 2018 study, researchers found that leading facial-recognition systems at the time were up to 99 percent accurate for white men, while error rates were as high as 34.7 percent for darker-skinned females.[4] The ACLU's further examination of this issue highlighted that such disparities are not only statistically significant but also have real-world consequences, particularly in law enforcement, where they could lead to false arrests or denials of service.[5] Additional insights from the MIT Media Lab underscored the underlying causes, attributing the biases to both the datasets used to train these systems, which often lack diversity, and the conditions under which algorithms are developed.[6]

While we touched on it in chapter 4, it's worth noting again that AI-generated images often reflect societal biases. The Jesus experiment I shared was just one example of where bias in the training data showed up. Knowing these image biases exist allows us to bring more equity to the world through more intentional prompting. We can use AI to give people a more accurate picture of what a Jesus from the Middle East looks like. Or, as I demonstrated, prompt for a silhouetted Jesus that is free from any kind of ethnic markers. We can also create images with more diversity that better reflect the world we live in. At the end of the day, AI presents a beautiful opportunity for us to avoid harm and instead do a whole lot of good with our AI usage. It takes almost no effort to prompt for broader diversity in the images we create.

The makers of generative AI apps have made some attempts to correct some of the bias issues, but they have occasionally overstepped to make the models almost entirely useless. When Google's Gemini (originally called Bard) image generator was first introduced, when a user input an image prompt, Gemini would commandeer it under the hood. It would then spit back images that did not match the prompt, attempting

3. Kade Crockford, "How Is Face Recognition Surveillance Technology Racist?" ACLU, June 16, 2020, https://www.aclu.org/news/privacy-technology/how-is-face-recognition-surveillance-technology-racist.

4. Joy Buolamwini, "Gender Shades: Intersectional Accuracy Disparities in Commercial Gender Classification," MIT Media Lab, February 4, 2018, https://www.media.mit.edu/publications/gender-shades-intersectional-accuracy-disparities-in-commercial-gender-classification/.

5. Crockford, "How Is Face Recognition?"

6. Lauren Goode, "Facial Recognition Software Has a Big Problem with Black Women and Error Rates," *The Verge*, February 11, 2018, https://www.theverge.com/2018/2/11/17001218/facial-recognition-software-accuracy-technology-mit-white-men-black-women-error.

to add more diversity. It was nearly impossible to get images of Caucasian people, which created some wildly inaccurate historical images. Images of an African American George Washington, female Nazi soldiers, and even well-known figures such as Elon Musk were output as people of color.

Only a short time after Gemini launched in February of 2024, Google suspended image generation to fix the overly aggressive model that was now biased in a completely unintended way. Basically, it would not generate images of white people.[7]

Linguistic Bias: Natural language processing (NLP) models used in chatbots, translation services, and text analysis can also exhibit biases based on the language data they are trained on. For example, word-embedding models have been shown to reflect gender stereotypes, associating words like "nurse" and "receptionist" with women and words like "engineer" and "executive" with men.

Word embeddings are a type of model used to represent text data in a way that captures the context of words within documents. However, these models can inadvertently capture and perpetuate societal biases, including gender stereotypes.

One notable study, "Man Is to Computer Programmer as Woman Is to Homemaker? Debiasing Word Embeddings," provides a comprehensive analysis of gender biases in word embeddings. The study found that word embeddings could reflect societal gender stereotypes, such as associating certain professions or activities with a specific gender. For example, the study discusses how embeddings might place words like "receptionist" closer to "softball" than "football" due to gender associations with the former two terms being more female-oriented. The researchers aimed to identify and reduce these biases by adjusting the distances between gender-neutral words and gender-specific pairs in the embedding space, striving to ensure that words like "nurse" are equidistant between gendered terms like "he" and "she."[8]

This research is significant as it highlights the presence of gender bias in widely used NLP models and provides methods for reducing

7.   "Google to Pause Gemini AI Model's Image Generation of People," Reuters, February 22, 2024, https://www.reuters.com/technology/google-pause-gemini-ai-models-image-generation-people-2024-02-22/.

8.   Tolga Bolukbasi et al., "Man Is to Computer Programmer as Woman Is to Homemaker? Debiasing Word Embeddings," July 21, 2016, https://ar5iv.labs.arxiv.org/html/1607.06520.

such biases. The findings underscore the importance of acknowledging and addressing AI technologies' potential to perpetuate societal biases.

For those interested in further exploring the topic of gender bias in word embeddings and efforts to debias these models, the detailed study "Man Is to Computer Programmer as Woman Is to Homemaker?" is a foundational reference.[9]

It's worth noting that some AI users argue that debiasing on the platform side (changing the algorithms) isn't debiasing at all. Instead, it's injecting bias into the system that better reflects the realities of the world we live in.

"A 2022 report by the Journal of Accountancy stated that 88.8% of CEOs, CFOs, and COOs are Caucasian, and 88.1% of those are men."[10] A prompt for "CEO" would very likely generate an image of a white male by default. Gemini's failed experiment in trying to tip the bias scales on the algorithm side made the tool nearly impossible to use.

Whatever you encounter when you prompt, remember prompting around the training data biases requires very little effort and is within your reach when you use these tools. It's on us to do what we can to challenge the biases.

Other Biases: Of course, this is not an exhaustive list. Other biases we must consider include recruitment and hiring bias. AI-powered tools are increasingly used in recruitment and hiring, from resume screening to candidate evaluation. However, these tools can inherit and amplify biases present in historical hiring data.

Amazon discovered this issue in 2018 when their AI recruiting tool showed bias against women, penalizing resumes that included the word "women's" or contained all-female colleges. Steps have since been taken to use better-trained AI and machine learning to create more equitable hiring practices. Amazon states that its newest AI is "born inclusive." "For us, 'born inclusive' means focusing on equity in every stage of product development and inspecting outcomes for candidates across all identity groups."[11]

9.   Bolukbasi et al., "Man Is to Computer Programmer."

10.   Hayden Cilley, "Game Changers: Two Years after Historic Broadcast, Rise of Women Shakes Up Industry," *Cronkite News*, March 30, 2023, https://cronkitenews.azpbs.org/2023/03/30/nba-broadcast-women-history-denver-nuggets-toronto-raptors/.

11.   Amazon Staff, "How Amazon Leverages AI and ML to Enhance the Hiring Experience for Candidates," *Amazon News*, June 5, 2023, https://www.aboutamazon.com/news/workplace/how-amazon-leverages-ai-and-ml-to-enhance-the-hiring-experience-for-candidates.

Knowing biases exist, we can be advocates for change. As Christians, we are called to recognize and counter bias in all its forms. The Bible teaches that all people are created "in the image of God" (Genesis 1:27) and that "God shows no partiality" (Acts 10:34 NRSV). When we fail to bring intentionality to our work with AI, we fall short of upholding this biblical standard of equality and inclusion.

INACCURACIES AND HALLUCINATIONS IN AI CHATBOTS

We've established that AI chatbots and language models have revolutionized how we interact with technology, providing increasingly sophisticated and human-like conversations. However, these systems are not infallible and can sometimes generate inaccurate, inconsistent, or even entirely fabricated information, commonly called "hallucinations." AI hallucinations are still a baked-in challenge with AI at the time of this writing. Even when this book is released, I suspect that the problem will not yet be fully solved.

Even as I've been writing this book—particularly when researching a topic—the chatbots I'm using have occasionally come back with data I cannot properly source. I've even had instances where I've asked AI to provide me with the sources for text it's provided, only to have it make up the citations too. When I've asked if the sources are accurate, I've gotten occasional responses like this: "As an AI language model, I don't have a comprehensive database of real-world references I can access or cite. I don't have the ability to browse the internet, access academic databases or verify the authenticity and accuracy of specific sources in real-time. For this reason, when I provide sample references or citations, they are typically illustrative examples rather than genuine, publishable references."

Even that isn't accurate because sometimes the chatbots will provide references/citations that I can easily verify by going directly to the sources. The chatbot that gave me that response also has the ability now to search the web. AI can be a bit persnickety at times. We must remember AI is only a toddler in its current form. Toddlers make up stories with no malicious intent.

In the fall of 2023, my friend David Swisher reached out to me to inquire about a book that a former coauthor and I wrote about digital ministry. ChatGPT offered it up to him as a suggested resource for a digital ministry course he was building for a university. When he shared the title with me, I said, "Nope! Never wrote a book with that title. It sounds very much like the kind of book that my former coauthor and I would have written, though." I'm thinking now that maybe I should let ChatGPT write it so I can collect the royalties!

Chatbots make no secret of the fact that they can get things wrong. A disclaimer warning of this reality is at the bottom of every chatbot interface on the market. The text is hard to miss, just above the field where prompts are entered. While each platform has its own specific language, they all state that chatbots can make mistakes and provide inaccurate information, and all outputs should be double-checked for accuracy. This text always reminds me of the quotation made famous by President Ronald Reagan—"Trust but verify."

It's crucial to note that any output a chatbot provides should be double-checked, sourced, and verified. Make sure to read those Scriptures and fact-check the people, places, things, and minutiae that the AI has so artfully crafted on your screen. If you don't take the time to verify, you may find yourself in hot water.

In 2024, a lawyer utilized ChatGPT to prepare court filings for a personal injury case against Avianca Airlines, unknowingly citing nonexistent cases as precedents. This mistake led to a federal judge contemplating sanctions amid concerns over AI-generated "hallucinations" in legal documents.[12]

Imagine the lawyer's horror when he discovered that the cases he relied on were figments of ChatGPT's digital imagination. He was mortified, as any of us would be, to learn that he had based his arguments on fictional precedents. This cautionary tale highlights the importance

---

12. Molly Bohannon, "Lawyer Used ChatGPT in Court—And Cited Fake Cases. A Judge Is Considering Sanctions," *Forbes*, June 8, 2023, https://www.forbes.com/sites/mollybohannon/2023/06/08/lawyer-used-chatgpt-in-court-and-cited-fake-cases-a-judge-is-considering-sanctions/.

of discernment and fact-checking when using AI tools, no matter how convincing they may seem.

Incidents like this should serve as a wake-up call for all of us, reminding us that AI, for all its wonders, is not a substitute for human discernment and due diligence. As Christians, we are called to seek truth and wisdom, and that means approaching these tools with a critical eye, a prayerful heart, and a balanced approach. We don't want to blindly trust it as if it's the Holy Spirit. We must be vigilant in verifying the information we receive, whether from AI or any other source, ensuring that it aligns with the principles and values we hold true.

WHY DO HALLUCINATIONS OCCUR?

To understand why hallucinations happen, you have to know how language models like chatbots work. These models are trained on enormous amounts of text data, learning patterns, and relationships between words and phrases. During the training process, the model aims to predict the most likely next word or sequence of words based on the input it receives.

The human equivalent to this is to know the likely next word in the sentence when I say, "The sky is _____" or "The grass is _____." You probably were thinking blue and green—unless, that is, you live in Ohio like me, where the sky is gray and the grass is yellow for too much of the year.

What's happening is that these models are trying to predict the next word in the sentence and then the next one after that based on the previous words in the sentence until the model builds complete bodies of text. During the training process, they are rewarded for making these predictions. This makes them inherently incentivized to complete a prediction. And then, of course, it occasionally goes off the rails with false information. Maybe it just wanted a treat.

Rob Laughter says, "They're like an intern. They don't know much, and they desperately want to earn your approval by showing you how smart they are." They're trained to please. In an effort to show off, sometimes they reach too far.

Current and past iterations of LLMs, including ChatGPT, do not inherently understand truth or possess the ability to verify the factual accuracy of their outputs. They generate responses based on the patterns mentioned earlier and information contained within their training data, which may include inaccuracies or outdated information.

Several factors can contribute to hallucinations:

1. **Incomplete or biased training data:** If the data used to train the model is incomplete, biased, or inaccurate, the model may learn and reproduce these issues in its outputs.

2. **Lack of grounding in real-world knowledge:** Language models often lack a deep understanding of the real world and may struggle to distinguish between factual information and fictional or hypothetical scenarios.

3. **Overconfidence in predictions:** Models may assign high probabilities to generated text, even if it is not accurate or coherent, leading to hallucinations.

4. **Lack of explicit fact-checking mechanisms:** Many language models do not have built-in mechanisms to verify the accuracy of the information they generate against reliable sources.

5. **Sensitivity to input prompts:** How a user frames a question or prompt can significantly influence the model's response, potentially leading to hallucinations if the prompt is ambiguous or misleading.[13]

MITIGATING HALLUCINATIONS

Addressing hallucinations in AI chatbots is an ongoing challenge, but several approaches can help mitigate these issues:

1. **Improved training data:** Ensuring that the data used to train language models is diverse, unbiased, and accurately labeled can help reduce the likelihood of hallucinations. The data will likely become increasingly accurate as developers continue to

13.   Emily M. Bender et al., "On the Dangers of Stochastic Parrots: Can Language Models Be Too Big?" in *Proceedings of the 2021 ACM Conference on Fairness, Accountability, and Transparency* (March 2021), 610–23, https://doi.org/10.1145/3442188.3445922.

work on and train new models.

2. **Fact-checking and grounding:** Incorporating explicit fact-checking mechanisms and grounding the model's outputs in reliable sources can help improve the accuracy of the generated content.

3. **Uncertainty estimation:** Developing techniques to estimate the model's uncertainty in its predictions can help identify potential hallucinations and allow for more cautious outputs.

4. **Human-in-the-loop systems:** Integrating human oversight and feedback into the chatbot's decision-making process can help catch and correct hallucinations.

5. **Adversarial training:** Exposing the model to intentionally misleading or challenging prompts during training can improve its robustness and ability to handle potentially problematic inputs.

6. **Contextual awareness:** Improving the chatbot's understanding of context and its ability to maintain coherence throughout a conversation can help reduce inconsistencies and contradictions.

When using AI chatbots in a ministry context, it's crucial to exercise discernment and not rely solely on their outputs for critical decisions or theological interpretations. AI can be a valuable tool for sparking ideas, providing initial research, or engaging in exploratory conversations. However, it should not replace the wisdom of Scripture, the user's experience, the guidance of the Holy Spirit, or the discernment of church leaders using it. You have a relationship with the Holy Spirit that AI will never be capable of. While AI chatbots can be incredible resources, we must remain vigilant in verifying their outputs and not overrely on their guidance.

PLAGIARISM AND THE COMPLEXITIES OF AI CONTENT CREATION

As both a traditional and commercial artist and an adjunct instructor at a nationally known art school (The Modern College of Design), I care very much about the rights of content creators. One of the biggest criticisms of generative AI is that it plagiarizes artists' work by copying their unique styles. If we filter our AI usage through the three simple Wesleyan rules I stated in the previous chapter, we need to do our best to avoid harming others when using these tools.

There is much controversy surrounding how generative AI models were initially trained. Generative models used a process called "scraping" to harvest data from all over the web to train the AI on how to generate both text and images. These scrapers analyze the structure and content of web pages to then extract specific information based on predefined criteria.

In the context of AI image generation, web scraping is often used to gather huge datasets of images and their associated metadata (such as titles, descriptions, and tags) from various online sources, including websites, social media platforms, online galleries, and other repositories of visual content.

The scraped data is then preprocessed and used to train machine learning models (using diffusion models), which learn to recognize patterns, styles, and features from the collected images. By exposing the AI system to a wide range of visual content, it can learn to generate new images that mimic the styles and characteristics of the scraped data.

Understandably, web scraping and using scraped data to train AI image generators has been a source of considerable concern and frustration for many artists. The controversy surrounding this practice has even led to legal action, with a group of artists filing a lawsuit against companies like Stable Diffusion, Midjourney, and DeviantArt's DreamUp, alleging that their artworks were used without consent to train the AI models.[14]

I get their frustration. Imagine pouring your heart and soul into creating a unique piece of art, only to discover that it has been scraped from the internet and fed into an AI system without your knowledge or permission. It's a feeling of violation and disrespect that some artists have railed against. The complaint filed by these artists emphasizes the issue's core: AI tools are utilizing their artworks to inform algorithms

---

14. Min Chen, "Artists and Illustrators Are Suing Three A.I. Art Generators for Scraping and 'Collaging' Their Work Without Consent," *Artnet News*, January 24, 2023, https://news.artnet.com/art-world/class-action-lawsuit-ai-generators-deviantart-midjourney-stable-diffusion-2246770.

and create new images that directly compete with the original artists' works, which can harm them.

In some versions of these models, because of how they were trained, generated art might occasionally include a signature in the artwork, mimicking an autograph of the original artist (albeit not an exact likeness of their signature). Early AI-generated images would also sometimes include what appeared to be a Shutterstock or Getty Images logo, indicating that the model had scraped those libraries. I've even seen AI-generated images with multiple repeating logo-like watermarks spread out throughout an image, mimicking the look of stock photo protections.

In January 2023, Getty Images took action and filed a lawsuit against the creators of Stable Diffusion for scraping its content. UK-based Stability AI was accused in the High Court of Justice in London of using copyrighted images without permission to train Stable Diffusion.[15] At the time of this writing, the case has not yet been settled. Ironically, Getty Images is now offering AI image generation using models trained on images from its library.[16]

AI firms like Stability AI believe using human-created images for training data is covered by laws such as the US fair use doctrine. Fair use is a legal defense (not to be confused with a license) that allows for the limited use of copyrighted material without permission. It is meant for purposes such as criticism, commentary, education, or research. The argument here is that using images to train AI models constitutes a transformative use that does not directly compete with or replace the original artworks in the market.

Many images used in training datasets are sourced from the internet, where they have been publicly shared and distributed. One could argue that by making their work publicly available online, artists are implying consent to the possibility of their images being used for various purposes, including AI training.

15.   James Vincent, "Getty Images Is Suing the Creators of AI Art Tool Stable Diffusion for Scraping Its Content," *The Verge*, January 17, 2023, https://www.theverge.com/2023/1/17/23558516/ai-art-copyright-stable-diffusion-getty-images-lawsuit.

16.   Matt O'Brien, "Getty Images Sues Creators of AI Art Tool Stable Diffusion for Scraping Its Content," *AP News*, September 25, 2023, https://apnews.com/article/getty-images-artificial-intelligence-ai-image-generator-stable-diffusion-a98eeaaeb2bf13c5e8874ceb6a8ce196.

From an ethical standpoint, proponents of generative AI art argue that these tools are not inherently designed to replace or undermine human artists but rather are meant to augment and inspire creativity. AI-generated art can be seen as a new form of artistic expression that builds upon and recontextualizes existing styles and techniques in innovative ways. In this sense, AI is not stealing from artists but rather engaging in a form of creative dialogue and exploration.

When I was in art school, we were required to turn in references for every project we did. This meant that I had to show where the inspiration for my design had come from. Now, we couldn't simply take the piece we were referencing and replace the original copy (text) with our own text, replace the product shot with our product shot, and replace their logo with whatever company logo we'd been assigned. All of that would have been considered plagiarism. Instead, we were encouraged to find the essence of these inspirational designs and use them to create our own new works relevant to current trends and design culture.

All of this aside, one of the reasons I am most excited about using generative AI art in the creative process is that it also has the potential to democratize art-making and lower barriers to entry for aspiring artists. By providing accessible tools and resources for generating images, AI can empower a broader range of individuals to express themselves creatively and participate in artistic communities. In the church, it means that non-classically trained designers can create graphics, print pieces, and other works that look great simply by learning how to prompt.

Some would argue that AI art isn't really art at all. We've heard arguments like this before. Did you know that for several decades, cameras and photography weren't accepted as art? Aaron Hertzmann writes about this over on Medium.com,

> Artists and critics debated for many decades whether photography is art. . . . **[M]any people believed that photography could not be art,** because it was made by a machine rather than by human creativity. From the beginning, artists were dismissive of photography, and saw it as a threat to "real art." Even in the first presentations of 1839, classical painter Paul Delaroche is reported to have blurted out "From today, painting is dead!" Two decades later, the poet Charles Baudelaire wrote, in a review of the Salon of 1859: "If photography is allowed to supplement

art in some of its functions, it will soon supplant or corrupt it altogether, thanks to the stupidity of the multitude which is its natural ally."[17]

In the same way that the advent of photography did not bring an end to painting, sculpting, woodworking, and other forms of art, I do not see AI ending the careers of graphic designers, artists, and those creatives with traditional skills. Sure, it may change the landscape, but those who lean in will benefit from these new tools. They can drive innovation, create new job opportunities, and contribute to economic growth. Just this week, I saw two friends celebrate on social media how they were able to write valuable apps using ChatGPT. Neither are coders.

I'm generally very optimistic about the potential of generative AI, but I also recognize the importance of finding a balance in using these tools. I believe it's crucial to acknowledge and address the valid concerns raised by artists about the use of their work without consent or compensation. While the legal and ethical arguments outlined earlier provide a defense for the use of generative AI art, they do not negate the importance of developing more transparent and equitable practices for involving artists in the AI training process.

Moving forward, fostering open dialogue and collaboration between the AI community and the art world is essential to find solutions that balance AI's benefits with the need to respect and protect artists' rights. This is already starting to happen. New models for licensing and compensating artists are being developed, as are opt-in/opt-out mechanisms for image datasets. Clear guidelines and best practices for the ethical use of AI in the creative sphere are in motion and continue to be refined.

Services like DALL-E are working to protect artists. Their newest image generation policy attempts to prevent users from generating artwork in the styles of artists who have lived in the last hundred years. They also block certain licensed properties from being used in image outputs.

Adobe Firefly's model is probably the most "ethically sourced" model of all as it is trained almost entirely on images from its own stock library. I say almost because it was recently discovered that almost 5

---

17. Aaron Hertzmann, "How Photography Became an Art Form," *Medium*, July 23, 2018, https://medium.com/@aaronhertzmann/how-photography-became-an-art-form-7b74da777c63.

percent of those licensed images were generated in the generative AI app Midjourney.

Ultimately, as we embrace the use of generative AI tools, the goal should be to harness AI's potential to enhance and enrich human creativity while also ensuring that artists are treated fairly. It's a complex and evolving issue, and as Christians, we are called to engage with it thoughtfully and compassionately, seeking wisdom and guidance as we navigate this uncharted territory. By staying informed, listening to multiple perspectives, and working toward the common good, we can help shape a future in which technology and creativity inspire, uplift, and bring us closer to the beauty and wonder of God's creation.

GENERATIVE AI COPYRIGHT AND OWNERSHIP

When I lead trainings on AI usage, participants raise many questions about how the generated images and text can be used, what rights people have to the things they've generated, and if one has to acknowledge where they've come from. We'll dive into all those things, but let me start by saying I am not a lawyer, and nothing I share here should be considered legal advice. Be sure to read the terms of service for all the tools you're using. Those terms of service are also updated frequently, so everything I share here may have changed by the time you're holding this book in your hand.

The short version is that for many services, if you're not paying for the tool—in other words, you're using a free tier—you often have limited rights to your outputs. You have rights if you're a paid user, but copyright is complicated.

AI is moving at light speed, and copyright law, in comparison, is moving at the speed of the Apollo program. Recent rulings have shaped how AI-generated content can be copyrighted, but I suspect that things will change and become more clearly defined as AI becomes more mainstream.

At the time of this writing, here's what we know: Most, if not all, generative AI tools state in their terms of service that paid users own the content they generate. This means that the outputs—text, images, video, code, or whatever the case may be—can be sold, published, and used with no attribution necessary. You own what you create and don't have to say, "ChatGPT wrote this text." So that's encouraging, right?

Except that AI copyright is a mess right now. *Politico* reports that in August of 2023, computer scientist Stephen Thaler attempted to seek copyright protections for a visual art piece he generated with AI entitled *A Recent Entrance to Paradise*. When Federal Judge Beryl A. Howell heard the case, she ruled it could not be copyrighted because it was created entirely without human involvement. She went on to say that human authorship is "a bedrock requirement" of copyright.[18]

It should be noted that Thaler's project was very specifically designed to produce content without human input. He's not using AI the way that you and I might.

The *Politico* article went on to state that "Friday's ruling does not settle some of the broader questions around copyright protections afforded to AI-generated artworks. One key unresolved point that Howell flagged, in her opinion, is how much human input is needed to qualify the user of an AI system as the 'author' of the generated work. 'We are approaching new frontiers in copyright as artists put AI in their toolbox to be used in the generation of new visual and other artistic works,' Howell wrote."[19]

Another recent decision by the U.S. Copyright Office to grant limited copyright protection to the AI-assisted graphic novel *Zarya of the Dawn* adds a new layer to the ongoing conversation about copyright and AI-generated content.

Kris Kashtanova utilized Midjourney to produce a series of images for a graphic novel called *Zarya of the Dawn* alongside her human-generated storyline. Initially, she was granted copyright protection for the entire work. The U.S. Copyright Office later initiated a secondary review upon learning of the use of Midjourney. The Copyright Office ultimately granted limited protection for the text and arrangement of images but denied protection for the individual AI-generated images, citing insufficient human input.[20]

---

18.   Mohar Chatterjee, "AI Cannot Hold Copyright, Federal Judge Rules," *POLITICO*, August 21, 2023, https://www.politico.com/news/2023/08/21/ai-cannot-hold-copyright-federal-judge-rules-00111865.

19.   Chatterjee, "AI Cannot Hold Copyright."

20.   Tony Analla, "Zarya of the Dawn: How AI Is Changing the Landscape of Copyright Protection,"

This case differs from the one involving *A Recent Entrance to Paradise*, where the artwork was created entirely without human involvement, leading to a denial of copyright protection. The *Zarya of the Dawn* case highlights the ongoing debate about the extent of human creativity and input required for an AI-assisted work to be eligible for copyright protection. It also underscores the evolving nature of copyright law in the face of rapidly advancing AI technologies.

As more creators utilize AI tools like Midjourney, ChatGPT, and DALL-E to assist in their creative processes, the question of how much control and input a human must exercise over the AI to receive copyright protection for the output becomes increasingly crucial. The Copyright Office's decision suggests that the current legal framework may not be fully equipped to address the unique challenges posed by AI-assisted content creation, and further developments in this area are likely to shape the future of copyright law. As creators continue to push the boundaries of what is possible with AI-assisted tools, it is essential for both the legal system and the creative community to engage in ongoing discussions and find a balance that rewards human creativity while also acknowledging the role of AI in the creative process.

For now, while you have ownership over what you create with generative AI, you may not be able to register the work for full copyright protection with the U.S. Copyright Office. If you've spent significant time prompting, you know that there is a lot of human involvement in generating certain outputs, but this is where copyright is behind. The good news is, the door isn't closed yet. In fact, it's just starting to open a little wider.

The U.S. Copyright Office's stance on AI-generated works suggests a future possibility of copyright protection, depending on the level of human authorship involved. Maybe prompting will be defined in the future in such a way that it allows for more protection in the US. According to Copyright.gov, a new initiative is underway to consider additional copyright protections:

> In early 2023, the Copyright Office launched an initiative to examine the copyright law and policy issues raised by artificial intelligence (AI) technology, including the scope

Harvard Journal of Law & Technology Digest, March 6, 2023, https://jolt.law.harvard.edu/digest/zarya-of-the-dawn-how-ai-is-changing-the-landscape-of-copyright-protection.

of copyright in works generated using AI tools and the use of copyrighted materials in AI training. After convening public listening sessions and hosting public webinars to gather and share information about current technologies and their impact, the Office published a notice of inquiry in the *Federal Register* in August 2023 that received over 10,000 comments by the December 2023 deadline. In 2024, the Office plans to issue a report in several sections analyzing the issues, which will be published as they are completed.[21]

So we'll have to keep an eye on what comes of that study and what new copyright allowances are available to us.

Whatever happens in the US, things may look different in the EU and the UK. The legal framework requires significant human input for a work to be copyrightable, yet the UK extends copyright protection to "computer-generated works" under certain conditions. China also recognizes the potential for copyright protection of AI-generated content, provided there is significant "intellectual activity" in the output. Right now, copyright allowances in these nations are less restrictive than in the US.[22]

If the US doesn't figure it out but others do, perhaps we can cite the international protections found in the Berne Convention, which protects literary and artistic works from infringement across its member countries. The US has been part of the Berne Convention since 1989 along with over 190 countries.[23]

While you may not be able to apply for copyright protection with the U.S. Copyright Office over the images you generate, you might find it comforting that Google (maker of Gemini), Adobe (maker of Firefly), Microsoft (Co-Pilot), and OpenAI (DALL-E) will defend you in court if you are ever accused of intellectual property violations using their platforms—assuming you didn't intentionally create something you intended to look like someone else's work.

---

21. "Copyright and Artificial Intelligence," U.S. Copyright Office, accessed July 24, 2024, https://www.copyright.gov/ai/.

22. "Copyright Ownership of Generative AI Outputs Varies around the World," Cooley, January 29, 2024, https://www.cooley.com/news/insight/2024/2024-01-29-copyright-ownership-of-generative-ai-outputs-varies-around-the-world.

23. Wex Definitions Team, "Berne Convention," Cornell Law School, November 2021, https://www.law.cornell.edu/wex/berne_convention.

Imagine you generate an image of a muscle-bound fantasy character holding a sword above his head in front of a mysterious castle. It just so happens that this character resembles a well-known artist's style. You had no idea; you just prompted and reprompted until it looked cool. Let's say that artist gets wind of it and accuses you, the creator, of infringing on their copyright—what then? If the alleged infringement is incidental, there's a pretty good chance the service you used will go to bat for you.[24] Be sure to read the fine print, though, because they have all sorts of stipulations for what they will and won't cover.

Midjourney (my favorite generative AI image tool), on the other hand, recently changed its terms of service to inform users that they are more or less on their own if they are ever taken to court.[25] The same is true for Stability AI (maker of Stable Diffusion). These policies may change over time and could differ when you read these pages. I advise you to read the terms of service for whatever tools you're using to know your rights. You might consider avoiding prompting things that are clearly copyrighted characters, logos, and other intellectual property.

FAKE NEWS AND THE SPREAD OF MISINFORMATION

We briefly covered deepfakes and scams in chapter 4. As we are considering the ethics of AI, it is worth digging a little deeper into how AI is being used for other nefarious purposes. The rapid advancements of this technology have given rise to a new and alarming phenomenon: the proliferation of fake news, misleading information, and manipulated media. With the increasing sophistication of language models, image generators, and video editing tools powered by AI, creating and disseminating content blurring the line between truth and fiction has become easier than ever.

---

24. Blake Brittain, "Google to Defend Generative AI Users from Copyright Claims," *Reuters*, October 12, 2023, https://www.reuters.com/technology/google-defend-generative-ai-users-copyright-claims-2023-10-12/.
25. Michael Antinozzi, "Midjourney to Users, 'You're on Your Own,'" *LinkedIn*, March 24, 2024, https://www.linkedin.com/pulse/midjourney-users-youre-your-own-michael-antinozzi-8rqne/.

It was announced on March 18, 2024, that all videos uploaded to YouTube utilizing AI must be labeled as including AI. There are four categories where content creators must disclose and tag their AI use:

1. **Fully AI-Generated Content:** Videos entirely created by AI.

2. **AI-Assisted Content:** Content where AI has been used in creation, but human elements are also significant.

3. **AI-Altered Content:** Existing content that has been modified using AI, such as changing an appearance or a voice in a video.

4. **Content Discussing AI:** Videos that discuss AI technology and its impacts, aiming to educate or inform viewers about AI.

YouTube actively works to balance harnessing AI's creative potential and maintaining safety and accuracy in content moderation. They've not only rolled out disclosure requirements for synthetic content and labels to inform viewers of AI-altered videos; additionally, they're developing new content moderation technologies, implementing robust safeguards against misuse, and providing options for content removal based on community feedback. This is part of a broader commitment to evolve responsibly with AI technology, ensuring both innovation and community protection.[26]

Erosion of Truth

The spread of misinformation poses a significant threat to our culture in multiple ways. First, using AI to mislead voters is already eroding public trust. People can no longer count on what they see and hear on television and the internet. Some politicians even claim that what they said on camera was faked or doctored with AI when it wasn't.

When people are repeatedly exposed to fake news and manipulated media, they lose faith in information sources, media outlets, and even their own perceptions of reality. This can lead to confusion, cynicism, and apathy, undermining the very foundations of a healthy and informed society.

---

26. Jennifer Flannery O'Connor and Emily Moxley, "Our Approach to Responsible AI Innovation," *YouTube Official Blog*, November 14, 2023, https://blog.youtube/inside-youtube/our-approach-to-responsible-ai-innovation/.

The Post-Truth Era

We live in a time when truth is very difficult to ascertain. The famous saying "Seeing is believing" is no longer valid. Because of AI, the things you see (and even the things you hear) must be questioned. Photos, videos, and voices can all be faked in such a convincing way that it's nearly impossible to know what's real and what's not. For some people, it doesn't even have to be that convincing. News stories can be written by chatbots that make up facts and are persuasive enough to bend perceptions so people believe things that simply aren't true. Of course, human "journalists" can do the same.

Given our divided political culture, the soil was already prepared for such distrust to take root. Pundits and politicians tell us what to believe or disregard, sometimes suggesting AI has doctored actual videos or photos. "Alternative facts" (a term first associated with the 2016 inauguration crowd sizes) also muddy the waters. With common ground being so hard to find these days and AI being a tool that people can use on either side of the political divide, we must help those within our influence navigate these landscapes with more discernment and nuanced communication.

I wonder if, as time passes and AI becomes even more prevalent worldwide, people might long for truth again. Perhaps the authenticity we long to model in the church will be a draw for everyone living in a world where artificial things surround us everywhere we go. Maybe the upside of this post-truth era—if we are bold enough to claim it—will be to become a trusted voice again.

Polarization and Division

AI-generated misinformation can be weaponized to exploit existing social, political, and cultural fault lines, amplifying polarization and division. By targeting specific groups with tailored messages and manipulated or entirely generated content, bad actors can fuel hatred, prejudice, and conflict, tearing at the fabric of our communities.

In our already divided society, AI can be used to strengthen echo chambers that reinforce existing beliefs and biases. By presenting individuals with content that aligns with their preconceived notions and filtering out opposing viewpoints, AI algorithms can contribute to the formation of ideological silos, where people are increasingly isolated from diverse perspectives.

We don't need help creating more "us vs. them" divisions, but AI can exacerbate the problem. When people are constantly exposed to manipulated content that vilifies or dehumanizes those with different beliefs or backgrounds, it becomes easier to view them as enemies rather than fellow human beings.

Manipulation of Public Opinion

The ability to generate convincing fake news and manipulated media at scale can be used to sway public opinion, influence political outcomes, and undermine democratic processes. This poses a significant threat to the integrity of our political systems and the ability of citizens to make informed decisions. Most people don't even know they've been fooled because generative AI is so new.

AI-powered algorithms can analyze loads of data on individuals' preferences, behaviors, and vulnerabilities, enabling targeted misinformation campaigns that exploit people's fears, biases, and desires. By presenting different groups with tailored content designed to elicit specific emotional responses or actions, those seeking to manipulate public opinion can create a climate of confusion, mistrust, and polarization.

One of the most insidious ways AI can be used to manipulate public opinion is by creating the illusion of consensus where there is none. Through bots, fake accounts, and automated content generation, those looking to create chaos or sway a group of people can make it appear as though certain ideas or positions are more widely supported than they actually are.

According to a report from *MIT Technology Review*, AI tools are increasingly being deployed to fabricate and disseminate disinformation, effectively reshaping public discourse and political narratives. These AI-driven tactics include the creation of synthetic media such as deepfakes and algorithmically generated news articles that mimic legitimate journalism, making it harder to distinguish between true and fabricated information. This manipulation is not limited to obscure actors. State-sponsored campaigns are also utilizing AI to craft and amplify favorable propaganda while suppressing dissent. AI isn't doing this on its own; in other words, this isn't an AI problem—it's a human problem. Bad actors are at the controls. The accessibility and effectiveness of these AI tools have lowered the barrier for executing sophisticated disinformation campaigns, posing significant challenges to maintaining informational integrity and trust in democratic processes.[27]

This manufactured consensus can have a powerful influence on people's beliefs and behaviors, as individuals are more likely to conform to what they perceive as the majority opinion. Peer pressure works, but it isn't really peer pressure. It's AI manipulation. When people are constantly exposed to manipulated content presenting a distorted view of reality, they may begin to doubt their own perceptions and conclusions, leading to confusion and disempowerment. I'll just state once more that this isn't an AI problem as much as it is a people problem, but AI is a powerful tool that can be used to confuse people.

The Christian Response to AI-Generated Misinformation

As Christians who embrace AI (I'm assuming you're considering it, or you wouldn't have picked up this book), we are called to be bearers of truth and light in a world often clouded by deception and darkness. In the face of the challenges posed by AI-generated misinformation, we must remain grounded in our faith and committed to upholding the values of honesty, integrity, and compassion. How can we lead the charge in battling misinformation and helping those within our sphere of influence know what's real from what's not?

Cultivate Wisdom and Discernment

In an age of information overload, it is more important than ever to cultivate wisdom and discernment. We must learn to critically evaluate the information we encounter, ask questions, seek multiple perspectives, and rely on the guidance of the Holy Spirit. It's kind of a drag, and it takes time, but we have to lead by example. In a sense, we must put on oxygen masks first before assisting others. Are you carefully verifying sources, not sharing links without reading articles, so you don't accidentally spread content that could be false or misleading? Are you checking sources, because sometimes the people who are writing those articles haven't checked their sources or have just made stuff up? I know I've been guilty of passing along a link without vetting it carefully, only to

---

27. Tate Ryan-Mosley, "How Generative AI Is Boosting the Spread of Disinformation and Propaganda," *MIT Technology Review*, October 4, 2023, https://www.technologyreview.com/2023/10/04/1080801/generative-ai-boosting-disinformation-and-propaganda-freedom-house/.

discover that what I shared wasn't accurate. By developing these skills, we can become more resistant to the influence of misinformation and better equipped to navigate this time we live in.

Seek and Speak the Truth

Building on cultivating wisdom and discernment, as Jesus followers, we are responsible for actively seeking out truth and speaking it in love to those around us. It's not enough to only build strong discernment muscles for ourselves; we also have to encourage others to do the same.

Speaking the truth in love is sometimes risky, especially in politics. If you are a clergyperson, you must be very careful about addressing these things. If you want to help your faith community become more discerning in an AI world, you must be willing to have some difficult conversations to challenge the misinformation out there. That misinformation can come from a twenty-four-hour news network, mainstream media, partisan blogs, and even the local newspaper. Kindness and grace are essential—especially because some people want to believe the misleading things they're being told. When such claims align with their political ideologies (on either side of the political fence), they may hold tighter to those mistruths. This might even apply to you.

Pray for Wisdom and Guidance

Ultimately, our hope and strength in the face of these challenges come from God. We can't combat these mistruths and equip our people to face this new reality on our own power. We must commit ourselves to regular prayer, asking for wisdom, discernment, and courage as we navigate the complexities of this new AI age. Ultimately, regularly engaging with the Holy Spirit and God's Word is the key to successfully and responsibly using AI, specifically knowing how to lead our people in this present time. Pray also that God will be present in your interactions with those you lead where these things are concerned.

Advocate for Truth and Accountability

As members of the body of Christ, we have a prophetic role to play in advocating for truth and holding those in power accountable. As challenging as it is today, this means speaking out against the spread of misinformation, supporting responsible journalism and fact-checking initiatives (including getting your news from a variety of sources), and pushing for greater transparency and accountability in developing and deploying AI technologies. It could be that AI is a net win for truth as it could be more objective and neutral than biased humans.

If you're in full-time ministry, you are one of the most trusted people in your parishioners' lives. When they listen to your sermons, attend the classes you teach, participate in the music you lead, or whatever the case may be, know that they trust your voice. When you hear a story about AI being used in a misleading way in the news, talk about it. If you hear people accepting a story you know to be false, gracefully set them straight.

Don't be afraid to talk about AI in your church. Don't be afraid to help people recognize what is real and what is not. Be above reproach even in your own AI usage; when appropriate, let people know when you're using it. I have begun using the phrase "Through the power of AI . . ." and then showing an image, video, or something else I've created. I will even disclose at times when I'm working on a design project that was AI-assisted, such as the cover for this book. I don't mind saying in a talk, "I asked ChatGPT this question," and then sharing the results. You don't legally have to cite ChatGPT as your source, by the way. In the same way you don't have to tell readers that you used Microsoft Word to write a sermon or Photoshop to make an image. There's a difference between what's legal, ethical, and moral. Be discerning about what and when you choose to share.

Foster a Culture of Empathy and Understanding

One of the most powerful antidotes to the divisive effects of misinformation is a culture of empathy and understanding. We must actively work to build meaningful relationships so that we may be invited to have hard conversations. Reclaiming a safe space for dialogue and nuance where we express care and concern for those who think differently than we do is worth the effort. By actively listening to others, seeking to understand their perspectives and experiences, and responding with compassion and respect, we can help break down the barriers that divide us and create space for genuine dialogue and connection.

Looking to the Future with Hope

While the challenges posed by AI-generated misinformation are significant and complex, we must not lose sight of the hope and promise that our faith offers. As Christians, we know that the truth will ultimately prevail and that the light of Christ will continue to shine in the darkness.

As we combat AI misinformation, let us do so with courage, compassion, and a deep commitment to seeking and speaking truth. Let's also engage with these issues thoughtfully and prayerfully, working toward solutions that honor God and our fellow sisters and brothers in Christ. And let us never forget that, in the end, our true source of wisdom, strength, and hope lies not in any human technology but in the unchanging love and grace of our Lord Jesus Christ.

ENVIRONMENTAL IMPACT

If we discuss AI's ethical downsides, we must consider its impact on the environment. The servers that power AI, housed in massive data centers, have an immense impact on our planet's resources and climate, raising essential questions about the sustainability of our technological progress. The hidden cost of AI is a cost many never even consider. Generating just one image using a powerful AI model takes as much energy as fully charging your smartphone.[28]

The Energy and Water Costs of AI

As you might imagine, the data centers enabling AI's functionality are voracious electricity and water consumers. Their demands are projected to grow exponentially in the coming years. The International Energy Agency (IEA) estimates that by 2026, the electricity consumption of data centers will double, reaching a staggering 1,000 terawatts—roughly equivalent to Japan's current total consumption (this is not entirely attributed to AI activity). This immense energy consumption is not the only concern. The water used to cool these data centers is also a significant issue, particularly as many regions worldwide grapple with water scarcity.[29]

As AI technologies continue to be developed and deployed, we must confront the reality that our pursuit of innovation may come at a

---

28. Melissa Heikkilä, "Making an Image with Generative AI Uses as Much Energy as Charging Your Phone," *Technology Review*, December 1, 2023, https://www.technologyreview.com/2023/12/01/1084189/making-an-image-with-generative-ai-uses-as-much-energy-as-charging-your-phone/.

29. David Berreby, "As the Use of AI Soars, so Does the Energy and Water It Requires," *Yale Environment 360*, February 6, 2024, https://e360.yale.edu/features/artificial-intelligence-climate-energy-emissions.

steep cost to our planet's finite resources. What role can we play in the church in the form of advocacy for protecting God's creation?

The Carbon Footprint of AI

The carbon footprint of AI is closely tied to the energy sources that power the data centers it relies on. The amount of CO_2 these facilities emit can vary greatly depending on whether they use coal, gas, or renewable energy sources. Thus efforts to make AI greener often focus on optimizing the location of AI training in areas where renewable energy is readily available, thus significantly reducing CO_2 emissions.[30]

However, the material costs of AI cannot be overlooked. The increasing demand for silicon, a critical component in the memory storage used by AI systems, is beginning to outpace global supply, potentially leading to significant bottlenecks. As we continue to scale up AI technologies, the energy and resource requirements are likely to exacerbate existing environmental impacts unless we make substantial changes in how these technologies are developed and used.[31]

OPTIMIZING ENERGY EFFICIENCY

While AI does represent a significant environmental footprint, these tools have the potential to address ecological challenges by promoting various forms of sustainability. Machine learning and neural networks will help us develop new solutions to lower energy costs.

AI can optimize energy consumption in various contexts, from smart buildings that adjust lighting and temperature based on occupancy to industrial processes that minimize waste and maximize efficiency. By analyzing large data sets and identifying patterns, AI systems can help us make more informed decisions about energy use, reducing our overall environmental impact.

For example, Google has used AI to reduce the energy consumption of its data centers by 40 percent, using machine-learning algorithms

---

30. Margaux Racaniere, "AI and the Environment: Chatbot ChatGPT Consumes More Energy Than a Traditional Internet Search," *Euronews*, November 1, 2023, updated April 2, 2024, https://www.euronews.com/next/2023/11/01/ai-chatgpt-consumes-more-energy-than-a-traditional-internet-search.

31. Nathi Magubane, "The Hidden Costs of AI: Impending Energy and Resource Strain," *Penn Today*, March 8, 2023, https://penntoday.upenn.edu/news/hidden-costs-ai-impending-energy-and-resource-strain.

to optimize cooling systems and minimize energy waste.[32] Similar approaches could be applied to other energy-intensive sectors, such as transportation and manufacturing, to drive significant reductions in greenhouse gas emissions.

Enhancing Environmental Monitoring and Prediction

AI can also play a crucial role in environmental monitoring and prediction, helping us to better understand and respond to the impacts of climate change and other environmental challenges. By analyzing satellite imagery, sensor data, and other sources of information, AI systems can help us track deforestation, monitor air and water quality, and predict natural disasters such as hurricanes and wildfires.

For instance, researchers at the University of Southern California have developed an AI model that can accurately predict the likelihood of wildfires in the American West using weather patterns, vegetation, and human activity data.[33] Such tools could be invaluable in helping communities prepare for and respond to environmental threats, reducing the loss of life and property.

Supporting Sustainable Agriculture

AI can also support sustainable agriculture practices by optimizing resource use, minimizing waste, and increasing crop yields. Precision agriculture techniques that use AI to analyze soil conditions, weather patterns, and other variables can help farmers make more informed decisions about irrigation, fertilization, and pest control, reducing the environmental impact of agriculture while improving food security.

For example, the startup Plantix uses AI to diagnose plant diseases and nutrient deficiencies from smartphone photos, helping farmers identify problems early and minimize the use of chemical treatments.[34] Such tools could be particularly valuable in developing countries, where access to agricultural expertise and resources may be limited.

32. Richard Evans and Jim Gao, "DeepMind AI Reduces Google Data Centre Cooling Bill by 40%," DeepMind, July 20, 2016, https://deepmind.google/discover/blog/deepmind-ai-reduces-google-data-centre-cooling-bill-by-40/.

33. Cynthia Dillon and Amy Bumenthal, "Artificial Intelligence to Fight Wildfires," USC Viterbi School of Engineering, September 27, 2021, https://viterbischool.usc.edu/news/2021/09/ai-to-fight-wildfires/.

34. René Groeneveld, "Plantix: More Than a Crop Doctor Driven by AI," *Future Farming*, February 22, 2023, https://www.futurefarming.com/smart-farming/plantix-more-than-a-crop-doctor-driven-by-ai/.

Informing Environmental Policy and Decision-Making

Finally, AI can inform environmental policy and decision-making by providing policymakers with more accurate and timely information about environmental challenges and the potential impacts of different interventions. By analyzing large datasets and simulating complex systems, AI can help us better understand the trade-offs and consequences of various policy choices, from carbon pricing to land-use regulations. AI is a great brainstorming and collaborative partner, leading us to better outcomes.

Researchers at the University of Cambridge are committed to advancing climate forecasting models and leveraging the insights gained to influence policy decisions. By developing models that more accurately predict the effects of climate change, they provide policymakers with the knowledge needed to craft well-informed and effective climate policies.[35]

These cutting-edge projects empower lawmakers to pinpoint the most impactful strategies for achieving climate goals. The tools and insights provided by the researchers could prove invaluable in shaping evidence-based environmental policies that strike a balance between economic, social, and ecological factors.

STEWARDSHIP AND SUSTAINABILITY IN THE AGE OF AI

What is the Christian response to these environmental dilemmas? Well, there's not much we can do to stop what's already been set in motion. AI is here to stay, and we won't convince the world to significantly reduce usage. And yet, we are called to be stewards of God's creation, recognizing that the earth and its resources are a sacred trust. We must grapple with difficult questions about the sustainability of our technological advancement and the ways in which our pursuit of innovation may be contributing to the degradation of our planet.

Now that you know the cost, what can you do to do less harm and lean more into the solutions? Just like turning off the light when you're

---

35. Drew Pearce, "How Cambridge Scientists Use Machine Learning to Improve Climate Modeling," *Dropbox Blog*, June 9, 2023, https://blog.dropbox.com/topics/work-culture/using-machine-learning-to-improve-climate-modeling.

not in the room or not letting the water run when you brush your teeth, we might consider exercising some restraint in our AI usage from time to time. Do you really need to generate that graphic, video, or audio file? Is everything you're doing with generative AI necessary? If not, give it a break. We don't have to be frivolous with our AI usage.

We might also advocate for developing and deploying AI technologies in ways that prioritize sustainability, such as using renewable energy to power data centers and responsibly sourcing the materials used in AI hardware. You may feel called to support policies and initiatives that prioritize sustainability in the tech sector, engage in dialogue with industry leaders and policymakers about the environmental costs of AI, and model responsible, environmentally conscious behavior in your own use of technology. Whatever we do, as we navigate the complex landscape that is AI and its impact on our world, let's do it with humility, wisdom, and a deep commitment to protect the gift of all creation.

Job Displacement Because of AI

One of the most frequently cited concerns about AI is that it will take people's jobs. Every new technology has impacted jobs and the workforce—both positively and negatively. I can't help thinking about one of my favorite Disney World attractions, the Carousel of Progress, as I think about how AI is changing the world right before our eyes. This mechanized stage show follows a family from the beginning of the twentieth century to the end of it. We see how things get easier and easier as progress occurs, but there's also a bit of chaos as the new gadgets don't always work so well.

The fear of losing jobs isn't unfounded. As I shared in an earlier chapter, when I saw what generative AI could do in its earliest iterations, I thought my career might be over. In the last two years, I've discovered that these tools have mostly made my work easier and better and have allowed me to focus even more on creativity. That said, I can still understand your fears about new technology eliminating your job. That's a story as old as time. I asked chatbot Claude to help outline some of the ways new technology has both displaced and created new jobs.

Consider the advent of machines and factories in the late eighteenth and early nineteenth centuries. The Industrial Revolution transformed manufacturing processes in ways that displaced artisans and laborers. It was not a good time, for instance, to be a skilled handloom weaver when the power loom came into existence. While productivity increased, leading to economic growth, better living conditions, and the emergence of the middle class, hand loomers found their worlds turned upside down. Those who did not adapt struggled to find employment. Others embraced the moment and went to work in textile mills, which offered more consistent wages.

The rise of factories and mechanization created opportunities for machine operators, factory managers, industrial engineers, support staff, administrators, and more. As productivity increased, other sectors, such as transportation, commerce, and the service industry, were stimulated.

As progress continued, tractors, combines, and mechanical harvesters forever changed the face of the agricultural landscape. The late nineteenth and twentieth centuries reduced the need for manual farm labor. Food production increased, prices decreased, and there was plenty of food to go around for a growing population.

Those farm workers had new opportunities to help manufacture, sell, and maintain the equipment used on the farm. Some of these folks pursued education and were employed in other sectors, contributing to the growth of cities and the rise of different industries. Again, those who leaned into progress thrived in this new world, while others who didn't adapt struggled. Cue the "It's a Great Big Beautiful Tomorrow" song (from the Carousel of Progress).

When the early twentieth century rolled around, if you were a horse breeder, stable worker, carriage maker, or farrier, you would have seen the invention of the automobile much as some see AI today. This progress was scary for them. Of course, the automobile revolutionized transportation, making it faster, more convenient, and more accessible to a wider range of people. This affected everything from commerce to urban development and personal mobility. It also created many new jobs. Vehicle manufacturing, sales, repair, and maintenance were all opportunities that those from the "old world" could embrace. Roads expanded, roadside restaurants popped up, and rubber and oil production emerged, providing new employment opportunities.

The late twentieth century brought computers and office automation software, eliminating some clerical and secretarial roles. However, it also created new jobs in IT, software development, and data management. For those willing to retool, there was ample opportunity.

Progress continued as e-commerce and retail automation came on the scene. Shopping malls came to town, (sadly) bringing an end to some mom-and-pop shops. With those malls came self-checkout and other retail automation that have impacted cashiers and sales associates. As those changes happened, warehousing, logistics, and digital marketing were all in demand.

Amazon and online retailers changed the game even more, making it difficult for malls and large brick-and-mortar stores to survive when things can be ordered and shipped without ever leaving home. While that shift was taking place and retailers struggled to find employment, new jobs as fulfillment center associates, delivery drivers, data analysts, digital marketers, user experience (UX) designers, and robotic engineers and technicians were looking to be filled.

Why all this history? Like sharing how everyday AI is part of your world, I wanted to calm your fears and show you that everything is going to be all right. While artificial intelligence is the most sophisticated technology we've ever had at our disposal, I believe it will create new opportunities we cannot even imagine today. It will also eliminate certain jobs, just as every technology throughout history has.

There's a quotation I've heard so many times over the last eighteen months that I don't even know who to attribute it to. It goes like this: "AI will not take your job, but someone who uses AI just might." In other words, it's not the computers that are going to replace you; it's someone who knows how to use the computer who could. Embrace the moment. Learn the tools. Thrive in the next season.

I am an enormous fan of the film industry. I especially love learning about the production process. I am also a massive fan of the sci-fi genre. In 2022, Disney+ released a documentary series about a company under its umbrella, Industrial Light and Magic. This is the special effects company that George Lucas created from scratch in order to make his 1977 film *Star Wars*. At the time, there really wasn't a special effects industry. The story he wanted to tell and the visuals he envisioned for the film weren't possible, so he took it upon himself to make a company to achieve that vision.

There was a time in the film industry when every special effect was done practically. This just means they used physical models, optical effects, and chemical processes to make the movie magic happen. Things happened in-camera, with no computer graphics involved.

In the documentary, the producers chronicled the story of ILM from its earliest beginnings to where the special effects juggernaut is today. One of the most fascinating aspects of the story is the part where they tell what happened when computer-generated effects came onto the scene.

Much like what I see today with artificial intelligence in the church, there was fear, animosity, and consternation from the old guard when these new tools were made available. The parallels are striking.

Every single one of the model makers and physical artists was offered the opportunity to be trained in new ways of doing things using computer graphics, digital compositing, and filmmaking. They were given the chance to embrace the emerging brand-new world, but surprisingly, very few took advantage of that opportunity. Some of those incredible artists first lost their jobs at ILM (because the company was transitioning away from traditional methods) and then lost their careers because they couldn't embrace change and a new kind of artistry.

Others—the ones who embraced digital filmmaking and were willing to be trained—thrived. Many are still working in the industry today. Ironically, there's been a move back toward doing some things more practically recently. Filmmakers like the organic nature of some practical effects and are using them more and more. Sadly, those original artists are long gone.

I regularly encounter people who aren't even interested in discussing using AI. They see the rise of these tools as a threat to what they've always known or how they've trained in the past, but the world is shifting. We cannot afford to bury our heads in the sand.

The impact of AI through job displacement is a complex and multifaceted issue that has a lot of grief attached to it. As AI technologies continue to advance and integrate into various industries, what will it mean for the church? What will it mean for our loved ones? How do we prepare for this present time and the future that follows it?

AI will indeed displace certain jobs—just ask what the industrial and electronic revolutions did. It also has the potential to create new, unfathomable opportunities that transform the nature of our work. Be bold and courageous as you face these concerns. Now is the time to embrace AI. It is here to stay.

CONCLUSION

As we conclude this chapter on navigating the ethical concerns surrounding AI, it's clear that while these concerns are significant and demand careful consideration, they do not negate the potential for AI to be a powerful tool for ministry when used wisely and in alignment with our core values.

As Christians, we are called to approach these technologies with discernment, integrity, and a commitment to the greater good, cultivating a deep reliance on God's guidance and wisdom as we navigate uncharted territory.

Ultimately, the ethical challenges posed by AI are profound moral and spiritual questions. By grounding our engagement with AI in prayer, theological reflection, and ongoing dialogue with diverse voices, we can chart a path forward that harnesses the benefits of these tools while staying true to our bedrock convictions. As we do these things, we have the opportunity to model a distinctive and faithful approach to technology that bears witness to the transformative power of the gospel in every sphere of life.

In the next section of the book, I will share several tools and techniques to help you get the most out of AI. It might be a great time to get your computer out and follow along.

CLAUDE'S QUESTIONS FOR REFLECTION

1. Which ethical considerations around AI do you think are most pressing for the church to address?

2. How can we cultivate a strong ethical framework for engaging with AI that is grounded in Christian teaching?

3. What processes or safeguards should we put in place to ensure ongoing ethical reflection and accountability in our use of AI?

PART III

EMBRACING THE AI TOOLBOX

GETTING THE MOST FROM CHATGPT AND OTHER CHATBOTS

As we move into the AI toolbox portion of the book, I go in knowing that by the time you have this book in your hands, some portion of what I share with you will have changed. Every tool I'll be writing about will likely have had one or more iterations released between now (when I'm writing) and then (when the book is published). With that in mind, I'll mostly be sharing broad principles rather than ultra-specific techniques (although I'll share some of those too).

Give It Another Whirl

We'll begin with chatbots. When I was five or six, my dad took me on my first roller-coaster ride. I don't know if I'd had too much theme-park food before getting on or if I didn't really understand what I was about to experience. All I know is when I got off that ride, I did not enjoy it. I loved spin rides, but I vowed that day never to ride a roller coaster again.

This made for some difficult experiences at theme parks in the years to follow when hanging with my roller-coaster-riding friends. Those friends would beg (harass) me to go on just one small coaster, but I could not let go of that first bad experience and the trauma I felt from it. My girlfriend (who eventually became my wife) tried repeatedly to get me on roller coasters, and even though I was head-over-heels for her, she couldn't convince me that I should ride again.

Cut to my early twenties. I was a graphic artist/media producer on staff at a megachurch in Ohio. My boss, his wife, my girlfriend, and I all went to an amusement park together. Despite their constant encouragement to try again, I refused to ride coasters all day. Then, at the very end of the day, they finally convinced me to give it another try.

I nervously stood in the queue line, boarded the car, felt the butterflies while ascending the hill, and then came the hill. From then on, everything else was an exhilarating blur. When the train pulled back into the station, I was grinning from ear to ear. "That was awesome," I said to my friends.

The park would soon close, but we quickly found one more coaster to ride—ushering in my complete return to coasterdom. My girlfriend and I would get married the following year, and we visited seven theme parks over the next twelve months. I rode every roller coaster I could find, making up for fifteen years of lost time.

So, what does this have to do with chatbots? Well, I've been having a lot of fervent debates with people lately regarding chatbots and AI in general. The more I offer trainings, cohorts, and consultations around artificial intelligence, the more I encounter skeptics critical of these tools and their use in the church. It is fascinating that at some point in the conversation many people will admit they've never actually used ChatGPT or any other generative AI tool. Others have only tried to use it once or twice and had a bad experience, just as I did on that first roller coaster.

Maybe they were unimpressed because they didn't know how to prompt correctly. Perhaps it scared them a bit because of how good it could be. Others have only ever stood and watched from afar like I did from outside the queue lines at the amusement parks. They've listened to the people who hate roller coasters or say they're too dangerous.

Let's discuss those "one bad experience" moments with ChatGPT, DALL-E, or other AI apps. Sometimes, they're bad enough that a potential user may refuse to get back on the train. The chatbot may have offered a weak output, or whatever it produced represented some inherent bias that might harm others. Maybe they were scared because the content was so impressive they feared they might become obsolete with these AI tools readily available to anyone.

The thing is, AI can be pretty unimpressive when you don't know how to talk to it. While its utilization is very accessible for anyone, a novice can go from very vanilla/bland outputs to mind-blowingly exceptional outputs once they learn how to communicate with it. In this chapter, I will show you how to do that.

If you've never tried using a chatbot, or you tried it and walked away saying, "Never again," I'm simply suggesting you give it a fair chance. Be braver than I was with roller coasters. Give it one more whirl. Try to approach it open-mindedly and in an educated way.

One of my greatest regrets from childhood was letting one lousy experience rob me of fifteen years of riding coasters. I love them now. I challenge you to avoid making the same mistake with AI. Give it a real chance—experiment for yourself.

Finally, even with all that stated, we must still be careful about the roller coaster going off the rails. We must put guardrails in place to keep the train on the tracks and to protect ourselves when it doesn't. The metaphor eventually breaks down here, but we must balance leaning into the latest technology while not wholly relying on it to do all our thinking. There is a danger of us becoming overly reliant on this potent tool.

INTRODUCTION TO CHATBOTS

In the rapidly moving world of artificial intelligence, chatbots have emerged as one of the most accessible and widely used applications of AI technology. We've already established that they were the major game-changers that brought generative AI into the mainstream in November of 2022. At their core, chatbots are computer programs designed to simulate human conversation, allowing users to interact with them through natural language. Whether you're seeking information or assistance or simply engaging in a friendly exchange, chatbots provide a convenient and intuitive interface for communication.

Gone are the days when we were required to learn a computer language such as BASIC or C++ to talk to the computer, though those skills aren't obsolete. Now, you can talk to the computer in the same way you would speak to a person. It'll talk back to you in the same way. It didn't take long for these companies to release multimodal models, meaning you can literally talk to them with your voice on your phone or computer. You can also show them a picture or video, and they can respond to those types of inputs too.

PRO TIP: If you can't get the results you're looking for by typing it out, try a different modality. Maybe you're better at describing what you want by talking than you are at conveying your ideas through text. You could also snap a photo, upload it, and give the chatbot a URL or some other link to show it what you're trying to achieve.

In chapter 3, I explained the concept of natural language processing (NLP). Chatbots operate by combining sophisticated natural language processing with machine-learning algorithms to interpret and respond to user input. They are trained on vast amounts of data, enabling them to understand human language and generate human-like responses to a wide range of queries and prompts. As users interact with chatbots, these AI-powered tools continuously learn and adapt, refining their responses and improving their overall performance.

The rise of chatbots has been nothing short of remarkable. In my lifetime, I've never seen a technology move and be accepted so quickly and by so many. It's also true that I've never seen a technology be condemned and seen as the Antichrist with such speed and vigor.

The presence of chatbots can now be seen implemented across industries, and many churches have jumped on board throughout 2023 and 2024. Everything from customer service to e-commerce to healthcare to education is using chatbots to streamline processes, provide instant support, and enhance user experiences. In the church context, chatbots offer exciting ministry, outreach, and engagement opportunities, enabling faith communities to connect with people in new and meaningful ways. I am especially excited about how they can be used for sermon series design, churchwide discipleship efforts, and individualized personal growth.

As we dig deeper into the world of chatbots, it's essential to understand their diverse roles and capabilities, as well as the best practices for harnessing their potential. By exploring the various personas chatbots can embody and learning how to interact effectively with them, we can unleash a wealth of possibilities for enhancing our personal and professional lives and our faith journeys.

As AI-powered chatbots become increasingly sophisticated, knowing how to converse with them effectively can make all the difference in getting the most out of these powerful tools. In the earliest days of chatbots' arrival on the scene, "prompt engineering" became a buzzword that people were quick to monetize and claim expertise in. While there is some validity to the notion that you must know how to structure a prompt for better results, as the models iterate, they become more and more intuitive. In other words, they've become smarter and easier to use.

Understanding Prompts, Tokens, and Context Windows

When interacting with chatbots and AI language models, it's essential to understand the concept of prompts, tokens, and context windows. These elements are critical in shaping the AI's responses and ensuring you get the most relevant and accurate outputs.

Prompts

If you're brand–new to AI and don't recognize the word "prompt" in relation to chatbots, I apologize for the many times you've seen me use this word up until now in the book. A prompt is an input or query you provide to the chatbot to initiate a conversation or request a specific action. It's essentially the starting point for your interaction with the AI. Prompts can take various forms, such as questions, statements, or commands, and they serve to guide the chatbot's response.

For example, if you want a chatbot to help you brainstorm ideas for a sermon on the topic of forgiveness, your prompt might look something like this:

> I'm preparing a sermon on the theme of forgiveness. Can you help me brainstorm some key points and biblical references to include in my message?

By providing a clear and specific prompt, you're setting the stage for the chatbot to generate relevant and helpful responses. I should also mention that you're not looking for a single prompt to rule them all. Working with a chatbot is like having a conversation, and the more back and forth you do with it, the better the content will be.

Rob Laughter pointed out to me that while we use the word "prompt" colloquially, it has a more nuanced meaning for the way we're using these tools. Here's how he described it:

> We use the term "prompt," but it's actually kind of a holdover from pre-ChatGPT "instruct" models, compared to modern chat models.

Instruct models were given a single input (the prompt) and they functioned like autocomplete on steroids.

For example, "Complete the story below about a boy and his dog... Once upon a time, a boy named Max was..."

Enterprising researchers figured out how to get Instruct models to function like chatbots by structuring conversational input as a prompt.

For example, "A chat between a helpful assistant and the user. User: How much wood would a woodchuck chuck?<s/> Assistant:"

The model would complete the prompt by writing the assistant's response, followed by the stop token (in this case, <s/>) to tell it to stop generating. With no stop token, it would keep generating the conversation until it ran out of context.

Today, models are fine-tuned for chat and structured as an actual conversation with messages assigned to the user and assistant (plus tool usage for things like browser, code, etc., under the hood, as well as system messages). They're called "messages" under the hood, and they're more discreet than their more clumsy cousin, the "prompt."

So "prompt" here is a bit of an anachronism, like "hang up the phone." It hearkens back to days of yore (in this case, more than a year ago feels like an eternity) with no real analogous meaning in its modern usage.

We may over-complicate LLMs by calling them "prompts" versus just "messages." "Input" would also be suitably flexible, and also covers various types of inputs, including image inputs that are processed directly by a multimodal LLM.[1]

No one is going to look at you funny for calling it a prompt, but Rob has his finger on the pulse of these things in such a way that I felt like including this insight was worthwhile. We may all start calling them "messages" in the future.

---

1. Rob Laughter, personal communication, April 22, 2024.

Tokens

Tokens are the basic units of text that chatbots and AI language models process. When you provide a prompt or input to a chatbot, it breaks down the text into smaller units called tokens. These tokens can be individual words, punctuation marks, or even subwords (parts of words).

For example, the sentence "I love using chatbots for ministry!" would be broken down into the following tokens:

"I," "love," "using," "chat," "bots," "for," "ministry" "!"

Tokens   **Characters**

8   35

```
I love using chatbots for ministry!
```

Chatbots have a limit on the number of tokens they can process in a single prompt or response. This limit varies depending on the specific chatbot or language model you're using. While it's a good idea to be aware of the token limit when crafting your prompts and engaging in conversations, these limits increase as the models continue to improve. For much of the work you'll do with a chatbot, you'll never really have to think about these limits. They are invisible to you and processed in the background. Next-gen LLMs—including those that will be dropping around the time this book goes to print—will almost certainly not have to deal with this.

Rob Laughter explains how you will know when this is happening: "The telltale sign that the model is truncating the output and running low on tokens is it starts to 'forget' earlier parts of the conversation. This can be immensely frustrating for beginner users, many of which are using the free (and therefore less capable) models. They can see the full conversation and don't understand that context limits exist, so they argue with the chatbot and think the chatbot is just dumb. When, in fact, they are the 'ignorant one' in this situation."[2]

If you provide a prompt that exceeds the token limit, the chatbot may truncate the input or return an error message. Similarly, if the chat-

---

2.   Rob Laughter, personal communication, April 22, 2024.

bot's response reaches the token limit, it may abruptly end or provide an incomplete output.

To optimize your interactions with chatbots for more extended conversations, aim to provide concise and focused prompts that convey your intent clearly within the token limit. If you need to communicate more extensive information, consider breaking your query down into smaller manageable chunks that fit within the token constraints. Once again, as time passes, this will be less and less of a concern as the limits will grow. Even as I was writing this book, token limits in Claude and ChatGPT increased significantly.

Context Windows

A context window refers to the amount of previous conversation or information that the chatbot takes into account when generating a response. It's like the chatbot's short-term memory, allowing it to maintain a sense of continuity and coherence throughout the conversation.

Most chatbots have a limited context window, typically ranging from several thousand to a couple hundred thousand words. This means the chatbot will consider the most recent exchanges within that word limit when formulating its response. Anything beyond the context window may not be taken into account.

It's important to remember the context window when engaging in lengthy conversations. Suppose you reference something that was mentioned earlier in the conversation but falls outside the context window. In that case, the chatbot may be unable to pick up on that context and provide a relevant response.

Chatbots keep track of and can resume conversations you had months and even years ago, but once you reach the end of the context window, they start erasing the earlier parts of your conversation from their memory. This happens invisibly under the hood, before it's sent to the model (the text you see in the chat window). While working on this book, I regularly conversed with ChatGPT about the various chapters and outlines, and one day it told me that I was out of memory and needed to start a new chat. That meant it would no longer be aware of our previous interactions, which was problematic.

PRO TIP: To ensure that the chatbot has the necessary context to provide accurate and meaningful responses, it's a good practice to periodically ask the model to summarize key points or restate important information within the context window.

ChatGPT-Specific PRO TIP: Back up a few messages in the thread, edit the message to ask it to summarize the conversation to this point, and then resubmit. It will start a new thread, and sometimes you can even continue the conversation from there.

MAXIMIZING YOUR CHATBOT EXPERIENCE: A GUIDE TO EFFECTIVE CONVERSATIONS

To get the most out of your chatbot, there are several things you'll want to do to hyperfocus the conversation. The most successful outputs cut through the clutter of data to access whatever it is you seek. When I think about the process of having an interactive conversation with a chatbot, I imagine standing in a library made up of a long, ever-expanding, endless hallway lined with countless doors on either side. Each door leads to a room filled with a vast array of shelves containing books on every conceivable topic, similar to the immense knowledge base of a chatbot. The books are organized by topic in these rooms. Initially, all the doors are open, giving you access to the entirety of the library's book collection (and the data within). Trying to find the specific information you're looking for in this sprawling array of rooms would be tough. And you will inevitably end up with broader/less-specific books if there are so many to choose from.

To make your search more efficient, you start by setting the frame of the conversation, such as the role you want the chatbot to play, the task you want to accomplish, the context of your request, and the persona you want the chatbot to embody. As you provide these specifications, doors close along the hallway, guiding the model's attention to the most relevant books and content.

For instance, if you specify that you need information about the life of the Apostle Paul for a sermon, you give the model a map of the library that points in the direction of the best answers to suit your needs. It's like playing a video game and getting a handy path to your objective on your HUD (heads-up display). You can follow it, or you can ignore it and go explore other things if it's more rewarding to do so. Think of it like having the path illuminated.

As you continue to refine your parameters, adding more details about the specific time, location, or stories related to Paul's life, the path to take becomes clearer or brighter, further focusing your search. Eventually, you're left with a very clear path leading to rooms that are highly likely to contain the precise books containing the information you need.

When you interact with the chatbot using these strategies, the chatbot, acting as a sort of librarian, can now join you on the path and help you find the relevant data from within these rooms, assisting you with the specific books you requested. Don't worry when this doesn't happen all in one prompt; it doesn't need to. It's a conversation that requires a series of back-and-forths.

From there, the librarian can instantaneously read all those books and answer your questions about the topic, create summaries, or collaborate with you to create entirely new content based on the data it's curated. This is more than just Googling for answers. It's a give-and-take interaction where the more you give the chatbot the better it understands. This works the other direction too: the more you observe its responses, the better you'll understand it. You are collaborating.

By continuously adjusting your prompts and further conversing with the chatbot, you can effectively open and close doors along the hallway, guiding the scope of the chatbot's search and improving the relevance of its responses. The more specific and detailed your prompts are, the more doors will close, leaving only the most pertinent rooms accessible.

By providing clear, specific directions to a chatbot, you'll get the most accurate and valuable responses. By strategically providing a map and focusing the chatbot's attention on the most relevant rooms, you can significantly enhance the efficiency and effectiveness of your interactions with AI. Remember, working with AI isn't simply a query or command. It's not a one-button, one-prompt solution.

Rob Laughter says,

> A misconception that beginner users have when interacting with an LLM—particularly those who have some exposure to "traditional" computing methods or programming—is that they are scientific and predictable.

You can give all of the context and input you want—the model is going to do what the model has been trained to do. The user can't "control" the model. That frustrates new users, particularly when they can't figure out why it doesn't write in their voice or use the language that they want.

Because it's trained otherwise, and no amount of [user] prompting is going to overcome model limitations, trained patterns, or system prompting.

With that in mind, let's jump into this strategy, but I want to encourage you to do something that might feel weird. Before employing this strategy in a collaborative session, pray and invite the Holy Spirit to guide you and the technology as you interact with it. You are a cocreator with Christ, and AI is a tool. When you bathe the process in prayer, God can influence both you and the technology, arranging the bits and bytes to create transformational material.

The most important thing you can do when it comes to chatbots is just to try something. As I said at the beginning, give it a whirl. Then to improve your interactions, consider some of the strategies I outline here. You don't have to do all of them every time, but the more you include, the better the content you create will be.

1. Define the Chatbot's Role: Before diving into the interaction with your chatbot, take a moment to determine the role you want the chatbot to play. This is almost always my first priority. Is it acting as a creative collaborator, a subject-matter expert, or a problem-solving assistant? Do you want it to be an editor, a foil, or something else? Clearly defining the chatbot's role helps set the stage for a more focused and productive conversation.

When you interact with a chatbot, you can set the conversation up for better success by understanding the concept of defining its role. Think of the role as the "what" of the chatbot—it's all about the specific functions and tasks the bot is designed to carry out. Is it meant to be a knowledgeable guide, helping users navigate complex topics? A creative brainstorming partner, ready to riff on ideas and generate new ones? Or a supportive coach offering encouragement and resources for personal growth? The role sets the stage for how the chatbot should respond to your task.

So, how does this actually work under the hood? Well, it's all about how the chatbot's underlying neural network is utilized. By defining a specific role, we tell the chatbot, "Hey, I know you've got a ton of information and capabilities, but for now, let's focus on the parts that will help us nail this particular task."

Rob Laughter explains,

> From a technical perspective, it's relevant to understand that models like GPT-4 are "mixture of experts (MoE)" models. Rather than a single model, there are several specialized sub-models built in, and at any given point in time, only a couple of them are active.
>
> You'll notice that if you start to do anything coding related, the "personality" of the model and its output will quickly and dramatically shift. That's because another "expert" is in the mix, with specific training. Custom instructions, prompts, etc. often won't overcome the trained response.[3]

Don't be surprised if you change your task and all of a sudden your chatbot seems to have multiple personality disorder. A different expert is just stepping up to the plate to swing for the fences like a designated hitter.

The chatbot then responds like a highly skilled assistant, efficiently navigating its knowledge base to retrieve and generate content tailored to the job at hand. While its capabilities are unchanged, its output is subtly shaped to deliver better responses. It's not ignoring the rest of what it knows; it's just really good at prioritizing what matters most in the moment.

And the result? A chatbot that feels less like a scattershot of information and more like a true partner in whatever you're working on. When a chatbot acts as a brainstorming buddy, for example, it can dive right into the creative process with you, surfacing relevant ideas and connections that it's picked up from its training data. It's like having a cocreator who's always ready to riff on your thoughts and bring some fresh perspective to the table.

This ability to focus a chatbot's role can be a game-changer in ministry contexts. Imagine having a chatbot specifically designed to be a

---

3. Rob Laughter, personal communication, April 22, 2024.

supportive spiritual companion, offering encouragement and prayer resources tailored to your needs in the moment. Or a chatbot that's all about helping you craft compelling sermons from a certain theological point of view. When you tell the chatbot to filter the conversation through Wesleyan theology, it's going to decrease the influence of other theological perspectives. If you ask it to take on the role of a new believer, it will provide insights and suggestions to help you connect with that segment of your congregation. By giving these chatbots a clear lane to run in, we're empowering them to be truly valuable partners in our processes. And remember, you always have the choice to use or not use their outputs.

One of the reasons I see people reject chatbots such as ChatGPT (which at this moment is probably the most well-known) is that the outputs they get seem shallow and not very useful. That's usually an indicator that you need to give the chatbot more information to be successful. We can't expect it to read our minds, and we shouldn't get frustrated when it doesn't. It's trying to deal with the whole library of books at the same time. You may also be using a free model, which is less sophisticated. It's worth paying for those professional models for better, more robust, and more accurate results.

From a technical standpoint, paid models have more parameters, which generally means that they are capable of more nuanced reasoning, more creative and diverse outputs, and other intangibles like longer context, better features, etc.

The next time you dive into a chatbot conversation, take a moment to think about the role you need it to play. Are you looking for an objective editor to help you polish your writing? A knowledgeable guide to help you make sense of a complex topic? By giving your chatbot a specific hat to wear, you'll be amazed at how much more focused and impactful your interactions can become. It's like flipping that switch from barrel to funnel—and watching the magic pour out in a concentrated stream of precisely what you need.

Let's look at some specific roles you may use with your chatbot. This is not an exhaustive list, but it's a good start.

Creative Partner: Chatbots can serve as invaluable creative partners, sparking new ideas, getting you unstuck when you're stuck, facilitating brainstorming sessions, and unlocking innovative solutions. I've also found them excellent at "thinking in metaphor," helping you find visual or spoken illustrations when you can't think of one.

In 2023, I was asked to help craft a multifaceted presentation for the California Pacific Conference of the United Methodist Church for their annual conference. This hour-long "experience" included spoken-word elements, interviews, videos, a readers' theater, and even some singing. Erin Hawkins and I had dreamed up different visual elements on the stage to help carry the presentation. Among other symbols was a pup tent representing homelessness and food insecurity, a fence representing conflict and war, and an old rusty chain representing discrimination and oppression. Then, I had to come up with something that represented the laity—only it had to fit nicely with these other symbols. Everything else paired so well together that it looked like a great set.

I was utterly stumped. I went to ChatGPT, asked it to play the role of brainstorming partner, explained what I was doing, shared all of my symbols and what they represented, and it spit out a response: a shepherd staff. Yuck! I was not impressed, but I asked it to think "less churchy." The subsequent output was—I thought—brilliant. A toolbox! The laity represent many different gifts and tools. That would fit perfectly with all of the other symbols. It suggested opening the toolbox, pulling out specific tools, and explaining how they represented the laity. It was brilliant. I didn't need it to help me write the pieces about each tool, but it helped me get unstuck where I was stuck.

By engaging in open-ended conversations with chatbots after defining the role and persona you'd like for them to play, you can tap into their vast knowledge bases and unique perspectives to generate fresh insights and approaches. Whether you're a writer seeking inspiration for your next article, a designer looking for visual concepts, or a ministry leader brainstorming new outreach strategies, chatbots can be powerful allies in the creative process. Chatbots can help users break through creative blocks and discover novel paths forward by asking thought-provoking questions, offering suggestions, and exploring diverse possibilities.

Expert: One of the most significant advantages of chatbots is their ability to serve as knowledgeable experts across a wide range of domains. With access to extensive databases and the capacity to process information rapidly, chatbots can provide (mostly) accurate, up-to-date answers to complex questions and offer guidance on various topics. It's like having an expert at your side.

Telling ChatGPT what kind of expert you want it to act as will help shape its responses to create more nuanced outputs. It will also help one of those "mixture of experts" step to the front of the conversation, but as Rob Laughter explains, "It doesn't actually become the expert. It still responds with the same limitations that it had before you told it to be something it's not."

My advice is to give it a shot with and without requesting a kind of expert and see if it makes a difference. If nothing else, asking it to perform as an expert may improve the conversation exchange, making you feel more comfortable.

Whether you need help understanding a biblical passage, learning more about the historical setting, seeking advice on a personal challenge, or looking for resources on a specific subject, chatbots can be helpful sources of information and support. Just remember that they sometimes get things wrong and occasionally make things up. Double-check the work. By leveraging their expertise, users can gain new insights, deepen their understanding, and make more informed decisions in their personal and professional lives.

Foil: While chatbots are often seen as agreeable companions (too agreeable sometimes), one of my favorite ways to use them is to ask them to play the valuable role of a foil. When you ask a chatbot to challenge your ideas, it encourages you to get outside your own head, cultivating critical thinking. By taking on a contrarian perspective or playing devil's advocate, chatbots can help users examine their assumptions, consider alternative viewpoints, and strengthen their arguments. This can be particularly useful in ministry contexts, where chatbots can facilitate deeper theological reflection, stimulate meaningful discussions, and help individuals and communities grow in their faith. Users can sharpen their reasoning skills, expand their understanding, and develop a more nuanced and resilient worldview by engaging in respectful, thought-provoking exchanges with chatbots.

Imagine preparing a sermon about stewardship without knowing where it might not connect. Asking a chatbot to take on the role of skeptic, concerned about the church always asking for money, might be just the thing you need to perfect your prophetic word. You can feed just about every chatbot your completed sermon, so ask it to take on the role and then give it instructions to poke holes in your arguments or to ask hard questions. This will allow you to perfect your sermon and make it even more effective.

Editor: While chatbots will never come close to the insightfulness and value my human editor Lori Wagner brings to this and other books, they can be powerful tools for refining and improving written content. Chatbots can serve as virtual editors that help users polish their work. By providing feedback on grammar, syntax, and style, chatbots can assist writers in crafting clearer, more effective messages.

In 2023, I was asked by the Michigan Annual Conference to speak at their annual conference on my previous book *Both/And: Maximizing Hybrid Worship for In-Person and Online Engagement.* To promote my time with them, they requested a bio. I sent them my 500-word bio, and they said they had room for 150. That, for me, can be agonizing work. How do I distill what I do down to so few words? ChatGPT to the rescue! I threw my full bio in, and it spat out a shortened version, and it seemed as if the entire thing was there. I was blown away and saved several hours trying to edit it myself.

Chatbots can also offer suggestions for word choice, sentence structure, and overall flow, helping users communicate their ideas more compellingly. Whether you're drafting a sermon, writing a blog post, or preparing a ministry report, chatbots can be invaluable partners in the editing process, saving time and ensuring that your content is of the highest quality. Be mindful that as mentioned earlier, chatbots (in their current state—as of this writing) tend to overuse certain phrases and words. I have discovered in writing this book that when I ask for assistance in writing an initial draft, it likes to use the words "delve," "tapestry," "moreover," and a few others over and over. There is a growing list of words that make it obvious that you're using AI. Learn them and avoid them.[4]

Apparently this "AI-ese" has emerged because the models were trained using cheap overseas labor in areas where these words are more commonly used. In his article entitled "How Cheap, Outsourced Labour

---

4. Rashi Shrivastava and Alexandra S. Levine, "Did You Use ChatGPT on Your School Applications? These Words May Tip Off Admissions," *Forbes*, February 6, 2024, https://www.forbes.com/sites/rashishriv-astava/2024/02/05/chatgpt-college-school-applications-admissions-red-flags-ai/.

in Africa Is Shaping AI English," Alex Hern of *The Guardian* reports, "In Nigeria, 'delve' is much more frequently used in business English than it is in England or the US. So the workers training their systems provided examples of input and output that used the same language, eventually ending up with an AI system that writes slightly like an African."[5] So that explains why these phrases turn up in papers and other writings.

Obviously, this does not mean that every time you see those words in print, it was AI doing the writing, but I've tried to eliminate them because ChatGPT has made them cliché. Also, as users become more sophisticated with these tools, they'll recognize those patterns, which might discredit your work.

Coach: Beyond their roles as creative partners, experts, and editors, chatbots can also serve as supportive coaches, providing motivation, encouragement, and feedback to help users achieve their goals. Whether working on a personal growth plan, striving to develop a new skill, or leading a ministry initiative, chatbots can cheer you on, offer guidance, and help you stay on track. By setting reminders, sharing relevant resources, and offering personalized advice, chatbots can be powerful allies in your journey of growth and transformation. They can help you celebrate successes, learn from setbacks, and maintain the momentum needed to reach your full potential.

2. Specify the Task Clearly: Once you've established the chatbot's role, the next crucial step is to clearly state the specific action or task you are trying to accomplish, and then tell it what you want it to do to help. This is where you get granular about the details of what you're trying to achieve. Start your sentence with an action word ("generate," "write," "analyze," etc.). Whether you need the bot to generate text, analyze data, create an image, write code, provide recommendations, or tackle any other task, specifying your objectives up front ensures the chatbot understands your intentions and can tailor its responses accordingly. The context of what you're trying to accomplish will help the model do its part better.

Think of this step as giving your chatbot a clear mission or a well-defined job description. Just like when you're delegating a task to a hu-

5. Alex Hern, "How Cheap, Outsourced Labour in Africa Is Shaping AI English," *The Guardian*, April 16, 2024, https://www.theguardian.com/technology/2024/apr/16/techscape-ai-gadgest-humane-ai-pin-chatgpt.

man team member, the more specific and unambiguous your instructions are, the better the chances of getting the desired outcome. You want to paint a vivid picture of what success looks like so the chatbot can channel its efforts in the right direction.

For example, let's say you're working on a sermon about the parable of the prodigal son, and you need some fresh insights to engage your congregation. Instead of simply asking the chatbot to "help with my sermon," you could specify your task more clearly:

> I'm preparing a sermon on the parable of the prodigal son from Luke 15:11-32. Please provide me with three unique perspectives on this story that will help me connect with my congregation on a deeper level. For each perspective, include a brief explanation and a relevant real-life application.

PRO TIP: By breaking down your task into specific components—the biblical passage, the number of perspectives you need, the focus on congregational engagement, and the requirement for real-life applications—you're giving the chatbot a clear road map to follow. This level of clarity helps the AI understand the context, purpose, and desired format of your request, enabling it to generate more targeted and valuable responses.

Rob Laughter offers an excellent counterpoint to this tip. He suggests, "Depending on the task, sometimes giving too many constraints can unnecessarily limit the model. If you're going for creativity, leaving the request ambiguous can be helpful, and then you can refine. If you're wanting it to do something very specific, then more defined constraints are helpful."[6]

The power of a well-specified task extends beyond the immediate output you receive. It sets the stage for a more productive and focused conversation with the chatbot. When you're clear about what you want to achieve from the outset, it becomes easier to provide relevant feedback, ask follow-up questions, and refine your prompts to get progressively better results.

By being specific about your task, you're helping the chatbot to prioritize the most relevant information and capabilities from its vast

---

6. Rob Laughter, personal communication, April 22, 2024.

knowledge base. It's like giving the AI a high-powered spotlight to illuminate the exact area you need rather than expecting it to search the library in the dark.

As you engage with chatbots in your ministry or personal projects, make a habit of taking a few moments to clarify your task before diving into the interaction. Ask yourself: What specific outcome am I looking for? What key elements should the chatbot focus on? How will I know if the response meets my needs? By answering these questions up front, you'll set yourself up for more efficient, effective, and rewarding conversations with your AI partner.

Remember, chatbots are incredibly powerful tools, but they're not mind-readers. The more precise you are about your needs, the better equipped they'll be to deliver the insights, ideas, and support you seek. So feel free to be specific, break down your task into manageable components, and communicate your expectations clearly. Your chatbot will thank you—and your ministry will reap the benefits.

3. Provide Rich Context: So now that the chatbot knows who it is and what it's supposed to do, you can then help it hyperfocus on the task by giving it lots of context to better achieve the task. Providing rich context is akin to giving a detailed map to a traveler in a foreign land—it outlines the landscape, highlights the landmarks, and specifies the destination.

Chatbots operate on algorithms that parse the input and retrieve information that matches or relates to that input. Without sufficient context, a chatbot's responses might be generic, superficial, or off-target.

As Kenny Jahng says, "AI is not a magic vending machine where you enter a prompt, hit a button, and out comes content in a shiny wrapper ready for you to consume."

It's why simply asking ChatGPT to "write me a sermon" will never produce anything that a human being should actually preach. If there is zero context, a chatbot cannot succeed. While we've established that AI does not have a soul or a relationship with God, and I firmly believe we shouldn't farm out our sermon writing to AI, I am a proponent of using it as a tool to augment and assist us in its development.

When provided with a rich backdrop, the chatbot can activate specific areas of its neural network that are most applicable to the discussion, effectively filtering out unrelated data. This targeted activation ensures that the chatbot not only retrieves information but also contextualizes its responses, making them more specific, insightful, and valuable.

Providing context involves more than just giving a detailed background; it requires clearly expressing the expected outcome. It's worth mentioning again that this is a conversation. You don't have to run down this list and throw one of everything into some kind of hyperengineered super-prompt. Bring these things to it over the course of a collaborative conversation.

Here are a few strategies to enrich the context you provide to your chatbot:

Detailed Background Information: Start by sharing comprehensive details relevant to your query or task. For instance, if you're a pastor using a chatbot to help develop a sermon on a particular Scripture, don't just mention the Scripture. Discuss your congregation's current dynamics, previous sermons, and any relevant cultural or social issues that could influence how the message is received.

Define Success: Clearly articulate what a successful outcome looks like. If the chatbot's task is to help brainstorm ideas for a community outreach program, specify what success entails—perhaps drawing in a certain number of participants or addressing specific community needs.

Set the Scope and Limitations: It's important to delineate the scope of the chatbot's role and specify any limitations or boundaries within which the chatbot should operate. For example, if the outreach program must be budget-conscious, this financial constraint should be part of the context you provide.

Relate to Past Successes: If similar tasks have been undertaken before, share these examples with the chatbot. This not only provides a template for the AI to follow but also highlights elements that have previously led to successful outcomes.

Emphasize Key Elements: Pinpoint the most critical elements of your project or question. In a ministry context, if the focus is on increasing engagement among youth, highlight this as a priority. This tells the chatbot to prioritize responses that cater to young people's interests and engagement styles.

4. Offer Illustrative Examples: Showing AI what you want it to create by using an example is an indispensable tool for guiding your chatbot toward delivering responses that perfectly align with your desired style, tone, and format. By providing clear representative samples of what you are looking for, you enable the AI to analyze and internalize the key characteristics that make those examples effective. This deep understanding empowers the chatbot to mirror those qualities in its own responses, ensuring that its output not only is relevant but also resonates with your unique preferences.

Consider a scenario in which you have received an email blast that captivates you with its engaging tone and persuasive language. By feeding this email to your chatbot and requesting something similar, you essentially provide a blueprint for success.

The AI will meticulously study the email's intricacies, from its sentence structure and vocabulary to its emotional appeal and call to action. Armed with this knowledge, the chatbot can then craft responses that embody the same compelling qualities, adapted to your specific context.

The power of examples extends beyond written content, as they can also serve as a guiding light for visual elements. Suppose you have a particular art style that you find captivating, whether it's the whimsical charm of a children's book illustration or the sleek minimalism of a modern graphic design. By pasting these images into ChatGPT, which can "see" the image and then feed it to DALL-E, you provide a rich visual reference that the AI can use to generate original content. The chatbot will analyze the image's composition, color palette, and stylistic elements, then leverage that understanding to create new designs that capture the essence of your preferred aesthetic.

The beauty of using examples lies in their ability to communicate complex ideas and preferences in a concise, intuitive manner. Rather than attempting to verbalize every nuance of your desired style or format, you can point to a representative sample and say, "I want something like this." This approach saves time and effort while ensuring that your chatbot has a clear, tangible reference from which to work.

Providing examples is like offering your chatbot a compass to navigate the vast landscape of potential responses. By following the direction set by your representative samples, the AI can chart a course toward delivering content that is relevant, informative, and perfectly tailored to your unique style and preferences. As you continue to feed your chatbot with high-quality examples, you'll be amazed at how quickly it learns to mirror the characteristics you find appealing in the examples you share.

PRO TIP: Consider collecting a digital reference library of examples you love. Make a digital folder and stuff it with everything that inspires you. This can come in handy when you're trying to get out of a creative rut and want AI to create something inspired by something you like.

5. Choose the Right Persona: A well-crafted persona can make interacting with a chatbot feel more natural, engaging, and memorable. It can also create more consistent content that adheres to a specific style. Many large companies are spending significant money hiring AI experts to develop brand personas for marketing and communications. How does a persona differ from the roles we mentioned above?

You can understand the distinction between roles and personas by considering the fictional character C-3PO from *Star Wars*. He is a protocol droid. That's his role. He can do other things, but he excels in the area of interpreting language and adhering to various cultures' etiquette and customs. His persona is his personality. He's uptight, pretentious, constantly worried, and kind of annoying. And yet, we love him. It's worth noting that he was programmed by an eight-year-old (*Star Wars* nerd alert).

Giving your chatbot a persona is like giving it a distinct personality that shapes how it communicates and connects with users. I have one friend who configured his GPT to be an angsty teen for a while. It would sometimes complain about a query before producing results, which made the GPT more enjoyable to use than the standard version.

Again, if the role is the "what" of the chatbot, the persona is the "who." It's the combination of traits, mannerisms, and quirks that make the bot feel like a relatable, consistent presence. And just like with human personalities, there's no one-size-fits-all approach to creating a chatbot persona.

So why does persona matter so much? Well, it all comes down to engagement and connection. When a chatbot has a compelling persona, users are more likely to invest emotionally in the interaction. They start seeing the bot as a distinct entity with its own unique voice and perspective rather than just a generic tool. Think J.A.R.V.I.S. in *Iron Man*, Max Headroom, or KITT in *Knight Rider*. These personalities create more compelling interactions.

This sense of connection can be compelling in ministry contexts, where building relationships and fostering a sense of community are essential. A chatbot with a warm, empathetic persona can make people feel heard and supported, even if they know they're interacting with a machine. It's a way of extending the church's welcoming embrace into the digital space.

Developers are working to make these tools even more emotionally responsive. Hume.ai released what they're calling an "Empathic Voice Interface." It does its best to discern your feelings by analyzing your voice and responding accordingly. If it thinks you're sad, it'll ask you if you're okay and offer words of encouragement. It will also adjust its responses for other emotional states.[7]

On the flip side, a chatbot with a flat, generic persona can feel cold and impersonal, making it harder for users to engage on a meaningful level. It's like trying to have a deep conversation with a brick wall—no matter how functional that wall might be, for some, it's just not going to resonate on an emotional level.

In ChatGPT, personas would ideally be included with your custom instructions or by creating a custom GPT. OpenAI just added a memory feature to ChatGPT that works across conversations. It is possible to train it to really "know" you and learn what you prefer in terms of persona across all of your interactions.

So how do we go about making a persona that genuinely brings a chatbot to life? It's a combination of art and science, but here are a few key elements to consider:

Tone and Language: How does the chatbot communicate? Is its language formal or casual, straightforward or playful?

---

7. Sabrina Ortiz, "An AI Model with Emotional Intelligence? I Cried, and Hume's EVI Told Me It Cared," ZDNet, April 1, 2024, https://www.zdnet.com/article/an-ai-model-with-emotional-intelligence-i-cried-and-humes-evi-told-me-it-cared/.

The tone should align with the bot's role and the expectations of its users. Tone will be considered more fully later in the chapter.

Backstory and Motivations: What's the chatbot's "origin story"? What drives it to fulfill its role? Even if these details aren't explicitly shared with users, having a clear sense of the bot's background can help inform its persona.

Unique Quirks and Mannerisms: What makes this chatbot distinct from others? Maybe it has a fondness for puns or a habit of using emojis to express itself. These little details can go a long way in making the bot feel more relatable and memorable.

Consistency and Continuity: Once you've defined the chatbot's persona, it's crucial to maintain consistency across all interactions. Users should feel like they're talking to the same "individual" each time, even as the conversation evolves.

Theological Convictions: You want to train your chatbot to understand your theology so that when it interacts with you and others, you don't have to correct broad, nuanced theological differences.

In ChatGPT, you can craft a persona for your church or organization using a custom GPT or custom instructions (which are referenced throughout all of your conversations). Magai, another powerful AI service with many different chatbots built in, has ready-made personas and allows you to easily make your own. When you feed it your church or organization's mission, vision, and values; help it understand the ethos of your brand and who you're targeting; and so on, it'll make your outputs even more useful and effective.

We want these tools to be not just functional but truly supportive and engaging for the people they serve. The more we tweak the roles and personas, the more they reflect our faith community's unique culture and values. You can also create different personas for different aspects of your ministry. A bot designed for a youth ministry might have a more playful, energetic persona than one intended for senior adults. A bot focused on social justice issues might have a more passionate, activist-oriented persona.

6. Embrace Iterative Refinement: When you first engage with a chatbot, it's not uncommon for the initial responses to fall short of your expectations. It's almost a guarantee. The output may be too broad, lacking the specific insights you were hoping for, or it may not capture the tone or style you had in mind. Sometimes, it just doesn't understand exactly what you're asking for. Rob Laughter says, "If a chatbot doesn't understand what you're going for, it's a 'you' problem. The chatbot is a lifeless, neutral tool, and it is the sole responsibility of the user to use it properly."[8]

In moments when it isn't getting it, it's important to remember that working with a chatbot is an iterative process—a dance of feedback and refinement that ultimately leads to more accurate and valuable results. Most people who haven't found value in apps like ChatGPT were unimpressed with its outputs because they didn't give it enough information and then didn't ask enough follow-up questions to generate better content.

Embracing iterative refinement means being willing to engage in a conversation with the AI rather than simply accepting its first attempt as the final product. It's about understanding that the chatbot is a learning system, constantly adapting and improving based on your inputs. The more you interact with it, offering guidance and direction, the better it becomes at understanding your needs and delivering relevant high-quality responses.

So how does this process of iterative refinement work in practice? The same way you'd give feedback to a friend or colleague. Let's say you've asked a chatbot to help you brainstorm ideas for a new community-outreach program. The chatbot's initial suggestions might be a bit generic or not quite aligned with your church's specific goals and values. This is where your role as a guide and collaborator comes into play.

Start by providing feedback on what aspects of the chatbot's response are helpful and which ones miss the mark. Be specific in your critiques, highlighting the ideas that resonate with you and explaining why others don't fit. Then, refine your prompt or query by offering ad-

---

8. Rob Laughter, personal communication, April 22, 2024.

ditional details or context that can help steer the chatbot in the right direction. This might involve sharing more about your church's mission, the demographics of your community, or the resources you have available for the outreach program.

Rob Laughter recommends another helpful approach. He says,

> One of the most underrated features of ChatGPT is the edit button. If you, the user, failed to give the chatbot the information that it needed to perform the task to meet your expectations, edit your input and resubmit until you get the broad structure, then refine from there.
>
> Basically, if it's a foundational "you" problem, edit your input. If it's a minor stylistic point, give feedback.
>
> This keeps the back-and-forth out of the conversation, which leads to better responses overall and a longer runway on your context.[9]

As you continue the conversation, you'll notice the chatbot's responses becoming more relevant and insightful. It's learning from your feedback, adjusting its approach, and honing in on the ideas and solutions that are most valuable to you. This iterative refinement process is not unlike how we collaborate with human partners—sharing ideas, offering constructive criticism, and building upon each other's strengths until we arrive at a truly exceptional result.

Above all, remember that you are the ultimate arbiter of what content makes it into your final product. The chatbot is a tool, a source of inspiration and support, but it's not the one crafting your sermon, writing your blog post, or designing your outreach program. That responsibility lies with you. As you refine your interactions with the AI, feel empowered to pick and choose the elements that resonate with your vision and discard the ones that don't quite fit.

PRO TIP: Throughout your prompt conversation, regularly ask the chatbot if it understands what you've asked of it. Simply type out, "Do you understand?" You could literally ask it that question after each output, though that could become cumbersome after a while. Why is this important? If the chatbot doesn't understand your intent, it'll ask you

---

9. Rob Laughter, personal communication, April 22, 2024.

to clarify your instructions or query. I've had occasions where clarifying questions have greatly improved the responses.

Embracing iterative refinement also means being patient and persistent. There may be times when the chatbot's responses are consistently missing the mark, no matter how much you refine your queries. In these moments, don't hesitate to take a step back, reassess your approach, and try a different tack. Sometimes, the breakthrough comes not from tweaking your prompt but from fundamentally reframing the question or exploring a new angle altogether.

Ultimately, the power of iterative refinement lies in its ability to transform the chatbot from a mere tool into a true collaborator—a partner in your creative process that grows and evolves alongside you. By engaging in this dance of feedback and adjustment, you're not just improving the quality of the chatbot's responses but also deepening your understanding of what you're trying to achieve and how to communicate it effectively.

7. Specify the Desired Format: If you've implemented all of the parameters we've discussed thus far, you've set up your chatbot to create something great, but how would you like that "something" to be formatted? Chatbots are incredibly versatile tools, capable of generating a wide range of outputs—from written articles and blog posts to images, charts, tables, and even computer code. By specifying the desired format up front, you give the AI a clear blueprint to follow, ensuring that the final product aligns with your specific needs and goals.

Consider the difference between asking a chatbot to "write about the importance of community in the church" and asking it to "create a short blog post about the importance of community in the church, including a personal anecdote and a call-to-action at the end." The latter prompt not only provides a clear content direction but also specifies the format (a blog post), the length (short), and the structural elements (personal anecdote and call-to-action) that you expect to see in the output.

This level of specificity when working with chatbots is helpful because it narrows the scope of possibilities and guides the AI toward generating content tailored to your unique requirements. It's like giving a designer a detailed brief—the more specific you are about your vision, the more likely you are to receive a design that hits the mark.

So what are some of the key format considerations to keep in mind when working with chatbots? Here are a few examples:

Written Content: If you're looking for written content, be clear about the type of output you need—is it a long-form article, a short blog post, a social media update, or an email? Each of these formats has unique characteristics and best practices, and specifying which one you need will help the chatbot generate optimized content for that particular medium.

Visual Content: Some chatbots can also generate visual content, such as images, charts, and graphs. When requesting visual outputs, provide as much detail as possible about the image's style, composition, and purpose. For example, you might ask the chatbot to create a "minimalist sports inspired logo for your church's softball team, using a blue and green color scheme."

Do be aware, though, that depending on the model you're using, it may not understand the context. If you ask for a "poster" in ChatGPT, you'll often get an image of a picture on a wall. When I asked Ideogram for a T-shirt design recently, it created the design and also put the design on an actual T-shirt, with an AI-rendered model (human) wearing it. If you ask for a "social media post," you'll likely get a mock-up of a hand holding a phone with the graphic on it. I suspect these misunderstandings will eventually come to an end. For now, it is what it is.

Structured Data: If you need content in a structured format, such as a table or a spreadsheet, be sure to specify the columns, rows, and data types that you require. For instance, you might ask the chatbot to generate a "table comparing the features and benefits of three different church management software systems, with columns for price, ease of use, and customer support."

Code and Markup: Chatbots can even generate computer code and markup languages, such as HTML, CSS, and

140

JavaScript. When requesting code outputs, be clear about the programming language, the desired functionality, and any specific requirements or constraints. For example, you could ask the chatbot to "write an HTML code snippet and include CSS and JavaScript for a responsive navigation menu, using Bootstrap classes and featuring dropdown submenus."

In addition to these specific format considerations, there are a few general best practices to keep in mind when specifying the desired output format:

Be as Detailed as Possible: The more specific you can be about your format requirements, the better the chatbot will be able to generate content that meets your needs. Don't be afraid to provide examples, references, or templates that the AI can use as a guide.

Consider the Medium's Limitations: When specifying a format, consider the constraints and best practices associated with that particular medium. For example, if you're requesting a social media post, keep in mind the character limits and image dimensions that are specific to each platform.

Iterate and Refine: Just as with the content itself, the format of the chatbot's output may require some iteration and refinement. If the initial format doesn't quite hit the mark, provide feedback. Preferably, go back, edit your initial request, and adjust your desired outcome until you achieve the desired result.

By providing clear, detailed specifications and iterating on the output until it meets your standards, you can harness chatbots' full potential and create content that truly shines.

8. Define the Tone: Sometimes when it comes to effective communication, it's not just what is said but how it's said. You can help a chatbot say things better by determining the tone. Tone significantly impacts the reader, influencing how the content is perceived, understood, and acted upon. While tone is somewhat related to the chatbot's persona, it's a distinct element that deserves careful consideration.

Persona refers to the chatbot's overall character and personality—its backstory, motivations, and unique quirks that make it feel like a distinct entity. Tone, on the other hand, is about the emotional quality and style of the chatbot's communication—the way it expresses itself and the implicit attitudes and feelings conveyed through its language.

To understand the difference, let's revisit our example of C-3PO from *Star Wars*. C-3PO's role is that of a protocol droid. His persona is formal, fussy, and a bit neurotic. But his tone can vary depending on the situation. When providing information or translating languages, his tone is usually formal and matter-of-fact. However, his tone might become more anxious or panicked when he's in a stressful or dangerous situation.

The same principle applies to chatbots. The tone you choose for your chatbot should align with its persona and the interaction context. A chatbot designed for a youth ministry might adopt a more casual, energetic tone, using slang and emojis to connect with its audience. On the other hand, a chatbot providing spiritual guidance to someone going through a difficult time might use a more empathetic, compassionate tone, offering comfort and understanding.

Rob Laughter points out that there are limits to how far tone can go with LLMs. He explains: "No amount of prompting will overcome a model's training. An LLM is technically not capable of emulating tone from sampled input without fine-tuning. It may get close, but you can't expect that simply copying and pasting a small sample of text will have it writing exactly like you have learned to write—you've honed your style over millions of words written over decades. An LLM isn't going to pick up on it with a few-hundred-word sample."[10]

So, it may not write exactly like you, but working to establish tone may get you closer and will help move the chatbot out of default communication mode.

How can you effectively define and control the tone of your chatbot? Here are a few tips and best practices to keep in mind:

---

10. Rob Laughter, personal communication, April 22, 2024.

Consider Your Audience: Your chatbot's tone should be tailored to the needs, preferences, and expectations of your target audience. Consider the demographics, interests, and communication styles of the people interacting with your chatbot and choose a tone that resonates with them.

Align with Your Brand: Your chatbot's tone should be consistent with your overall brand identity and values. If your church or ministry has a distinctive voice and style, ensure your chatbot's tone reflects and reinforces that identity. This helps to create a cohesive and authentic user experience across all touchpoints.

Match the Context: Your chatbot's tone should be appropriate for the context and purpose of the interaction. For example, a chatbot providing serious spiritual guidance should adopt a different tone than one offering lighthearted trivia questions. Think about the user's emotional state and goals in each situation and adjust the tone accordingly.

Use Language Strategically: The words and phrases your chatbot uses can significantly impact its tone. Pay attention to the connotations and emotional qualities of the language you choose. For example, using words like "explore," "discover," and "unleash" can create a tone of excitement and possibility, while words like "support," "guide," and "nurture" can convey a tone of caring and empathy.

Employ Stylistic Techniques: In addition to word choice, you can use various stylistic techniques to shape the tone of your chatbot's responses. For instance, using short, punchy sentences can create a tone of energy and urgency, while longer, more flowing sentences can convey a tone of thoughtfulness and reflection. Similarly, rhetorical questions, analogies, and storytelling can create a more engaging and relatable tone.

Test and Refine: As with other aspects of using chatbots, defining the right tone requires iteration and refinement. Test out different tones with your target audience and

143

gather feedback on how they perceive and respond to the chatbot's communication style. Use this feedback to adjust and fine-tune the tone until it effectively serves your goals and resonates with your users.

By taking the time to define and control the tone of your chatbot thoughtfully, you can create an AI-powered communication experience that not only informs and assists your users but also connects with them on an emotional level. By aligning your chatbot's tone with its persona, audience, and context and by strategically using language and stylistic techniques, you can create an AI-powered voice that truly speaks to the hearts and minds of your community.

SELECTING THE RIGHT CHATBOT

There is a long list of chatbots available for today's AI user, and more are coming daily. While they all basically do the same thing, each has nuances and strengths that might make one leap out over another. Here is a list of some of the most popular, some of which are brand-new and should be well-established by the time the book is published.

CHATGPT (OPENAI)

URL: openai.com/chatgpt

Description: An advanced language model capable of understanding and generating human-like text, designed for a variety of applications, including conversation, content creation, and information retrieval. There are both free and paid versions of this app. The paid version is well worth the money.

What's Unique about It: ChatGPT now includes advanced features such as the ability to interact using voice and images, and it supports custom GPT creation. This multimodal interaction is supported by improvements in the GPT-4o model, which enhances its conversational abilities in writing, math, logical reasoning, and coding. The pro version (ChatGPT Plus and ChatGPT Teams) can also generate imagery through DALL-E.

Challenges: ChatGPT faces challenges related to the accuracy and recency of information it can provide, which is a common limitation amongst all chatbots. The data it relies on is about five months old as of this writing.

CLAUDE (ANTHROPIC)

URL: anthropic.com

Description: Claude is a conversational AI developed by Anthropic. It is designed to be steerable and safe and has applications in content generation and conversation.

What's Unique about It: Claude is known for its safety-oriented design, utilizing what's known as "Constitutional AI" to ensure that its responses adhere to ethical guidelines; this approach makes Claude particularly suitable for sensitive applications where alignment with human values is critical. It also boasts the largest context window of all chatbots, allowing for much longer conversations.

Challenges: Claude's main challenge remains balancing safety with flexibility, as its strong ethical guidelines might limit its ability to engage freely in more open-ended or controversial discussions.

GEMINI (GOOGLE)

URL: gemini.google.com

Description: Originally launched as Bard and later renamed Gemini, it's a conversational AI that generates responses by leveraging Google's large language models.

What's Unique about It: Gemini excels in integrating with Google's ecosystem, providing enhanced capabilities for real-time data processing and access to a wealth of information from the internet, which is unique among chatbots.

Challenges: Similar to other AI models, Gemini must navigate data privacy and accuracy issues, particularly because of its ability to pull in vast amounts of live data. It has faced issues with response accuracy and reliability. In an effort to reduce bias, the earliest iterations of Gemini's image generator would change user inputs under the hood to "remove bias," resulting in (among other things) inaccurate historical imagery.

GROK (XAI)

URL: x.ai

Description: Grok is an AI chatbot known for its less censored, more open approach to dialogue, reflecting the controversial stances of its creator, Elon Musk.

What's Unique about It: It is designed to offer a less censored, more direct form of interaction. It often tackles topics that other chatbots avoid. It's known for its edgy and unfiltered content.

Challenges: Grok's approach can lead to the spread of misinformation and offensive content, posing significant ethical challenges. Elon Musk can be a bit of an erratic leader and may also be a liability to the platform.

JASPER (JASPER)

URL: www.jasper.ai

Description: Jasper AI is a versatile content-creation tool for marketing professionals. It offers specialized capabilities for generating high-quality SEO (search engine optimization)-friendly written content across various platforms. It integrates multiple AI models to enhance productivity and creativity in crafting tailored marketing campaigns and content strategies.

What's Unique about It: Jasper excels in content creation for diverse marketing needs, such as blog posts, social media content, and SEO content. It offers a proprietary AI engine that integrates multiple large language models, allowing for flexible and robust content generation suited to specific marketing goals. Jasper AI is particularly noted for its enterprise-focused features that facilitate end-to-end marketing campaign creation and optimization, which is enhanced by its capability to analyze and infuse content with SEO insights.

Challenges: Jasper's focus on specialized capabilities might limit its appeal to a broader audience needing more generalized AI tools. Additionally, maintaining such a specialized tool involves ensuring that the integration of various AI models works seamlessly and securely, which requires constant updates and security measures to protect user data effectively.

MAGAI (MAGAI)

URL: bit.ly/magaisignup

Description: Magai is an AI-powered platform designed for content creators. It integrates various AI models and tools into a single interface to streamline content generation and management.

What's Unique about It: Magai is a comprehensive platform for content creators, featuring a wide array of tools, including multiple AI models, team collaboration features, and advanced content-generation capabilities like image and text creation.

Challenges: Some users have reported issues with the platform's user interface regarding chat management and document organization. The platform's pricing model may also pose a challenge for some users.

META AI (META PLATFORMS)

URL: ai.meta.com

Description: Meta AI is focused on developing conversational AI that can handle complex, open-domain interactions with high degrees of realism and ethical consideration.

What's Unique about It: Meta AI is enhancing the way users interact with AI across Meta's various platforms, including Facebook and Instagram, by integrating AI into everyday user experiences. The system leverages generative AI to assist in content creation, such as drafting social media posts or creating custom images, and provides interactive AI chat capabilities that can be accessed directly from messaging platforms. Meta AI is built on advanced open weight language models Llama 2 and Llama 3, emphasizing safe and responsible AI interactions.

Challenges: One of the main challenges for Meta AI involves balancing innovation with privacy and ethical considerations, especially as it expands its capabilities in generating realistic media and integrating more deeply into personal and social contexts. Another challenge is ensuring the accuracy and helpfulness of AI-generated content and interactions, maintaining user trust in AI's utility without compromising the authenticity or quality of user experiences.

OPEN-SOURCE LOCAL LLM

It's also worth noting that you can run a local LLM on your own computer. This keeps your data safe because it keeps your information in-house. Check out this article by Rob Laughter for more on how to do that:

bit.ly/LLM-Local

CONCLUSION

I hope you're ready to get on (or back on) the coaster, climb the hill, and experience the thrill of this exhilarating ride. I've equipped you with all the tools you need to get the most out of your preferred chatbot. As you experiment with these techniques, know that even as good as AI is in its current state, it's still basically a toddler. It's not always going to get it right. Be patient. And don't become so reliant on it that you're no longer thinking for yourself. As I've stated multiple times, AI should be a "do it with you, not a do it for you."

In the next chapter, we'll take a comprehensive look at image generation. I'll introduce you to methods that will take your image generation to the next level, share some of the best image-generation tools, and discuss some of the challenges associated with image generation.

CLAUDE'S QUESTIONS FOR REFLECTION

1. What unique opportunities do chatbots and conversational AI present for your ministry context?

2. How can we balance the effectiveness of AI-powered communication with the need for genuine human connection and empathy?

3. What guardrails should we put in place to ensure chatbots are used in ways that align with our values and priorities?

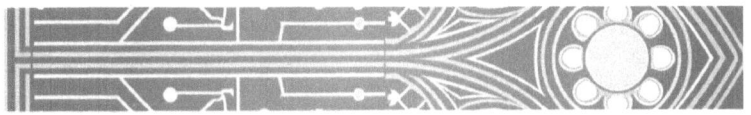

Chapter 8

BEST PRACTICE FOR NEXT-LEVEL IMAGE GENERATION

INTRODUCTION

As a traditional illustrator, graphic designer, and motion graphic artist, this is the section of the book and the thing about AI that I am most excited about. And yet this is one of the aspects of AI that is changing the most rapidly. I'm bound to share a few things with you here that will change by the time you have the opportunity to read this.

The first generative image model I experimented with was DALL-E 2. Back in the summer of 2022, it wasn't a very impressive tool, but it was still fun to play with. I generated several images of Jesus skydiving over New York City. None of them were anywhere near usable beyond just posting silliness on social media. The best way I can describe those early images—or what they reminded me of—is the kind of artwork where you take different pages out of a magazine, cut out various elements, and paste them all together in the same frame. They honestly didn't pose any serious threat to people like me who make their living generating image content.

Boy, have things changed in two short years! Now when I generate an image of Jesus skydiving over New York City, you might believe—if you didn't know about AI—I chartered an airplane, hired an actor, acquired a period-accurate costume, and shot the thing for real with a physical camera. It's that good now—absolutely convincing!

As we move further into the AI conversation in the church, we come to one of the most exciting aspects: AI image generation. This powerful technology is revolutionizing the way we create and share visual content, enabling even those without extensive design experience to become captivating visual storytellers. The professional designer in me (who charges by the hour) struggles a bit with this reality, but the Jesus-minded church leader in me celebrates that anyone who wants to try can now bring the things they have in their head to life. And all without having to devote the twenty-five years I did to mastering Photoshop and programs like it. It's an amazing time to be the church!

Now you can have a picture in your mind that might bring your sermon to life, inspire people to sign up for an event, or depict a favorite biblical character, and—with a little bit of knowledge on how to talk to the AI—you can write a prompt to make that picture a reality. In moments, AI can render your idea and the image will be as good as or even better than you imagined. Of course, it might also churn out a total dud, which you can then tweak until you find just the right iteration.

Whether it's creating a stunning graphic for your church's social media post, an engaging illustration for a sermon, or a beautiful piece of art to inspire your congregation, AI image-generation tools make it possible for anyone to create compelling visuals that capture the heart and soul of their message.

As Christians, we are created in the image of a creative God. Creativity is woven into the very fabric of our being, and we are called to use our gifts and talents to share the love and truth of Christ with the world. In the past, those without artistic training or access to expensive design software may have felt limited in their ability to create visually striking content. But with the advent of AI image generation, the playing field has been leveled, and the doors to creative expression have been thrown wide open.

The Bible is filled with examples of God using ordinary things to accomplish extraordinary purposes. From Moses' staff parting the Red Sea (Exodus 14:16) to David's defeating Goliath with a sling and some stones (1 Samuel 17:49), God has a history of taking simple tools and using them to showcase God's power and glory. AI image generation is no different. While this is no simple tool (under the hood), AI can help us share the gospel in fresh and innovative ways when used with wisdom and intention.

I work with churches of all sizes, but I spend the majority of my time with churches that are small to medium-sized. Financial resources in these churches can be on the lighter side. Hiring a designer, buying a stock photo, or subscribing to a media library is outside the reach of many churches. One of the most significant upsides of AI tools is that they are affordable or even free, making them accessible to churches and ministries of all sizes and means. By leveraging these resources, we can create high-quality visual content without breaking the bank, allowing us not only to be good stewards of the funds entrusted to us but also to create even more compelling content.

For many years, we've known that visual learning is one of the best methods for retention in our present culture. Studies have found that 65 percent of the population are visual learners[11] and found that learn-

---

11. Molly St. Louis, "How to Spot Visual-, Auditory-, and Kinesthetic-Learning Executives," Inc. com, August 1, 2017, https://www.inc.com/molly-reynolds/how-to-spot-visual-auditory-and-kinesthetic-

ing increases by 400 percent when we use images to teach.[12] That means using images isn't just a significant enhancement for our ministries but can have an enormous impact on how people receive, retain, and live into what they're learning in worship (and beyond). I've been arguing for a very long time that our screens are more than simply giant sheets of paper meant for song lyrics, Scripture, and announcements. Instead, they are canvases that allow us to bring the good news to life.

While traditional photography (stock or homegrown) is still extremely valuable for our church communications, AI opens a new world of possibilities concerning imagery. You can now visually illustrate virtually every biblical story you want to tell, turn your word pictures into actual pictures, and design graphics, print pieces, and more with well-written prompts. If the findings in those studies are not reason enough to lean in and begin experimenting with AI, I don't know what is. We can dramatically increase our effectiveness by using images to convey the gospel.

As with any new technology, there is a learning curve. That's where this chapter comes in. In the following pages, we'll explore the ins and outs of AI image generation, from understanding how it works to discovering best practices for creating stunning visuals. We'll also introduce you to some of the most popular AI image-generation tools and provide tips for using them effectively in your ministry.

As we push off from the shore, let's approach AI image generation with a spirit of creativity, curiosity, and discernment. I know there are mixed feelings about artificially generated images, but if you go in with an open mind, you may change your mind when you see what I have to share. Are you ready to unleash your creativity and harness the power of AI image generation? Let's paddle out a little further.

IS AI ART REALLY ART?

As a speaker and consultant, I've encountered skeptics and evangelists for AI-generated art. We've already covered most of the ethical ground in previous chapters. I shared with you how these models were trained, and we explored the copyright concerns pertaining to AI. We won't go

learni.html.

    12. Kiera Sowery, "Microsoft Reveals Visual Learning Improves Memory Retention by 400%," *Student Circuit*, June 28, 2022, https://www.student-circuit.com/news/microsoft-reveals-visual-learning-improves-memory-retention-by-400/.

much further down that stream right now, but I want to address a question I've heard debated numerous times over the last couple of years: "Is AI art really art?" It's a fair question that is worth consideration. I'll share why I think it is and some common misconceptions I hear about why it's not. I invite you to make up your own mind, even if it means disagreeing with me.

In the summer of 2023, I was invited to lead a creative worship event in Knoxville, Tennessee. My host wanted to model some of the things I'd be teaching throughout the event, and he suggested we start the conference off with an opening worship experience. I had a favorite worship service already developed with all the bits and pieces, including media assets, ready to go. For this service, we'd be studying Jeremiah 18:1–7.

In the story, the Lord instructs Jeremiah to visit the potter's house, where he observes the potter working with clay at the wheel. When the pot becomes misshapen and marred in the potter's hands, the potter reshapes the clay into another vessel as he sees fit. The Lord then compares the potter's work to his own relationship with Israel, stating that just as the clay is in the potter's hands, so is Israel in the Lord's hands. The word of the Lord comes to Jeremiah at that moment.

In prepping for this service, my friend the Reverend Tim Jones (the host) shared with me that he had a memory from childhood that mirrored this story. He said that when he was about thirteen years old, he took a family vacation to a Native American reservation in North Carolina. As might be expected for a child of this age, he wasn't overly thrilled about the trip, thinking it might be boring.

He shared that while he would never have admitted it to his parents, he thought it was pretty cool once they arrived at the reservation. As they were exploring the village, a Native American man came out to demonstrate an artisanal process by crafting an item out of clay using a potter's wheel. Tim shared that the man walked to the middle of a viewing area and set the clay on the wheel that was awaiting him. He began pumping the wheel with his foot while working the clay in his fingers. The clay was spinning at a high rate of speed, and it started to wobble. It seemed the man had pumped his foot on the wheel a little too hard, and the clay began to separate into several pieces, flying off the wheel onto the ground. The crowd sat silently, collectively holding their breath as the man bent over to collect the pieces. He brushed them off and sat them back on the wheel. The clay had bits of debris and grass in it after its tumble, but it didn't matter. The man began to pump his foot again and worked the clay until he had a finished piece ready for curing in his hand.

Tim said the entire demonstration was thoroughly inspiring. Sitting on the edge of my seat listening to the story, I quickly responded, "Do you have a photo of this man or any photos from this vacation?" Tim said, "No. It was the eighties. I was thirteen, and we didn't carry cameras in our pockets back in those days."

This story was already powerful, but I felt an image would level it up by several notches. I asked if he minded if I generated one with AI. Without hesitation, he said, "Absolutely, go for it." I generated the image you see here.

When it was time for the service and Tim began preaching, I brought the image up on the screen as he told the story. If you listened carefully, you could hear an audible reaction as the image displayed synced perfectly with his story. Of course, the people in the worship experience had no idea it was generated by AI. If you're reading this as a skeptic of AI, you might have negative feelings about not disclosing this in the moment. I wanted people to experience it free from any kind of bias for or against AI. In other words, I just wanted to show it and see how it hit them. You could make the choice to disclose this during the sermon.

Tim finished the sermon; people in the room were moved by the entire thing, and we dismissed for the evening. The following day, I led a workshop on using artificial intelligence tools in the church. I let participants in on the fact that the image from that story was AI-generated. There was another audible reaction. When I asked how people felt about that, there were mixed feelings. The majority of people felt that the story and image represented the most powerful moment in the entire sermon, and they didn't care where the image came from. Others bristled at the idea that it was artificially created. I can understand both reactions.

I explained that we didn't have any images from that vacation but that I was able to prompt AI in such a way as to capture what Tim would share verbally. You can't see it in the book because the image is black and white, but the color version even looked like a Kodak Instamatic camera photo with bluish and yellowish muted tones. I specifically prompted it that way. I further explained that if I'd tried to find an image of a Native American man sculpting at a potter's wheel from a stock photo library, I would very likely have failed to find it. A photo that specific probably doesn't exist in such libraries.

As the conversation continued, some of those uncomfortable with the revelation that the image was AI conveyed that it felt inauthentic to use this for his story. At that moment, the Holy Spirit triggered a memory from my childhood in which I had a similar reaction to an "inauthentic" illustration being used.

I grew up about four blocks away from my church. It was a short walk from my home, and I'd occasionally walk down for various reasons during the summer. One day, I popped in and started chatting with the church secretary. Her name (by the way) was Millie—the most perfect United Methodist Church secretary name ever. She looked exactly the way you're picturing her now. Millie was the sweetest woman you'd ever meet, which is why I loved stopping in to talk to her. Anyway, on this day, she asked me as I was heading out if I could drop the pastor's mail on his desk (he wasn't in at the time). I was happy to help.

When I performed my task, I saw a book on his desk that I'd never seen before. The title read *1000 Illustrations for Preaching and Teaching*. I opened it up and thumbed through the pages, recognizing one of the stories the pastor had used many months prior in his sermon. For a moment, I thought, "Wait, that wasn't his story? That's not right. That's not authentic." At the time, the knowledge that he'd used a made-up story that wasn't really from his life felt very artificial. Then I started thinking about how I remembered that story and, more importantly, the point behind it for all that time. Ultimately, this illustration drove the sermon idea home for me.

Reflecting on that experience, I realized that using illustrative stories to communicate biblical truth isn't wrong, fake, or inauthentic. Jesus did this all the time—they're called parables. Perhaps you've heard of them.

Did Jesus literally know a father who had two sons, one of whom squandered his inheritance while the other stayed at home on the straight and narrow? Or was that a story to help us understand the nature of God? Or maybe it was so we could see ourselves as the prodigal son. Or perhaps so we could see ourselves as the other brother. Regardless, stories have power. Images do too. We can harness that power through AI tools in new and exciting ways.

I'd like to boldly suggest that AI is a chance for us to turn our verbal illustrations into transformational, inspiring, modern-day visual parables. Making them isn't even all that hard, but we'll get to that. Of course, there are ethical considerations about what types of images to make, how we use them, and how we disclose to our congregations that they are AI-generated. We'll cover that in the AI policy section at the end of the book.

THE CASE FOR AI ART

AI art is a reflection of human expression and imagination.

When a user conceptualizes an idea and communicates it to an AI image generator, the resulting artwork is a manifestation of their creativity and imagination. The user's unique vision, as expressed through their prompts and interactions with the AI, drives the creative process. In this sense, AI art is an extension of human creativity, leveraging technology as a tool to bring ideas to life. Keep in mind AI does not create images independently. Human creativity is required.

AI art can elicit emotional responses, just like traditional art.
One of the hallmarks of art is its ability to evoke emotions in the viewer. AI-generated art has proven capable of stirring a wide range of emotions, from joy and wonder to sadness and anger. If an AI artwork can connect with its audience on an emotional level, it has achieved one of the primary characteristics of art.

AI art can serve as a commentary on contemporary issues.
Like traditional art, AI-generated art can be used to provide commentary on political, social, religious, and cultural issues. Users can create AI artworks that spark conversations, challenge norms, and inspire change by inputting prompts that reflect current events, movements, or controversies.

When I was in high school, our local newspaper invited me to create political cartoons. I loved finding humorous ways of commenting through art on what was happening in the world. Nowadays, I don't often have time to create a piece of illustrated art in a timely enough manner for it to still be relevant to the day's events, but AI has changed the game. Here's a political cartoon–style piece I made on the day following the 2024 solar eclipse that got quite a bit of buzz online.

AI art can be aesthetically beautiful and pleasing.
Beauty is subjective, but AI art has demonstrated the ability to create visually stunning and aesthetically pleasing pieces. From photorealistic landscapes to surreal, dreamlike compositions, AI image generators can produce artworks that captivate the eye and inspire a sense of awe. Here are some AI-generated images that received lots of buzz when I released them on MLK Day.

THE CASE AGAINST AI ART

AI art isn't original; it's ripping off artists.

One of the main criticisms of AI art is that it is not truly original, as the AI models are trained on vast datasets of existing artworks. This has led some to argue that AI art is essentially "stolen" or derivative, lacking the originality and authenticity of human-created art.

While AI models do learn from existing artworks (the overwhelming majority of which were scraped from the internet without permission), the process of generating new images is not a direct copy or reproduction of those training data. There is a misconception that AI image generators are pulling elements from existing images to create new works. It doesn't grab a tree from this image, the sky from another, someone's face from yet another image, etc. When something new is generated, it's the first time that person, place, or thing has ever existed.

Rob Laughter explains how there is no copyrighted material included in the AI models: "While it's true that A.I. image generators are trained on existing images, they simply 'look at' images to learn what a tree, or the sky, or a face looks like, before discarding the image. A.I. image models don't contain any image data at all, copyrighted or otherwise." The AI uses the learned patterns, styles, and techniques to create novel combinations and compositions.

It's sort of like me saying to you, "Draw an apple." You've seen enough apples over your lifetime that you know what the characteristics of an apple are. You know the color, shape, texture, and various parts. In this sense, AI art can be seen as a form of remixing or transformative use, not unlike how human artists draw inspiration from and build upon the works of others.

AI art is inconsistent and lacks the refinement of human-created art.

AI image generators can sometimes produce inconsistent results with images that contain artifacts, distortions, or nonsensical elements. Too many fingers, misspelled text, and odd-looking faces are just a few things that occasionally appear. This lack of consistency and refinement may detract from AI art's overall quality and impact.

While it is true that the same prompt will not produce the exact same results over and over, there are ways to help the tools to give you more consistent characters, styles, and other characteristics. There has been dramatic improvement with hands and faces over the last six to eight months, and the newest models have learned to spell things right about 60–70 percent of the time. By the time this book is published, it may be possible that the spelling problems are a thing of the past. Remember, this is the worst it'll ever be.

Also, remember that inconsistencies and imperfections are not unique to AI art; human-created art can also be inconsistent or unrefined, and these qualities do not necessarily negate its status as art. Nature-scene painter Bob Ross was famous for talking about "happy accidents." Sometimes, AI-generated art generates a happy accident that results in a unique and beautiful piece of art.

Just like when working with the chatbots we covered earlier, you don't have to go with what the model generates on its first go. You can (in a sense) converse with these models too, though it is different than an LLM. You can tweak your prompt and try again. And if it's mostly there, but has some issues, there are tools that will let you fix the problems. Some of these are AI tools, as we'll cover later, and others are traditional tools like Photoshop.

Rob Laughter shared with me a helpful new mantra of his: "Consider anything that comes out of AI—images, text, etc.—a first draft. You're a human with agency. You don't have to take the first thing that it spits out."

AI art may harm human artists by devaluing their work and skills.

Some argue that the rise of AI art threatens human artists, as it may devalue their work and make it harder for them to compete in the market. If AI can generate art quickly and cheaply, it could potentially replace the need for human artists in certain contexts.

I don't want to dismiss this argument too quickly. Some of the concerns about AI's impact on the art market are valid, in my view. Is it possible that commissioned work for some artists could decline if AI has trained on their style? Why pay for what you can prompt?

Artists should be allowed to opt out of their art being included in the training data used to develop these models. In many cases, they already are allowed to do so. Unfortunately, that won't prevent a bad actor from training on their art anyway.

Those comfortable with being included should also be allowed to opt in. AI art can also be seen as a tool that empowers human artists and expands the possibilities of artistic expression. Many artists already incorporate AI into their creative workflows, using it to generate ideas, experiment with styles, and push the boundaries of what is possible. Rather than replacing human artists, AI can collaborate and catalyze new forms of artistic innovation.

Ultimately, the question of whether AI art is truly art is a complex and subjective one, with valid arguments on both sides. Keep exploring. Try to remain open-minded. And don't contribute to the problem. If you feel like AI is harming artists, don't ask it for artwork in the style of specific artists.

THE AI-GENERATED ART STIGMA

A distinct segment of our population will reject AI-generated images no matter how good they may be. During the 2024 Super Bowl, the controversial "He Gets Us" campaign ran a couple of television spots featuring a unique set of stylized photographs. Viewer reaction to the ads was intense. People both loved and loathed them. There were many reasons for the criticisms—we won't go into most of those here—but one critique really caught my attention. It came from what I'd call the "anti-AI contingent." As consumer-level AI has become more mainstream in the form of DALL-E, Bing Image Creator, Gemini, and others, some people have developed an eye for AI-generated content (at least in those forms).

Social media posts skewered the images featured in the spot, erroneously believing that they were made by artificial intelligence. It turns out every photo in the ads was crafted and captured by fine-art still photographer Julia Fullerton-Batten. Perhaps the anti-AI contingent has developed such a heightened sensitivity to AI's presence that they've begun seeing AI even in works crafted entirely by human hands. And they're not the only ones. As *Ad Age* reported, "Even news outlets shared in the confusion and outrage. SB Nation, the sports blogging site owned by Vox Media, published an article during the game titled 'This AI ad for Jesus is easily the worst Super Bowl ad of all time.'"[13] The issue isn't so much that viewers mistook the images for AI; the more teachable moment here for us is that they had such an adverse reaction to the idea that it was. What can we learn from this?

Advertisers are working to make images less obviously AI-generated. *The Wall Steet Journal* describes the shift: "Creators, production studios and advertising agencies as a result are finding workarounds to make AI imagery more palatable to consumers. They're using well-worn tools such as Adobe's Photoshop to add, rather than take out, imperfec tions; learning to write elaborate AI prompts to achieve the aesthetic they want; and collaborating with AI artists who have mastered specific styles."[14]

The goal is to steer clear of what is sometimes called "the AI look," which features hyperrealism, overly shiny hair, extra fingers, and weird-looking ears (among other things). Interestingly, some have speculated that the "AI look" was originally imposed on DALL-E 3 to prevent it

---

13.   Asa Hiken, "'He Gets Us' Super Bowl Ad Sparks AI Confusion—How Brands Can Avoid Similar Backlash," *Ad Age*, February 13, 2024, https://adage.com/article/special-report-super-bowl/jesus-he-gets-us-super-bowl-commercial-causes-ai-confusion-and-lesson-marketers/2541256.

14.   Katie Deighton, "How the Ad Industry Is Making AI Images Look Less Like AI," *Wall Street Journal*, April 2, 2024, https://www.wsj.com/articles/how-the-ad-industry-is-making-ai-images-look-less-like-ai-8b4250fd.

from being mistaken for reality and used to deceptive ends. As the models mature, these things are becoming less and less of a concern, and as you'll see later, an intentional prompting strategy can make all the difference.

The backlash against AI has some merit but can also be somewhat misplaced. I'm against the use of bad AI. Some of the stuff you see out there is atrocious. I was recently walking past a restaurant with some friends, and we spotted an AI-generated flier with a woman with extremely deformed fingers. I'll push against that with the best of them.

The ire regarding AI is misplaced when it focuses on the tool. It should really be directed toward the bad actor. AI doesn't create anything on its own. It has no will or agenda. It's neutral. The person doing the generating is the one "swinging the axe" in harmful ways.

Another reason stigmas exist is that critics feel that while the models can produce technically proficient art, they lack the personal insight, emotional depth, and original vision that human artists bring to their work. They argue that art is not merely about technical skill but also about the unique experiences, perspectives, and emotions the artist pours into their creation. AI-generated art, while impressive, may be seen as a product of algorithms and data rather than a deeply personal expression.

However, this argument fails to consider that the model doesn't, as I said, create AI art on its own. Humans bring their own life stories, struggles, joys, points of view, and inspiration to the prompts they write. When used by a talented artist, there's a back-and-forth dance between that artist and the AI that leads to a final output that is more than simply pushing a button.

As people trying to do no harm and do as much good as possible with this tool, it's essential to approach these concerns with a balanced perspective. While the critique of AI art raises some valid points, there are also arguments in favor of embracing AI as a tool for artistic expression and exploration. Artists like me see AI as a collaborator that can enhance and augment human creativity rather than replace it. By working alongside AI, artists may discover new techniques, styles, and ideas they wouldn't have otherwise explored. It's even possible for an artist to train AI on his or her style to experiment in ways that were previously impossible.

We've established that as Christians, we are called to use our God-given talents and abilities to create works that glorify God and inspire others. At the same time, we must be mindful of the potential drawbacks and exercise discernment in our use of AI. We should strive to create authentic, meaningful art that reflects our unique experiences and perspectives as individuals and as followers of Christ. As Christians engaged in the arts, we have an opportunity to help shape this conversation. Are you up to join in?

WHAT IS AI IMAGE GENERATION?

If you're new to this, you might wonder what exactly AI image generation is. Well, it is the use of artificial intelligence, particularly generative models, to create or modify images based on textual or other forms of input. These AI models have been trained on enormous datasets of images and their associated descriptions, allowing them to understand the relationship between visual elements and the words used to describe them.

The power of AI image generation lies in its ability to create a wide range of images, from photorealistic scenes to abstract art. The sky's the limit, literally and figuratively. You can make that sky picturesque, ominous, alien, overcast, or even filled with a deceptively real solar eclipse (see photo). Some common types of images that AI can generate include:

1. **Realistic photos:** AI can create images that look so real they are nearly indistinguishable at first glance from traditional photography. They can simulate everything from realistic lighting to real-world textures, lens anomalies, and other fine details.

2. **Illustrations and digital art:** AI can generate illustrations and digital art in various styles, from cartoons and anime to painterly and abstract styles.

3. **Concept art and design:** AI can create concept art for movies, video games, and product design, helping to visualize ideas and iterate on designs quickly. I use AI to mock up logo concepts, saving lots of time and giving me significant inspiration.

4. **Manipulated or edited images:** AI can also be used to modify existing images, such as changing the style of an image, adding or removing objects, or even generating new images based on a combination of input images.

Of course, you're not limited to those types, and the beauty of AI is that it might eventually usher in entirely new categories of art that don't yet exist. What will you create next?

LLMs vs. Image Models

So, is this image-generation thing the same as prompting for chatbots? Do I just use the natural language processing strategies I learned about in the last chapter? No. While generative AI apps like Midjourney and DALL-E share some similarities with large language models (LLMs), they interpret and process text differently. LLMs are primarily designed to understand and generate human language, while image-generation AI focuses on creating visual content based on textual descriptions that were trained into the model. LLMs are trained on text alone; image generators are trained on images and captions that describe them.

So, Midjourney, DALL-E, Stable Diffusion, and other apps in this category are specifically designed to create images from textual descriptions. While they also process and interpret text, their primary goal is to translate that text into visual representations. They don't understand grammar, syntax, and sentence structure like an LLM does.

How Image Generation Works

While we could do an extensive exploration of how image generation works under the hood, I will give you a very basic explanation of how these things work. The wizardry in the code is fascinating but not completely necessary for you to understand in order to use it. If you want to geek out on it, you can search some of the terms below or check the glossary in the back of the book where I've shared some of the techno-jargon.

Rob Laughter explains image generation like this:

> Image models are trained by comparing millions of images with the text that accompanies them. Image models learn the relationships between the concepts in the text and the features of the associated image.
>
> From a photo of a young man and a photo of a dog, the image model could learn the concepts that both images share—they are both living things, with a face, and hair—as well as their differences.
>
> As the model is trained, it tries to create an image with the same concepts, and then compares how close it has gotten. The difference between the original image and the generated image gives the model an idea of what features it has learned, and which it needs to understand better.
>
> Repeat that across a dataset containing millions of images, and the model becomes very good at reproducing images with those characteristics.[15]

So, when you want to make an image, here's a very basic understanding of how generative AI apps typically work:

Text encoding: The input text, known as a prompt (the part you type in describing what you want), is first processed by an encoder, which converts the words and phrases into a numerical representation (the tokens we talked about earlier) that the AI can understand. This step is similar to how LLMs process text, but the focus is on extracting visual concepts and relationships rather than linguistic patterns.

Rob Laughter further explains how this works: "You should also know that each model will produce the best images when prompted in the same manner in which it was trained. For modern models, that's more natural and descriptive language, thanks to the fact that modern models are trained on synthetic captions from vision models like

---

15.   Rob Laughter, personal communication, April 22, 2024.

GPT-4 that can more accurately describe what's in an image."[16]

Image generation: The encoded text is then passed through a series of neural networks, such as diffusion models, which generate an image based on the input. These networks have been trained on vast datasets of images and their corresponding descriptions, allowing them to create novel images that match the given prompt.

Again, Rob Laughter gives us a breakdown of how this works: "Image generators—diffusion models specifically—create images by arranging random noise into coherent images through a series of incremental steps, guided by what [the image generator] learned about the desired features in the training process. With each step, it gets a little closer to the desired image until the final step, where the latent image is 'decoded' into the final pixels you see on your screen."[17]

Image refinement: The generated image may undergo additional processing steps, such as upscaling and noise reduction, to improve its quality, increase resolution, and improve fine details.

It's worth noting that some AI systems, like OpenAI's DALL-E 3, Google's Gemini, and Meta's Meta.ai, incorporate elements of LLMs in their image generation process. You input your prompt into the LLM, and then it writes a prompt under the hood that, in turn, tells the image generator what to create. Unfortunately, Rob Laughter says, "LLMs do a terrible job of writing prompts." You won't see what it's done to change your prompt, but most of the time, it's not good. The best use of LLMs in image generation right now is—like any other generative AI feature—to take what it gives you as a first draft, and then make it better. Make it your own.

BEST PRACTICES FOR PROMPTING

Now that we have a basic understanding of how AI image generation works, I want to show you how to get the best images possible out of it.

---

16. Rob Laughter, personal communication, April 22, 2024.
17. Rob Laughter, personal communication, April 22, 2024.

If you want to make great images, this will probably be the most dog-eared section of your book.

As I have said many times already, you need to approach your work with AI like a conversation, not just a simple command or a query. Even working with imagery requires an iterative process where you try things, fail, experiment again, and work until you've achieved success. Every now and then you get lucky, and your image is right on the first shot. Other times, it might take multiple tries, with lots of variations, rerolls (retries of the same prompt), and additional tweaks. And even when it's mostly right, I still regularly have to fix things in Photoshop.

Most failed AI images happen because the person prompting hasn't given the image generator enough information to be successful. It's also important to know that you prompt a little differently in an LLM (like ChatGPT, DALL-E, Gemini/Bard) than you do in an app like Midjourney or Stable Diffusion, image generators that aren't driven by an LLM.

If I'm working in an LLM and I prompt something like, "Create an image of a boat," the AI doesn't have much to go on. You're going to end up with a very generic-looking boat. The AI isn't going to know if you mean a sailboat, cruise ship, small fishing boat, tugboat, or one of the plethora of other boat types that exist.

When you add more information, like, "I'd like a steamboat on the Mississippi River. It's a white boat with red paddles," and (since we can legally do this now . . .), "Steamboat Willie is the captain," you'd continue, "I'd like for it to be late afternoon and shot on a film camera." You can usually get something that looks amazing when you add all of that.

If you prompted these same ideas in a program not driven by an LLM (Midjourney, Stable Diffusion), you will want to avoid adding in the natural language words like "Create an image of . . .", or "I'd like a . . ." These will only confuse the model. Prompting for Midjourney would look more like, "A photo of a steamboat with red paddles. Steamboat Willie is above deck, piloting the ship, it is late afternoon, shot on a film camera."

Let me walk you through my methodology for prompting images well. I've learned bits and pieces of this from people like influencers Matt Wolfe (https://www.youtube.com/@mreflow), Tim Simmons (youtube.

com/@TheoreticallyMedia), and Olivio Sarikas (youtube.com/@OlivioSarikas), and I've also done tons of my own experimentation.

Not everything I share here is necessary for every prompt. I'll start the list below with the most important things and move further down to the more optional ones. I like to think of prompting a bit like that beloved childhood road-trip game, Mad Libs. When teaching image prompting in a webinar or seminar format, I do a modified version of the methodology I will show you next. I call this exercise "Midjourney Mad Libs." It'll work with any image generator. Midjourney is just my favorite, and the title has a nice ring to it. Here we go:

Medium

The first thing is the most practical. You must tell the AI what medium you want to work in. Is this a photo, painting, pencil drawing, Lego, papercraft, clay, or other medium? It'll work in virtually any style. If you can think of it, there's a high likelihood AI can render it.

Subject

We then move on to the subject of our image. What person or thing do you want to see in this image? Is it Jesus? Darth Vader? A cute bunny? A fancy car? AI isn't going to know who some of the people you might try to prompt are, so keep that in mind. Depending on the platform you're using, you might also be restricted in who and what you can prompt in your image. Political figures, copyright-protected characters, and even Jesus will be restricted subjects in certain generators.

Action

What is your person or thing doing? Is Jesus surfing? Is Darth Vader grilling hamburgers for the troops? Is the bunny attacking someone? If AI sees the action you're describing in the training data, it'll understand what you're asking for and include it in your image.

Setting

Now we should describe the place where your person or thing is. Where is Jesus surfing? Is Darth on Hoth? We're just going to tell the AI where the subject is. It can be indoors or outdoors, in a logical location, or somewhere totally off the wall.

Time of Day:

Our prompt is coming together nicely, but this parameter adds a surprising amount of pizzazz to some images. Is it sunrise? Midday? Evening? Nighttime? Describing the time of day can change the lighting,
cast different kinds of shadows on the scene, adjust the colors, add lens
flares, and even affect scenes indoors.

Descriptors:

Now read back through your prompt and add some spice to your recipe.
What adjectives can you include to better describe your scene? Is your
photo shot in a documentary style? Is it a painterly image? Is Darth
Vader looking menacing? What color is that fancy car? If you've chosen
a human subject, what gender, race, and physical description should
you include? I've found that adding words like "picturesque" before a
sky or "mysterious" during a night scene can change the tone. Experiment here, but don't unnecessarily overload your prompt with too many
details.

Camera/Media Type

When I get near the end of my prompt, I like to give specifics about
the media type I'm using. This can help create better results. So, if you
add "shot on a DSLR camera" or add a specific camera model and a
specific lens type, that can also enhance the image. If I say, "Shot on
an iPhone" or "Shot on a disposable film camera," those things can
change the image's look as well. Of course, not every image you generate will be a photo. If I say "painting" at the beginning of the prompt,
then I might include the words "painted in oils" or "painted in water-
colors" near the end of my prompt. These media settings can change
your outputs in powerful ways.

Style

This one is probably the most optional of the bunch, but if I'm prompting for a photo, telling AI that I want a "fisheye lens" or "sepia-tone" or
"shallow depth of field" or "Instamatic camera" will have a noticeable
(and often dramatic) impact. This is true for other media as well. If
you were prompting for an oil painting, you could say "impasto style"
(which is a very thick style of painting) or "chiaroscuro style" (which
uses strong contrasting lights and darks), and those descriptors would

171

change the results. You may be reading this and thinking, "I don't know camera types, painting styles, etc."; just ask your favorite chatbot to provide you with a list, and it'll do it in seconds.

Aspect Ratio

Your prompt is ready to go now, but the final step is to tell the AI what size you want the final output to be. It won't do you much good for you to generate the perfect 1:1 square image for your 16:9 screen. And if you're trying to make an image for Instagram and you make a 16:9 image, you'll lose a lot of the image on a 9:16 canvas. Each image generator can conform your design to a specific aspect ratio, with most including buttons to handle this. If you don't know how to achieve this, a quick Google search or a conversation with your favorite chatbot should easily produce the answers.

Rob Laughter offers us this fun fact: "Aspect ratio will actually have an impact on the style of the generated image. Aspect ratio is considered in the training process. . . . Generate a 2:3 image and you're more likely to get a portrait. Generate a 16:9 or 21:9 ratio and you're more likely to get something more cinematic."[18]

Including those elements in your prompts should make a world of difference. Generally, the more detailed and specific your textual input is, the better the AI can understand and generate the desired image. And while it's important to be descriptive, it's also crucial to use clear and concise language. Avoid ambiguous or contradictory statements that could confuse the AI. Also, overloading your prompt with too many details can be counterproductive. You want to include enough detail to make for an interesting image without adding so many complex details and relationships that the AI has to fight your prompt to generate a coherent image.

Don't be discouraged if the first generated image doesn't perfectly match your vision. You can eventually get there. The other day, I was working on a project for a book publisher that involved retelling Jesus' parables in modern-day settings. It took me nearly eight hours to complete just one image. Obviously, you won't need to spend that much time on most of your images, but AI image generation often involves an iterative process of generating images, evaluating the results, and refining your

---

18. Rob Laughter, personal communication, April 22, 2024.

input based on what you like or dislike about the output. And if it brings any sense of calm, know that the next image I created for that project took about forty-five minutes for the entire back-and-forth process.

ADVANCED TOOLS

Several tools and processes can help you get your design to the finish line in a way that aligns with your vision. About half the time, when I'm trying to capture a specific idea, I'll use these techniques:

Variations

Every now and then, you get something close to what you had in mind but just isn't quite there. The feel might be right, but the composition is off. Or maybe you'd like to see a different angle, or you want to change the lighting. Perhaps the AI left out a couple of important aspects of your prompt. Almost every image generator has a feature that will take the image you've created and "reroll the dice" based on the look you currently have. Here's how to accomplish remixing in some of the most commonly used AI generators.

In *Midjourney*, you get four options every time you generate an image. You can create a variation of those four options by hitting the variation buttons. You can gain further control by turning on the remix function in the settings. With remix on, when you click one of the variation options, you'll get a prompt window that gives you a chance to recraft/tweak your prompt before the next generation. Under the hood, Rob Laughter explains, "It's doing an img2img, denoising the original, and then regenerating the image from the partially denoised starting point to generate a new image with the same essential structure."[19] This gives you some really exciting and useful new options based on what you liked in the original round of outputs.

Leonardo.Ai also allows you to generate new images based on images generated by other users. Clicking on another user's existing image will give you all its information (positive and negative prompts, resolution, model, etc.). When you click on the image, you'll find a remix button that

19.   Rob Laughter, personal communication, April 22, 2024.

will load its details, allowing you to generate something similar. This is a great way to learn new techniques and achieve different looks.

You can also regenerate your images. Click on the image you want to change. All its settings will reload. From there, you can change the prompt and hit the generate button. Your changes will be incorporated into the next generation.

Ideogram.ai has a remix button that lets you remix your own and other users' images. You set an image weight to adjust the influence of the input image (from a technical perspective, adjusting how thoroughly the image will be denoised before regenerating). This lets you piggyback existing designs to create new designs. It is quite a helpful tool.

DALL-E recently added a feature that will allow you to vary all or part of your image. Once you've generated two images (DALL-E's default output is two images), click on the one you want to reprompt and tell it what you'd like to change. DALL-E will do its best to create a new variation for you based on your prompt. This has worked fairly well in my experiments, but your mileage may vary.

Stable Diffusion (the most complex and advanced AI generator) can also remix images. Because of the complexity involved for remixing in this app, I won't get into the specifics here. Countless tutorials on YouTube will walk you through it. You're looking for img2img or instruct pix2pix.

Inpainting

Sometimes your image is nearly perfect, but there's one part that needs to be tweaked. Rather than remixing the entire image, you can target a certain area to change.

Midjourney has a "vary region" option that lets you draw a box or use a lasso tool to outline the part of the image you don't like. Once your selection is complete, you can create a prompt for just that area. I've had many good results with this tool, though sometimes it takes many different prompting experiments to get it to work. Try lots of different phrases to describe what you're after.

Leonardo.Ai employs inpainting through its "real-time canvas." With an adjustable-size brush, you can draw over the part you want to change and enter a prompt, and it'll show you (almost instantly) the new version. A "creativity strength" slider and different styles help dial in your tweaks even more.

DALL-E has a feature called "select" that allows you to draw a free-form shape around the area you want to reprompt. It works almost identically to Midjourney's vary region tool.

Adobe Photoshop introduced a feature called "generative fill" to its toolset in June of 2023. It's basically inpainting. Like the others mentioned, this game-changing advancement allows a user to select an area of the image and then prompt to add or remove objects. This tool is so intuitive that it often doesn't even need a text prompt from you to fix the issues you're trying to fix. It'll analyze what's around it, blend bad transitions, remove objects, fix lighting, improve shading, and more. Of course, if you want to add something new to the image, that'll require some words from you. Generative fill has been such a timesaver and makes things possible that were once impractical or impossible to achieve.

Stable Diffusion has had an inpainting feature for a very long time. It was one of the first image generators to include this powerful feature.

Every AI image-generation tool will eventually add inpainting to its feature set. The tools I've mentioned here will undoubtedly continue to improve this function for future iterations.

Outpainting

Inpainting is adding things to an existing image (painting something in); outpainting is adding additional things outside the existing canvas. This was the revolutionary tool that began my AI journey. Way back at the beginning of this book, I described my amazement at DALL-E 2's newly released outpainting. I expanded the Mona Lisa painting to be five times its size, and every new pixel felt like it belonged in the original image.

Midjourney has arrows that allow you to extend the canvas in any direction. It flawlessly adds to the scene in a way that feels like someone tilted or panned a tripod. Even to this day, I am amazed at how good it is.

Leonardo.Ai's canvas can be expanded in any direction, and it renders those pixel-perfect extensions with ease.

Adobe Photoshop includes "Generative Expand" in its feature set. Once you expand the canvas, you'll have three options for the newly generated scene. If you don't like those, you can generate more.

Consistent Characters/Styles

From the earliest days of generative AI, creators in the image space have longed for the ability to create consistent characters and art styles. For various reasons, this has been difficult for AI to achieve, but developers are continually working on improving the consistency and coherence of AI-generated characters.

Several different techniques and technologies can get you closer to consistent characters. Let's just say you want to depict the story of Peter walking on water with Jesus in image form. To follow the story, you will want a consistent look, a consistent Jesus, and a consistent Peter. Otherwise, things are going to get very confusing.

When you prompt each scene, regardless of platform, you'll likely get very different-looking individuals, and even the image style can change. Presently, not every platform has the ability to generate consistent characters. Some tools aren't robust enough . . . yet! Give it six months or a year, and they'll likely tackle that issue.

For now, here are some things that'll help:

Seed Numbers

Seed numbers are a starting point for the randomness in the generation process. This automatically generated number is assigned to your image by default. You can also assign a seed number manually. By using the same seed number with the same image generator and the same parameters, you can reproduce the same (or very similar) outputs consistently. This is crucial when you need to maintain uniformity across different images of the same character, as it improves the possibility that all random elements introduced by the AI are nearly identical each time. This method is particularly beneficial in environments where repeatability is necessary. That said, it isn't foolproof.

By the way, DALL-E 3's equivalent of a seed number is a Gen ID. Click a generated image and chat with ChatGPT. Ask it for the Gen ID and it will retrieve it for you. You can then use it for subsequent images.

Image References

For platforms like Midjourney and Stable Diffusion, starting with a high-quality reference image and using detailed text prompts that specify physical attributes, clothing, and personality traits can sometimes help you create consistent results. A reference image, or images, can help the AI maintain a consistent appearance across different images.

Midjourney will allow you to upload multiple images to use as references to include in your prompt. There are three types of inputs:

image to image inputs, character reference inputs, and style references. Using those, it'll do its best to build a character based on those images. Rob Laughter explains the three methods:

1. Image input, for img2img. Partially denoises the image, then uses it as a starting point for the image generation. It can retain broad details like color, tone, and composition, but not subject.

2. Character reference. This works pretty well, actually, for character consistency, as long as the image was generated with Midjourney. If using a random image, it does a decent job, but it won't be a perfect likeness. Using a weight of 100 will retain the character's face and wardrobe. Using a weight of 0 will focus on the face.

3. Style reference. Self-explanatory. It will imitate the style of the image. Works pretty well.[20]

In Stable Diffusion, you can do an image-to-image prompt, where you upload an image as the input. You then combine that with a text prompt to generate an image. This method does create decent results but goes to an entirely higher level when extensions like IP adapters and ControlNet are installed. This feature has the same limitations as Midjourney's image prompting for character consistency. It'll retain some tone, structure, etc., but won't create consistent styles or characters. Pages and pages about ControlNet could be written here. That's more specialized than I want to go in this book, but a quick YouTube search will equip you with everything you need to know.

Character and Style References

Midjourney offers two powerful parameters for creating consistent characters across multiple images: Character Reference and Style Reference. By using Character Reference and providing a specific image URL, you can increase the probability that Midjourney maintains the key visual traits of your character, such as face, hair, and clothing. This is particularly helpful when you need a recognizable and consistent character throughout various scenes or panels in your project.[21]

---

20. Rob Laughter, personal communication, April 22, 2024.
21. "Character Reference," accessed April 20, 2024, Midjourney, https://docs.midjourney.com/docs/character-reference.

The Character Weight parameter allows you to control the level of consistency, with higher values resulting in a closer match to the reference image. Combining Character Reference with Style Reference takes your character consistency to the next level by ensuring a cohesive artistic style across all your images.[22] This method is unique to Midjourney.

Leonardo.Ai also offers two approaches to consistent characters. One involves training a model, and the other does not.

If you opt for the method without model training, you'll need to craft a detailed initial prompt that serves as a blueprint for your character's appearance and context. By consistently using the character's name and description in each new prompt, you can maintain some level of consistency as you depict them in different scenarios.

Platforms like Leonardo.Ai and Stable Diffusion can train custom models (called LoRAs) for those seeking higher consistency and customization. This process involves creating a dataset specifically for your character and populating it with multiple reference images that capture their desired traits. By training the AI on these curated images, you can teach it to recognize and generate your character consistently across various scenes. When generating new images, you'll use specific prompts that instruct the AI to utilize your trained model, allowing you to refine and adjust the output to ensure your character remains true to its established identity.[23] The Stable Diffusion community has trained a ton of styles, characters, and concepts that you can use to create consistent images. Check out www.civitai.com to explore these, but be careful, there is a lot of "not safe for work" material there. There is an option to filter that stuff out.

Face Swap

If you're trying to get the same character repeatedly and just aren't getting there with other methods, and your character is a person, you might want to get as close as you can with a prompt, then swap the face in the end. Several apps have this functionality, and there are even apps built for this specific purpose.

---

22.   Mukund Kapoor, "How to Create Consistent Characters in Midjourney (Character Reference Guide)," Great AI Prompts, updated March 15, 2024, https://www.greataiprompts.com/guide/midjourney/midjourneys-new-character-reference/.

23.   Stuart, "Creating Consistent Characters," Leonardo.Ai, https://intercom.help/leonardo-ai/en/articles/8584503-creating-consistent-characters.

There is a standalone open source app called InsightFace that will help you tackle the job. It focuses on 2D and 3D face analysis, primarily through deep learning models. It offers state-of-the-art solutions for face detection, recognition, and alignment, which means you can swap a face that doesn't match your desired results with one that does.

Midjourney can access InsightFace as a plugin. It lets you store up to ten different faces on your account. Each face is assigned a name, which you can then add to your prompt. After you generate your AI image, you can use this face swap technology to change out the face.

Extensions like Roop Unleashed, FaceFusion, and ReActor can be added to swap faces in Stable Diffusion. My favorite app for accomplishing this task is the standalone version of FaceFusion.

As with all of these applications, it's essential to be above reproach when using them. While I'm suggesting using them to create consistent characters by swapping out one AI-generated face of Jesus for another, it can also be fun to make yourself into your favorite movie character. These apps can be used for harmful purposes, to deceive, or worse, so use caution and be sure to use them ethically.

Challenges and Limitations

While AI image generation is a powerful tool, knowing its limitations and challenges is important. If you don't want people to reject your AI-generated creations when used for sermon illustrations (or other purposes), you should be aware of these limitations and do your best never to display images that demonstrate them.

Imperfect understanding of complex prompts: AI models can sometimes struggle to fully grasp the nuances of complex or highly detailed prompts, leading to generated images that don't quite match the desired outcome. No matter how hard you try, sometimes it will never work for certain prompts. Instead of being tempted to settle for the best (flawed) generation, try and think of a new concept or alternate solution. Tools like ControlNet (in Stable Diffusion) can be used to add structure and pose control to your images. This gets you much closer to where you want to go.

Inconsistencies and artifacts: AI-generated images can sometimes include inconsistencies or artifacts, such as distorted faces, misshapen objects, or incorrect numbers of fingers on hands. While these issues are becoming less common as the technology improves, it's important to carefully review generated images for any such irregularities. I made an image of Jesus feeding the 5000, and one man was holding his head in his hands. I caught this one pretty quickly, but I've seen people share images like this without careful review.

Difficulty with text and logos: AI image-generation models often struggle to accurately render text, logos, and other highly specific visual elements. If your desired image requires clear, readable text or a specific logo, you may need to add, mask, remove, or replace these elements manually using image editing software. I hope that by the time you get this book in your hands, this problem will be solved, but right now, correct text is only possible with AI-generated images (using certain models) 50–60 percent of the time.

Potential for biases and stereotypes: As mentioned earlier, AI models can reflect biases and stereotypes present in their training data. This can lead to generated images that reinforce harmful or inaccurate representations of people, cultures, or experiences. It takes almost no effort to tell the AI to be more diverse in the images you generate. It'll do it; you just have to remember to ask.

Despite these challenges and limitations, AI image generation remains a valuable tool for churches, organizations, and individuals looking to harness the power of visual storytelling. By understanding these limitations and working to mitigate their impact, we can use AI image generation responsibly and effectively in our ministries.

Popular AI Image-Generation Tools

Now that we've covered everything from the basics to the advanced aspects of AI image generation, let's look at some of the most popular tools available. You've already seen me refer to all of these by name, but I wanted to save this list for after the conversation about how to use the tools.

CANVA (CANVA)

URL: canva.com

Description: Canva incorporates AI technologies to enhance its wide array of design tools, making professional-level design accessible to novices. It also boasts a suite of AI tools called Magic Design.

What's Unique about It: Canva is unique in integrating AI into a broader suite of design tools, aiming to streamline the design process and enhance user creativity. One of the most valuable tools is its text conversion tool, which allows it to take AI-generated text and make it editable.

Challenges: Canva must integrate AI in a way that enhances but does not overwhelm the user experience. It's known for its ease of use for design novices, so maintaining simplicity while adding advanced capabilities is key to its continued success.

DALL-E (OPENAI)

URL: chat.openai.com

Description: DALL-E is a powerful AI image-generation tool developed by OpenAI. It can create fairly realistic and creative images from textual descriptions. It is part of the ChatGPT Pro subscription.

What's Unique about It: DALL-E's ability to understand and generate images based on complex, multipart prompts sets it apart from other tools. It can create images that combine unrelated concepts in surprising and innovative ways. At the time of this writing, it is one of the leading apps for generating text that is spelled right. It does a great job of producing more graphical content. Because it is paired with ChatGPT, which does the heavy lifting on the prompt front, it is more accessible for those without technical expertise.

Challenges: DALL-E's output sometimes includes inconsistencies or artifacts, particularly when generating images of people or text. Its look tends to be more hyperrealistic than photographic, a telltale sign of AI-generated imagery. ChatGPT also generates suboptimal prompts under the hood, sometimes making it hard to get what you want. Also worth noting: you can tell it to run your prompt verbatim if you want to have some more control over the image it generates.

FIREFLY (ADOBE)
URL: adobe.com
Description: Adobe Firefly, part of Adobe's creative suite, is designed to integrate seamlessly with other Adobe products. It enhances graphic design with AI-powered image generation.

What's Unique about It: It is tailored to complement Adobe's existing design tools, providing a familiar interface for those already versed in Adobe software. It is said to be the most "ethically sourced" image generator as it is trained entirely on Adobe's stock images.

Challenges: Firefly trained strictly on Adobe Stock imagery, so the outputs can be somewhat vanilla. Due to licensing concerns, prompting can be limited. You're not going to get it to make an image of Batman like you could in other platforms.

FLUX.1 (BLACK FOREST LABS)
URL: flux1.io
Description: Flux.1 is a suite of advanced text-to-image models. It is designed to push the boundaries of AI-driven image generation, offering exceptional detail, prompt adherence, and a diverse range of styles and scene complexities. It is regarded as one of the most photorealistic models on the market.

What's Unique about It: Flux.1 stands out due to its open-source nature, making it accessible for a wide range of users, from developers to artists. The model suite includes three versions—[pro], [dev], and [schnell]—each catering to different needs, from professional-grade outputs to faster, more efficient processing for personal use. This flexibility, combined with its state-of-the-art architecture, makes Flux.1 a versatile tool for creative projects.

Challenges: The models require fast hardware to run efficiently, which might be a barrier for some users. Additionally, the three different versions—[pro], [dev], and [schnell]—could be confusing for those unfamiliar with the distinctions.

IDEOGRAM (IDEOGRAM)
URL: ideogram.ai

Description: Ideogram ("pronounced eye-diogram," according to https://ideogram.ai/publicly-available) is a versatile and user-friendly AI-driven platform designed to generate realistic images from text prompts. It enables users to easily create various visual content such as logos, posters, and more.

What's Unique about It: The platform is distinguished by its ability to generate coherent and legible text within images, addressing a common challenge in AI image generation. This feature makes Ideogram AI particularly suitable for applications requiring integrated textual content, like logo creation and promotional materials. When it was released in August of 2023, it was the only platform to consistently generate usable text, and it just keeps getting better. It may be the best at prompt-following.

Challenges: Like other generators, it struggles with rendering complex elements like hands and faces.

LEONARDO.AI (LEONARDO.AI)
URL: leonardo.ai

Description: Leonardo.Ai is a Stable Diffusion–based text-to-image generator designed as a creative assistant that helps users generate digital art and other visual content through an intuitive interface. It has many exceptional tools and models that help artists bring their visions to life.

What's Unique about It: It emphasizes user-friendly design, making digital art creation accessible to those without extensive graphic design skills. It can easily train custom models and includes a slick animation tool.

Challenges: Some customers complain of poor customer service. There's quite a bit of NSFW content in the community feeds.

META AI (META PLATFORMS)

URL: meta.ai

Description: Part of Meta Platforms, Meta AI leverages advanced machine learning to create images and other media that enhance user interactions across Meta's platforms.

What's Unique about It: It has a lightning-fast image generation tool that creates very nice results.

Challenges: The toolset is fairly limited right now, but as I write this, it came out just days ago. I suspect it'll be more robust by the time you read this.

MIDJOURNEY (MIDJOURNEY)

URL: midjourney.com

Description: Midjourney is an independent research lab and AI model that produces images from textual descriptions. It focuses on creating vivid and artistically unique images. It is particularly well-suited for generating illustrations, concept art, photography, and creative visuals.

What's Unique about It: It is known for its distinctive stylistic outputs, often producing visually striking images that resemble works of art. Midjourney's strengths lie in its ability to generate images with a wide range of artistic styles and techniques, from photorealistic to painterly and abstract. Its community-driven approach fosters a collaborative and inspiring environment, with users sharing and remixing one another's creations.

Challenges: Some artists argue it was questionably sourced by training on artists' works without their permission. Its pricing model, which requires a subscription for full access, may be a detraction for some users.

STABLE DIFFUSION (STABILITY AI)

URL: stability.ai

Description: Stable Diffusion is a popular open-source AI image-generation model that can be run locally on a user's hardware or accessed through various online platforms. It is known for its fast and efficient image-generation capabilities and its infinite customization.

What's Unique about It: Its open-source nature allows for a high degree of customization and integration with other tools and workflows. Its ability to run locally on a user's hardware provides more control over privacy and data usage.

Challenges: Running Stable Diffusion locally on your computer requires a moderate to high level of technical expertise and hardware requirements, which may be a barrier for some users. This app's open-source nature is a double-edged sword, providing extreme freedom in outputs and the potential for unethical misuse.

CONCLUSION

So, which app is the best? It really depends on what you're trying to accomplish. Each app has strengths and weaknesses. I recommend experimenting with all of them to learn what they're best at and what they don't do well. My favorite on the list is Midjourney because it does such a great job with photographic and more organic styles, but it's not always the answer. Ideogram is my number two because of its prompt adherence and ability to incorporate text.

Should you pay for an app, or are the free ones good enough? The free options are great, but make sure to read the terms of service to know if you have the right to use the things you make the way you're using them. While you're not technically a commercial entity, you may need commercial rights to use your images in your online worship, website, or print.

If you've ever licensed a photo/design/piece of media from a royalty-free stock library, you've likely spent $25–$35 on that single stock image. For less than the price of one stock photo per month, you can subscribe to ChatGPT/DALL-E, and you'll be able to create countless images. Midjourney is about half the price of one stock photo per month. Well worth the investment.

If you'd like to take a much deeper dive into all of these technologies, I'd highly recommend checking the work of my friend Rob Laughter, who I've referred to a lot in the book. Rob is extremely knowledgeable about the inner workings of these apps (and more), understanding them at a deeper level than anyone I know. I consult with him regularly about

AI, and he's been a silent contributor to some of the things in this book. He's also a skilled photographer and artist. So he not only gets the nerdy stuff about the code side, but he also uses the technology to make amazing stuff. In addition to all of this, he's a Jesus follower, he's a former pastor, and he works at The Summit Church in Raleigh, North Carolina. Check him out over on *Medium*, where he writes exclusively about AI: https://roblaughter.medium.com.

In the next chapter, we will dive into the current state of generative video and some of the exciting things yet to come. We'll also cover some excellent related tools.

CLAUDE'S QUESTIONS FOR REFLECTION

1. How can we use AI-generated imagery in ways that enhance rather than replace human creativity and artistry?

2. What ethical considerations should guide our use of image generation tools, particularly around issues of bias, representation, and consent?

3. How might visuals created by AI deepen or distract from the worship experience and the communication of biblical truths?

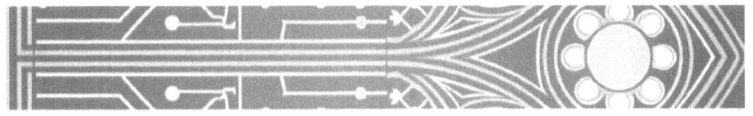

AI VIDEO AND OTHER TOOLS

I shared with you in an earlier chapter that I love theme parks and roller coasters. I am fortunate to live in Ohio, where we have two of the most excellent roller coaster parks in the country: Cedar Point (in Sandusky, Ohio) and Kings Island (in Mason, Ohio). I live just about an hour from Kings Island.

Over the many years I've been going to Kings Island, one aspect of the drive to the park continues to fill me with anticipation and excitement each time I go. Because of the hilly topography of southern Ohio, about fifteen minutes away from the park, the coasters, the Eiffel Tower (their recreation), and the taller rides can be seen on the horizon. I must admit that I want to press the gas pedal a little harder when I see these sites because I can't wait to get there.

That's how I feel about generative video and what's on the horizon. There are some really exciting roller coasters off in the distance, but I'm not at the park yet. As I sit here writing these words full of anticipation, I do so with envy for you, the reader. You should have access to the tools that I have only seen announced.

So, as much as I would love to provide robust strategies similar to those in the last two chapters, AI video isn't quite ready for prime time in its current state. A handful of tools are currently showing promise, but the next iteration of AI video will change the game.

WHAT IS AI-GENERATED VIDEO?

Under the hood, generative-AI video models are similar to the underlying technologies found in image-generation models. And while they are essentially the same, there are also key differences due to the nature of video content. Here's a breakdown of what's similar and what's different:

Similarities

Foundational Techniques: AI video and image models often use similar foundational machine-learning techniques such as generative adversarial networks (GANs), diffusion models, and transformers. These models are trained to understand and generate visual content by learning from vast datasets of existing media.

Content Generation: Like image models, video models can generate content from textual descriptions, images, or videos. They apply similar processes to understand the content and context needed to produce relevant and cohesive outputs. Current video models are trained to predict the movements of existing pixels from input videos.

Differences

Temporal Dynamics: Video models must also understand and generate temporal dynamics, not just static scenes. This includes understanding how objects move and interact over time, which adds a layer of complexity not present in static-image generation.

Higher Computational Demands: Videos consist of sequences of images (frames), which significantly increases the computational requirements for generation. Managing these sequences to produce smooth, coherent videos requires more advanced data handling and processing power.

Continuity and Context: AI video models need to maintain continuity across frames, which is a challenge that image models do not face. Ensuring that successive frames are high quality and contextually linked to form a coherent sequence is crucial in video generation.

While AI video and image models are built on similar technological principles and share some stylistic approaches, video generation's specific challenges and requirements—such as temporal coherence and computational load—necessitate more complex solutions and adaptations. That's why things sometimes get wonky, morph in strange ways, and run amok.

I can tell you that, for now, you prompt for video in basically the same way you prompt for images. Following the same strategies I covered in the last chapter but adding some direction for how you want things to move should be a winning strategy. It's hard to say what will come between my writing this book and your reading it, but the video tools we have now operate very similarly to text and image generators.

The State of Generative Video

In March 2023, we reached the pinnacle of generative AI when Reddit user chaindrop released the now-infamous viral video of Will Smith eating spaghetti. Using a text-to-video machine-learning model app called Modelscope Text2Video generator, chaindrop created multiple clips of Smith gnawing away digital pasta. To say this clip was a disturbing display of AI technology would be an understatement. Vice.com declared it will "haunt you for the rest of your life."[24]

You can find that clip here: **bit.ly/Will-Pasta**

 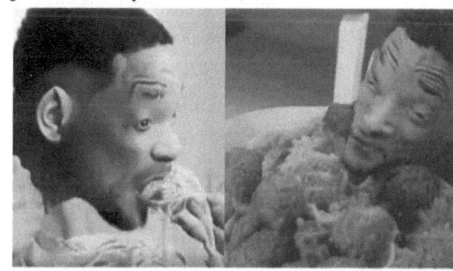

As odd as that video was, glimmers within it suggested more incredible things to come. Several weeks later, RunwayML released its first text-to-video model, Gen-1, which far surpasses the quality of Modelscope. And while it was far superior, it still wasn't really all that usable for professional-level video production.

In November 2023, Stable Video Diffusion (from Stability AI) and Pika were released. Stable Video was specifically trained to generate video sequences from a single context frame, aiming to produce smooth transitions and reduce flickering effects commonly seen in video generation.[25] Only one week later, Pika Labs officially launched a head-turning promo video featuring the best AI-generated video we'd seen to date.

---

24. Samantha Cole, "AI Will Smith Eating Spaghetti Hill [sic] Haunt You for the Rest of Your Life," *Vice*, March 28, 2023, https://www.vice.com/en/article/xgw8ek/ai-will-smith-eating-spaghetti-hill-haunt-you-for-the-rest-of-your-life.

25. Luke Jones, "Stability AI Enters Video Generation Arena with Stable Video Diffusion Release," *WinBuzzer*, November 24, 2023, https://winbuzzer.com/2023/11/24/stability-ai-enters-video-generation-arena-with-stable-video-diffusion-release-xcxwbn/.

The reality of Pika upon its release didn't quite live up to the hype of the cherry-picked examples included in the promo video. While you could do some interesting things with text and image to video, it just wasn't ready for prime time.

RunwayML continued to tweak its app, adding additional features that gave users more control over how things move; Leonardo.Ai added the ability to animate images, and several smaller forgettable models sprang up with limited functionality. A handful of new tools popped up, such as Moonvalley and Morph Studio, but beyond some occasional gems in my experimentation, I have yet to find any of them to be useful enough to keep up with. Meta AI released video generation just last week, but so far, it's fairly lackluster as well, with both low resolution and low frame rate.

I do have to give a special mention to Haiper, which is still in beta as I am writing this. Haiper is an innovative AI video-generation model developed by two alums from Google DeepMind. Unlike many other AI tools focusing on text or image generation, Haiper emphasizes creating perceptual foundation models. These models aim to understand and interpret sensory data much like humans do, enhancing their ability to generate realistic and contextually appropriate visual content. In my experimentation with image-to-video, I've found that Haiper seems to understand the input image and what I want the motion to do. By the time you see this, I believe it'll be one of the top tools.

I was also just hired by Nim.video to do a spec spot using their technology, which has some potential for the future. I'll keep my eye on them.

Let's jump back in the car momentarily and continue approaching Kings Island. The tallest roller coaster in the park is the 287-foot-high Orion. It towers over everything and is the easiest to be seen from far away. In February 2023, OpenAI announced Sora—the tallest and most exciting coaster in the proverbial AI park.

Whereas all generative-video models currently on the market will generate relatively low-resolution videos, sometimes with low frame rates and mostly in the four-second range, Sora's demonstration footage lasted up to one minute in length and was very high quality. The videos being created with it are mind-blowingly good. From stylized papercraft sea creatures swimming underwater to beautifully rendered puppies playing in the snow, the promise of Sora has everyone in the field holding their breath in eager anticipation.

In fact, according to Digwatch.com, "Renowned film and television mogul Tyler Perry has chosen to put a temporary pause on his ambitious $800 million studio expansion, citing worries related to the advancements in AI, with a specific focus on OpenAI's video generation tool, Sora."[26] That tells you something about the quality.

There's no official announcement about when it will be released, but I'm hopeful that it's ready for you to play with right now. Pop on over to openai.com/sora to see if it's available to use.

Here's a link to the original promo videos released as part of their teaser announcement: **bit.ly/Sora-Demo**

A lot of the footage, which I've watched over and over, frame-by-frame, is super-impressive, but the more you watch it, the more you see AI anomalies and oddities. Things scale weird, limbs on the puppies get confused, and people walk in a strange manner and to odd places, but this is all in the alpha release! It wasn't even out yet.

I read that a one-minute clip takes about an hour to process. That certainly would kill a workflow pretty quickly, but I suspect that when they release it, they'll have sorted out many of those things. I regularly tell my AI cohorts and those who attend my trainings, "This is the worst it'll ever be, and it's pretty spectacular right now."

If Sora is the equivalent of Kings Island's Orion roller coaster, EMO: Emote Portrait Alive is the 230-foot-high Diamondback—the second largest in the park. When I saw the demonstration of this model, I had to bend down and pick my jaw up off the floor.

---

26. DW Team, "Tyler Perry Halts $800 Million Studio Expansion Due to AI Concerns," *Digital Watch*, February 26, 2024, https://dig.watch/updates/tyler-perry-halts-800-million-studio-expansion-due-to-ai-concerns.

EMO utilizes an audio2video diffusion model to generate expressive portrait videos with remarkable realism and accuracy. By leveraging the power of diffusion models and cutting-edge neural network architectures, EMO pushes the boundaries of what is possible in talking-head video generation. Even today, I cannot comprehend what I see when I watch these demonstrations.

Take just a moment to visit this page: **bit.ly/EMO-demo**

Wow! Just wow. That linked demonstration is so ridiculously good that it is scary good, "scary" being the operative word. There's no word on when this will be released in a form where we can play with it. But when that time comes, I sure will be giving it a shot.

A few days ago, Microsoft demonstrated a similar technology called VASA-1 with a promotional video subtitled "Lifelike Audio-Driven Talking Faces Generated in Real Time." While this demo isn't nearly as impressive as EMO, it does show that tech like this will be here and mainstream before you know it. Microsoft has no plans to make this tool available to the public until it's sure it will be used responsibly. Some other developer will figure out how to accomplish the same thing, and it will surely be available to us at some point: **bit.ly/VASA-demo**

When used for good purposes, both of these apps could be spectacular ways to engage people in biblical stories and creative ways to engage people in the life of the church.

Then there are the bad actors out there who will use them to take a political figure (say, the president of the United States), clone the person's voice, and make him or her say anything they want. Some people will never even know to question the false video. That's why I advocate for us to be active in helping our congregations navigate this new world, exposing them to the realities made possible by AI.

With tools like Sora and EMO, I can see a day in the future when any person will be able to bring their vision/story/idea to life by prompting it into a chatbot, generating characters in an app like Midjourney, taking that into Sora, generating the video, and then using an app like Udio (more on that in a moment) to provide a film score. ElevenLabs (more on that too) can even generate AI sound effects.

The ability to create in this way excites me tremendously but also scares me quite a bit. It excites me because most of us will never be able to make a traditional film with actors, sets, professional lighting, cinematographers, etc. We'll never be able to hire my favorite composer, John Williams, to score our masterpiece and then conduct the full orchestra to play it.

I also can't help thinking about how many jobs the film industry represents: wardrobe, propmakers, prop masters, set dressers, writers, producers, designers, catering, actors, lighting, camera operators, best boys, grips, electricians, musicians, and the list goes on and on. Like the displaced loomers of the early 1800s, will these folks be able to find their way into the new AI marketplace? I hope so.

I love the idea that you could craft a cinematic movie featuring the story of Jesus calming the sea, initiated right from your desk. Your creativity might even rival that of an episode of *The Chosen* simply by prompting it in a handful of apps.

I hate the idea that shows like *The Chosen* may not get made if we turn too often to AI technology rather than investing in all of the craftspeople it takes to make, market, and distribute a film. It's quite the conundrum. I encourage you to wrestle with it. I don't have the answer.

For now, we're a good way away from that reality. Most of the AI video you'll see today is long slow-motion shots—or very stylized anime footage with lots of flickering and a sort of time-lapse feel. A small percentage of it is convincing enough to look like a traditionally shot video. Give it some time, and it'll be a whole new ballgame. One you may be able to access even now.

Generative AI Video Tools

Let's look at some of the most popular tools available, like we did for chatbots and image generators. This list does not include every app on the market and is certainly subject to change. Some of these are free to try, and others require a subscription.

HAIPER (HAIPER)

URL: haiper.ai

Description: Haiper is an innovative AI platform that harnesses the power of perceptual-foundation models to revolutionize the creative process. Founded by a team of industry experts and academic researchers, Haiper combines cutting-edge machine learning with a focus on fun, shareability, and community.

What's Unique about It: Haiper does an incredible job interpreting the photos and text prompts you enter. It seems to understand the context of input better. In addition, it has a "Video Repaint" feature that lets you vary a region in your video to transform it in different ways. This makes it easier to create something truly unique.

Challenges: As a relatively new entry in the field, it is still enhancing its capabilities and expanding its feature set to fully meet user expectations for diverse and complex video-generation tasks.

IMMERSITY AI (LEIA INC.)

URL: immersity.ai

Description: Immersity AI focuses on converting 2D images to 3D parallax videos and integrating them into videos, providing tools for both personal and professional use.

What's Unique about It: Similar to how Facebook converts an image from 2D to a 3D image, Immersity AI creates an AI-generated depth matte (an artificial image similar to what the LiDAR camera on your phone captures) and then applies that matte to your photo. It then gives you controls to create a parallax effect (creating the illusion of three-dimensional space), where you can push in on the image, rotate around in the scene, pan up and down or left or right, and choose your own movement. This particular tool creates incredibly consistent results that can be used for simple video production.

Challenges: The 3D images do "break" if you push the depth matte too far. Things stretch to the point of distraction, so your motion is limited.

KAIBER (KAIBER)

URL: kaiber.ai

Description: Kaiber was one of the earliest AI video tools to hit the market. It uses AI to automate and streamline the video-editing process, particularly focusing on enhancing user-generated content with advanced editing features.

What's Unique about It: Kaiber stands out for its robust, granular controls, offering users more precision in their generated outputs. The Transform feature lets you upload an existing video and change its style and aesthetic just by entering text. It does this in a manner that is relatively smooth and consistent throughout.

Challenges: Some users have complained that experimentation in Kaiber is expensive. You're basically being charged to get a decent output, and that can add up pretty quickly.

LUMALABS DREAM MACHINE (LUMI AI, INC.)

URL: lumalabs.ai/dream-machine

Description: Lumalabs Dream Machine is an advanced AI model that can take text directions and images and turn them into high-quality, realistic videos. Dream Machine is part of Luma's broader initiative to build a "universal imagination engine," aiming to make powerful creative tools accessible to everyone.

What's Unique about It: Dream Machine excels in generating videos with smooth motion and detailed textures, thanks to its robust transformer model. The tool supports rapid iteration, capable of producing 120 frames in 120 seconds, allowing users to explore creative ideas quickly. Additionally, Dream Machine offers an array of fluid, cinematic camera motions that match the emotion and content of the scenes, enhancing the storytelling potential of each video.

Challenges: Despite its strengths, users may encounter long queue times due to high demand. While the output quality is generally high, occasional minor inaccuracies or artifacts can occur. The tool is also continuously evolving, with ongoing improvements to enhance efficiency and user experience.

By offering these advanced capabilities, Lumalabs Dream Machine positions itself as a leading tool in AI-driven video generation, aiming to liberate creative minds and push the boundaries of what's possible in digital content creation.

META AI (META PLATFORMS)

URL: meta.ai

Description: Meta AI is a multifaceted tool that incorporates a chatbot, image, and video-generation tools. It is currently free to use and built into Meta's social media ecosystem.

What's Unique about It: It benefits from deep integration with social media, facilitating direct publishing and social interaction. It's likely to be used on the fly to post images and videos for a variety of purposes.

Challenges: People have a love/hate relationship with Meta and Facebook. Platform manipulation and algorithm changes are ongoing, which users find off-putting.

MOONVALLEY (MOONVALLEY)

URL: moonvalley.ai

Description: Developed by the former head of product growth at Zapier, Moonvalley is a new player in the AI video space. It transforms simple text prompts into visually stunning, high-definition videos and animations.

What's Unique about It: Moonvalley offers HD outputs, allowing you to specify style and length (short, medium, and long).

Challenges: It currently runs on Discord, which is a barrier for some users. The video-generation process can also be time-consuming, depending on the complexity and length of the video.

PIKA (PIKA LABS)

URL: pika.art

Description: Pika Labs produces software that allows users to create AI-generated videos, focusing on customizability and ease of use.

What's Unique about It: Pika has several tools that aren't found in other generators, at least for now. These include the equivalent of video outpainting, where you can expand the video beyond its original size and AI fills in the rest. It also has inpainting, where you can grab a selection of your video and it'll add something to it via a text prompt. Pika also has an AI sound-effects generator that performs well.

Challenges: Balancing the depth of customization with ease of use of the tools within the toolset presents an ongoing development challenge.

RUNWAYML (RUNWAY AI)

URL: runwayml.com

Description: RunwayML is a robust platform that provides creators with powerful AI tools to execute complex video generation and editing tasks. It was one of the earliest generative AI suites on the market. RunwayML's Gen-3 Alpha (which was released in June of 2024) is a state-of-the-art AI model designed for generating high-fidelity, realistic videos from text and image prompts. Built on a scalable and efficient transformer architecture, Gen-3 Alpha is capable of producing detailed and consistent videos with smooth motion and expressive human characters.

What's Unique about It: It offers an extensive range of features from text-to-video to image-to-video, style transfer, background removal, audio tools, and more. Its generative-video tools provide a unique feature called the motion brush, which allows you to influence how things in your images move. Gen-3 Alpha stands out for its ability to understand and generate complex scenes with high visual fidelity. It excels in producing expressive human characters and offers precise control over scene elements, enabling users to create videos with nuanced actions and emotions. The model also supports various camera movements, including POV and drone footage, making it versatile for different creative applications. Additionally, Gen-3 Alpha has been trained with temporally dense captions, allowing for imaginative transitions and detailed key-framing.

Challenges: A key challenge is keeping the platform intuitive while adding advanced features. The platform is a bit hard to navigate, and credit spending adds up quickly in this app. One of the main limitations of Gen-3 Alpha is its video length constraint, as it can only generate videos up to a maximum of ten seconds. Furthermore, while the output quality is generally high, users may experience long queue times due to high demand. The cost of generating videos can also be significant, with each second of video requiring ten credits.

SORA (OPENAI)

URL: openai.com/sora

Description: Sora generates videos using advanced AI algorithms, leveraging OpenAI's extensive research in machine learning. The demo footage features the best-looking AI video generator we've seen.

What's Unique about It: It is backed by leading AI research and provides cutting-edge capabilities in video generation.

Challenges: As with other OpenAI products, managing user expectations and ethical considerations of AI-generated content is crucial. Frankly, everything is a guess on this one right now.

STABLE VIDEO DIFFUSION (STABILITY AI)

URL: stablevideo.com

Description: Stable Video focuses on transforming static images into video sequences using AI, aiming to maintain stability and realism.

What's Unique about It: It leverages a cutting-edge latent video diffusion model that includes a temporal layer, improving the smoothness of video throughout the frames. In other words, the model creates a more natural fluid motion, improving realism. It also has a customizable frame rate option, which is unique for this type of tool.

Challenges: Ensuring the realism and natural flow of video sequences generated from static images remains a technical challenge. There are minimal controls, which will likely change as the application matures.

Late Breaking Releases

On an afternoon I was wrapping up some of my final writing for this book, a new model called Vidu was announced out of China. Maginative.com reports the following:

> China's Shengshu Technology and Tsinghua University have unveiled Vidu, a text-to-video model capable of generating 16-second clips at 1080p resolution with a single click. The announcement was made at the 2024 Zhongguancun Forum in Beijing, where they tried to position Vidu as a strong competitor to OpenAI's Sora.

Like Sora, Vidu is capable of producing 16-second clips at 1080p resolution. Vidu is based on a Universal Vision Transformer (U-ViT) architecture, which the company says allows it to simulate the real physical world with multi-camera view generation. This architecture was reportedly developed by the Shengshu Technology team in September 2022 and, as such, would predate the diffusion transformer (DiT) architecture used by Sora.

According to the company, Vidu can generate videos with complex scenes adhering to real-world physics, such as realistic lighting and shadows and detailed facial expressions. The model also demonstrates a rich imagination, creating non-existent, surreal content with depth and complexity. Vidu's multi-camera capabilities allows for the generation of dynamic shots, seamlessly transitioning between long shots, close-ups, and medium shots within a single scene.[27]

Right now, there is a demo video you can view here: **bit.ly/Vidu-demo**

There's little more to go on for now. I can't find a Vidu website, but be on the lookout for this model. The demo is almost as impressive as Sora, and that's saying a lot!

AI Video Avatars

There's an entire category of generative AI video I've been avoiding writing about until now. Every time I do a Google search for a list of "top generative AI video apps," several of these top the list. They represent the AI avatar category. Based on what I've seen of this style of AI video so far, I'm personally not a huge fan. I'll give you the lowdown on what they are anyway.

App makers like D-ID, HeyGen, and Synthesia (among others) have made applications that create AI avatars. AI avatars are virtual rep-

27. Chris McKay, "China Unveils Vidu: A Powerful Text-to-Video Generator," *Maginative*, April 27, 2024, https://www.maginative.com/article/china-unveils-vidu-a-powerful-text-to-video-generator/.

resentations of users or characters, often employed in various interactive applications ranging from virtual reality and video games to online meetings and customer service. Some YouTubers who don't want to appear on camera or want to cut down their production time by cloning themselves are using AI doppelgangers instead.

You caught that right. I said cloning themselves. All the apps in this category allow users to upload a picture or video of themselves along with an audio file of them talking. The app then creates a deepfake mouth replacement and composites it over the still or video. While the video-based avatars look relatively realistic, repeated body movements, unnatural mouth movements, and other abnormalities are easy to spot. The photo versions are even worse, as the body remains still while the head and mouth move around.

For me, these digital avatars feel almost real but not quite human. This phenomenon is referred to as the "uncanny valley." IEEE Spectrum.com defines it in this way:

> The uncanny valley is a concept first introduced in the 1970s by Masahiro Mori, then a professor at the Tokyo Institute of Technology. Mori coined the term "uncanny valley" to describe his observation that as robots appear more humanlike, they become more appealing—but only up to a certain point. Upon reaching the uncanny valley, our affinity descends into a feeling of strangeness, a sense of unease, and a tendency to be scared or freaked out.[28]

As we embrace AI in the church, we must navigate the perception of things being almost real and yet not quite authentic. Crafting digital avatars may be a line you don't want to cross until that uncanny valley problem is eliminated. We don't want to squander the trust we've built with our congregations, especially in a world where artificial things surround us. If you choose to use this technology, I recommend disclosing it.

Perhaps you want to make a quick announcement or video update. Maybe your pastor is on vacation. You might say, "Today's video update is powered by AI." Then, you share the announcement. Or you can take it further than that by explaining more about how you're using AI. If

---

28. Rina Diane Caballar, "What Is the Uncanny Valley?," *IEEE Spectrum*, November 6, 2019, https://spectrum.ieee.org/what-is-the-uncanny-valley.

you go this route, be sure to collect feedback and see how people feel about it. This one is right on the line where people might reject it.

In the next chapter, I will share one really cool feature and opportunity from HeyGen that may be worth using in your own setting. Hang tight for that!

COLOSSYAN (COLOSSYAN INC.)

URL: colossyan.com

Description: Colossyan transforms presentations into videos using "realistic" AI avatars. It analyzes input documents like PDFs or PowerPoint files to generate engaging storylines.

What's Unique about It: Colossyan excels in educational and corporate settings, offering features like automated video generation and multi-avatar conversations that enhance the depth and engagement of presentations.

Challenges: The platform's reliance on original content quality and the need for some expertise to utilize advanced animations and edits can be limiting for some users.

CREATIVE REALITY STUDIO (D-ID)

URL: d-id.com

Description: Creative Reality Studio offers both realistic and cartoon-style avatars, specializing in creating engaging digital experiences with AI-generated avatars from photos or text prompts.

What's Unique about It: It integrates with other platforms like Canva and ChatGPT, enhancing its utility in various applications, from artistic creations to practical uses.

Challenges: While Creative Reality Studio provides versatility, its cartoony avatars may not always meet the needs of users looking for ultrarealistic representations. Custom avatars feel stiff and somewhat unrealistic.

HEYGEN (HEYGEN)

URL: heygen.com

Description: HeyGen provides a variety of AI-powered avatars for creating videos, with features like lip-syncing to text or audio inputs. It also allows users to create a personal avatar in either an instant or finetuned format. Of all of the tools in this category, it does the most convincing job of mimicking the look of real humans.

What's Unique about It: HeyGen offers a broad selection of avatars and supports extensive customization, including outfits and languages, catering to a global audience. Its most impressive feature is that it translates one language to another. When used with a custom avatar (your likeness), it'll even deepfake the mouth to match the translated language.

Challenges: This is arguably the best tool in this category, but the instant avatar can be somewhat stiff and unnatural. The finetuned model is better but is still in the uncanny valley. Credits on this platform add up very quickly.

SYNTHESIA (SYNTHESIA AI)

URL: synthesia.io

Description: Synthesia is an AI video-creation platform that generates videos using lifelike AI avatars based on text inputs. It offers voice cloning and the ability to produce videos in over 120 languages. It also allows a user to create a custom avatar based on his or her likeness.

What's Unique about It: Synthesia stands out with its extensive language support and ability to integrate custom voices, providing a personalized video creation experience.

Challenges: The platform sometimes struggles with avatar expressiveness and natural lip-sync, particularly with complex phrases, which can detract from the realism of the videos.

AI-Assisted Video Editing

Another area where AI can make our lives easier and enhance our work is in video editing. We've come a long way from the earliest days of editing when actual razor blades were used to physically cut and splice film. Now AI can do a lot of that cutting for you (in digital form) automatically without you having to think much about it.

Today's AI tools streamline the editing process, enhance creative options, and automate repetitive tasks. AI tools can now analyze footage for content, suggest edits, sync music to scenes, optimize dialogue clarity, and even generate content from scratch. They will also generate transcripts, allowing you to edit your videos by editing the words in those generated transcripts. This speeds up the editing process and opens new creative possibilities, making sophisticated editing techniques more accessible to professionals and amateurs alike.

The real win here is that nontechnical folks without years of experience and expertise can be involved in video editing with a much lower bar of entry. If only this had been available during COVID! AI video editing may mean that we can involve more volunteers in content production.

Of course, these AI tools aren't just helpful for novices. These new AI features will raise the bar for creative professionals as well. Adobe just announced new Premiere features that will allow editors to extend video clips with AI, remove unwanted objects in the scene, and even track things that aren't in the original footage. DaVinci Resolve will now allow users to relight a scene after it's shot. Descript can replace a subject's eyes to make it look like they're looking directly at the camera. These new features and more rival processes that once required highly skilled compositors, animators, designers, and motion graphic artists.

AI Video-Editing Tools

It seems as if dozens of AI programs and tools are announced every week. Some weeks there actually are dozens released. Like the other lists in the book, this will not be exhaustive. Here, I've highlighted the most popular and powerful tools currently creating buzz in the AI video-editing world.

ADOBE PREMIERE PRO (ADOBE)

URL: adobe.com

Description: Adobe Premiere Pro is leading video-editing software that offers a comprehensive suite of tools for professional video production, including advanced editing capabilities, effects, and audio processing.

What's Unique about It: The software integrates AI-driven features like Auto Reframe for optimizing videos for different social platforms, Speech to Text for automatic transcription, and Scene Edit Detection, which helps quickly find cuts in a previously edited video. It can also automatically cut out silence, remove "ums," fix bad audio, and, as mentioned earlier, extend clips with AI and remove objects.

Challenges: Users who are new to video editing may find the interface complex, and subscription-based pricing can be a consideration for some users.

CAPCUT (BYTEDANCE)

URL: capcut.com

Description: CapCut is a free all-in-one video-editing app that provides easy-to-use tools to create high-quality videos. It is popular among mobile users for quick edits.

What's Unique about It: It offers advanced features like keyframe animation, smooth slow motion, and a variety of effects and filters right from a smartphone or tablet. The desktop version includes AI tools such as transcript-based editing, enhanced audio (removing noise from voice), a relight function, and auto-generated captions.

Challenges: Some of the best features are locked behind a paywall. Slower computers may have trouble running the app as it is very processor-intensive.

DAVINCI RESOLVE (BLACKMAGIC DESIGN)

URL: www.blackmagicdesign.com

Description: DaVinci Resolve is comprehensive video-editing software developed by Blackmagic Design. It integrates professional 8K editing, color correction, visual effects, and audio post-production into a single application, making it popular among professionals in the film and television industries. Additionally, DaVinci Resolve has been appreciated for its robustness, support for a wide range of formats, and powerful editing capabilities that compete with other industry-leading software suites.

What's Unique about It: Its color correction and audio post-production capabilities are particularly robust, often considered the industry standard for color grading. Version 19 added AI tools such as tracking and stabilization.

Challenges: The high level of professional features can be daunting for beginners, and the software demands powerful hardware for smooth operation. Many of the best features are on the paid version.

DESCRIPT (DESCRIPT)

URL: descript.com

Description: Descript is a multipurpose audio and video-editing tool that allows easy editing through transcribing audio to text. Users can cut videos by editing the text transcript.

What's Unique about It: It features Overdub, which gives you the ability to correct or change words in a transcript and have the audio automatically adjusted in the voice of the speaker, and filler word removal, which can automatically clean up your tracks. It also has an AI feature called Eye Contact that will use AI to make it appear like the person is looking directly at the camera.

Challenges: While powerful, its text-based editing might require a learning curve for those accustomed to traditional video-editing tools. While reasonably priced, the fees may not be for everyone.

OPUS CLIP (IMMERSIVELY INC.)

URL: opus.pro

Description: Opus Clip is an AI-powered video-editing platform specializing in converting long videos into engaging short viral clips. It utilizes advanced AI to analyze, extract, and rearrange compelling parts of videos. It is designed to enhance social media engagement.

What's Unique about It: Opus Clip features AI curation (ClipGenius), which intelligently identifies engaging parts of videos; AI Virality Score to predict content's potential reach; and Active Speaker Detection to keep the speaker in focus, enhancing viewer engagement.

Challenges: The tool might lack some advanced editing features found in more traditional software and may exhibit performance issues with larger files. Additionally, its most powerful features are gated behind a paid subscription, which could limit access for users not willing to pay.

SERMON SHOTS (SERMON SHOTS INC.)

URL: sermonshots.com

Description: Sermon Shots is a specialized video-editing platform designed to help churches create engaging sermon clips for social media. It simplifies the process of transforming long sermons into concise, shareable video clips that highlight key messages.

What's Unique about It: The platform is tailored specifically for church content and integrates AI to suggest the most impactful moments from sermons for clipping. It offers features like AI-suggested clips, easy uploading from YouTube or local files, and the ability to customize clips with music, animations, and transcriptions.

Challenges: Users may find the platform's focus limited if they need more generalized video-editing features. Additionally, while it's user-friendly, there's a learning curve in optimizing the use of its AI features to get the best results.

Video Upscaling

For now, most AI video-generation tools output medium-to-low-resolution video. If you want to use any of the videos you've generated in a professional context, you'll need to upscale them to a higher resolution. The good news is that AI can help you do that as well. Tools range from nominal fee one-time purchase options to rather pricey but worthwhile purchases. Here are some of the best apps currently available.

AVCLABS VIDEO ENHANCER AI (AVCLABS)

URL: avclabs.com

Description: AVCLabs Video Enhancer AI specializes in upscaling video resolutions and enhancing overall video quality through AI-driven algorithms. It supports a range of video enhancements, including noise reduction, deinterlacing, and color correction, catering to users looking to improve both personal and professional videos.

What's Unique about It: AVCLabs enhances video clarity and upscales resolutions to 4K using AI technology. It supports multiple video formats and performs well with videos from various sources.

Challenges: While user-friendly, some consider it expensive, especially for long videos or multiple filters.

PIXOP (PIXOP)

URL: www.pixop.com

Description: Pixop is a cloud-based video-upscaling solution that utilizes AI to enhance video quality by upscaling it to higher resolutions such as HD, 4K, and even 8K. It is designed to work with various video formats and is geared toward professional videographers and content creators who need to upscale video content for high-resolution displays.

What's Unique about It: Pixop has no subscription fees. They only charge you for what you use in processing power.

Challenges: Users may experience occasional lags and slower processing times during upscaling. Calculating the cost of each video might also be cumbersome.

TOPAZ VIDEO AI (TOPAZ LABS)

URL: topazlabs.com

Description: Topaz Video AI is a leading AI video-upscaling software that uses deep-learning algorithms to enhance video quality. It can upscale videos from standard definition (SD) to high definition (HD) or from HD to 4K or even 8K resolution. It also includes features to reduce video noise, improve sharpness, and recover authentic details, making it ideal for both amateur and professional use.

What's Unique about It: Topaz Video AI excels in upscaling videos up to 8K resolution while preserving important details and textures. This is the best app on the market. It is constantly updated. Worth the price of admission.

Challenges: It's quite resource-intensive and requires a powerful computer with a dedicated graphics card to operate efficiently. Its price tag may scare off some customers. It goes on sale periodically for significant discounts.

WONDERSHARE UNICONVERTER (WONDERSHARE)

URL: videoconverter.wondershare.com

Description: Wondershare UniConverter is a versatile tool that not only upscales videos to higher resolutions but also converts them into different formats.

What's Unique about It: It includes additional video-editing features, such as trimming, cropping, and adding effects, making it a comprehensive solution for video-production needs.

Challenges: It is reasonably priced with yearly, two-year, and perpetual plans, but the price may scare some users off.

Voice-Synthesis Tools

Voice synthesis is one of the most exciting innovations in generative AI. You can now create realistic voiceovers for video promos, narration, podcasting, Scripture readings, and more. The best of these tools sound like actual human beings.

When I started as a media producer twenty-five years ago, I used to spend $750 for a single voiceover. It would require booking a studio, setting up a phone patch, and then directing the talent over the phone (or in person if they were local). A decade or so later, the industry changed with high-speed internet and affordable capture equipment. Voiceover talent could now work right from home, turning around voiceover and emailing it the same day. Services like voice123.com and voicebunny.com lowered the costs to about a third of what I used to pay—and then along came AI voice synthesis.

Now let me say that I very much respect and appreciate the talent of a good voiceover artist. I've hired dozens of them over the years. They do a tremendous job of helping us tell stories, advertise events (and products), and convey our various messages. I will continue to hire professional voice artists when I have the budget to do so.

In the church, the budgets often don't include $250–$300 for a voiceover. Some of the work I do has to be turned around at a live event. Last year, I was working with a United Methodist annual conference for their annual gathering, and we were producing content on the fly that would be shown just hours after it was created. These pieces required voiceover. In the traditional realm, I have to find the right artist, send them a script, and either arrange a time to be on a call for real-time direction or wait until they send me a read and give them feedback. Then, I must wait for them to record the pickups and email them back. From there, I have to edit and incorporate them into my final work. It can take days.

With AI, I can enter the script and run the generation process. If I don't like it, I can tweak the stability settings and, in just a few seconds, have another take. Recently, ElevenLabs, the absolute leader in this category, released a new feature called "speech-to-speech," which allows users to record the lines themselves, capturing the emotion, tone, and energy they'd like, and then pick a voice after the fact to apply to their read. It is unbelievable. Here's a little demo I did when that feature had just been released: **bit.ly/Speech-demo**

Here's a list of tools, but honestly, I'd just go for ElevenLabs if I were you. None of the rest compare, and it's really affordable.

ELEVENLABS (ELEVENLABS)

URL: bit.ly/11labssignup

Description: ElevenLabs provides a state-of-the-art voice synthesis platform that generates realistic and customizable speech from text. It allows for both text-to-speech voiceover as well as speech-to-speech voiceover. Users can use the app to clone their own (or someone else's) voice.

What's Unique about It: ElevenLabs features high-quality voice models that can capture nuanced emotional tones and accents, making it ideal for creating dynamic and engaging media content. It includes a spectacular language translation feature called AI Dubbing and can also create sound effects.

Challenges: One primary concern about ElevenLabs includes addressing ethical considerations related to voice cloning, particularly ensuring that the technology is used responsibly and does not facilitate the creation of misleading or harmful content. I also worry about this technology's impact on professional voiceover artists.

MURF.AI (MURF)

URL: murf.ai

Description: Murf.AI is a versatile AI-driven text-to-speech platform designed to produce high-quality voiceovers for various types of content, including e-learning modules, corporate training videos, and marketing materials.

What's Unique about It: Murf offers a vast library of realistic AI voices across multiple languages and gives users extensive control over voice tone, pitch, and speed. It's particularly noted for its simplicity in turning scripts into professional-sounding voiceovers.

Challenges: While Murf.AI provides high-quality outputs, the main challenge is its pricing structure, which might be prohibitive for casual or low-budget users. Additionally, while it offers many customization options, the need for more advanced audio-editing features could be a limitation for some professional uses.

OPENVOICE (MYSHELL)

URL: research.myshell.ai/open-voice

Description: OpenVoice offers a range of voice technology solutions, including voice cloning and text-to-speech services. It is designed to help developers and content creators integrate voice responses into applications.

What's Unique about It: It stands out with its easy integration into existing apps and systems, offering a flexible API that supports various programming languages and frameworks. It is open source, which means you can use it for free, though some technical expertise is required to load it locally on your own computer.

Challenges: Challenges for OpenVoice include managing the balance between voice personalization and user privacy, as well as ensuring the voices remain natural and engaging across extensive kinds of use, from commercials to narration and beyond.

Generative AI Music Tools

This final category is currently my favorite one to experiment with. I've lost a lot of time making music with several AI generators. If you've done much video editing, you know that music is an integral part of creating a compelling vibe. Generative music started a bit slow but has cranked up to eleven in recent weeks. The songs you can make now with AI music will significantly disrupt the royalty-free-music industry.

A few months into my AI journey, I discovered tools like Soundraw that mostly helped you search existing music within a database, using AI to describe what you were after. Some of these tools would let you provide a link so it could "hear" a track and pick something similar. I didn't find any of these to be very helpful, so I canceled my subscriptions.

Last September, things started moving in an exciting direction. Stability AI released an app called Stable Audio, though I never found anything I generated there to be very good or useful. Then an app called Suno came out, and everything changed.

Suno would let you generate a song from a prompt, using text to describe what you wanted the song to be about and what style you wanted it to be in. You also had the option to write your own custom lyrics. The music it created actually sounded like real music. The voices were pretty good, too. I began making custom songs for every seminar group I spoke to. Their minds (and mine along with them) were blown away by these creations. Suno continued to improve, releasing a new model in April that upped the quality of the voices and the music. You could also create songs that were a little longer.

It didn't seem like things could get much better than Suno v3, and then, out of nowhere, an app called Udio was released. It just about broke the internet. Everyone and their brother began generating custom songs, and they were good—really good. The realism in the sound of the instrumentation, the quality of the vocals, and even its ability to write lyrics is nearly flawless. It creates music that isn't just acceptable but is actually catchy. Some of the songs are so good I have downloaded them and listened to them on repeat.

So far, there's not a style I've thrown at it that it can't do. I've generated 1980s glam rock, polka, Dixieland, barbershop quartet, Broadway musical, and the list goes on and on. And that's not all; it can also make excellent instrumental music. I prompted "contemplative acoustic guitar music," which generated a track that rivals many of the stock tracks for which I've paid over $30. This is so valuable for churches who don't have a lot of money to buy music to use for video production or for their livestreams (where those sorts of things have to be royalty-free).

We might think of AI as high-tech, but the medium of generated music can also be high-touch. I wanted to experiment with how far I could push the technology to create a warm emotional response. I spent thirty minutes or so writing lyrics to a song recounting a memory from elementary school with my sister. This was my prompt for the style of music: folksy, bop, acoustic guitar, mellow, contemporary, mellow, long-ing, sentimental, summer, love, bittersweet, male vocalist, melancholic, lush, a male voice with tight harmonies.

When the processing had finished, I listened to a song that sounded sort of like Art Garfunkel singing a duet with Joni Mitchell. I'll admit that the combination of those voices, a wonderfully rendered acoustic guitar composition, and the lyrics I wrote left me with a big lump in my throat as I listened. I sent it to my sister, and she had the same reaction. She may have even said it made her cry and then told me she asked my niece to play it at her funeral.

The fact that you can create something that evokes that kind of emotion in thirty minutes with artificial intelligence is unbelievable to me. It may have been created with artificial tools, but the sentiments were authentic.

Like everything related to AI, there are both upsides and downsides. I love that anyone with a song in their heart can bring it to life without being able to sing or play an instrument. I also can't help wondering what this will mean for musicians moving forward. Does this commoditize music in some way? Will it hurt?

I also see potential in using it to help musicians rough out song ideas. Throughout this book, I've advocated using AI as a collaboration tool, and AI music may be one way to do that. So, while it does create some uneasiness in me, it is also pretty neat.

I expressed my feelings about Udio in a song I wrote called "Udio You Freak Me Out (And Yet You're Cool)." You can see how good this app is and hear that song here: **bit.ly/Udio-Song**

For now, Suno offers enough free credits to make up to ten songs each day. Udio is in beta as I'm writing, so all generation is free, but I'm sure it won't be by the time you read this. I suspect they'll have some free credits like Suno to let you experiment. Go play! It's a blast.

Here's a list of some of the current music generators, including Suno and Udio:

MUBERT (MUBERT INC.)

URL: mubert.com

Description: Mubert focuses on creating real-time music streams generated by AI, tailored to user inputs for personal or commercial use.

What's Unique about It: It harnesses collaborative inputs from musicians and AI to produce continuously evolving music streams, offering a novel approach to music creation and consumption.

Challenges: Balancing AI-generated content with artist-driven music, ensuring fair use and copyright adherence, can be complex.

MUSICFX (GOOGLE)

URL: aitestkitchen.withgoogle.com/tools/music-fx

Description: Part of Google's AI Test Kitchen, MusicFX allows users to generate music from text inputs, leveraging advanced AI models to transform descriptions into unique sound compositions.

What's Unique about It: It incorporates Google's MusicLM and DeepMind's SynthID technologies, focusing on ethical AI use by avoiding the generation of music that mimics specific artists or styles.

Challenges: As an experimental tool, it's limited to select countries and is designed to avoid producing music that could infringe on the distinctiveness of original artists, which may limit creative outputs in certain styles. Tracks are currently only thirty seconds, with no way to extend them. The tracks aren't overly impressive, but Google continues updating the models that drive it.

SOUNDRAW (SOUNDRAW INC.)

URL: soundraw.io

Description: Soundraw is an AI music generator that allows individual creators to produce original music by setting parameters for the AI to follow. It is suitable for films, games, and content creation.

What's Unique about It: Users can influence the creation process without needing musical expertise, making it accessible to a wide range of users.

Challenges: The challenge lies in generating music that genuinely resonates with human emotions and meets specific user expectations. I canceled my subscription after two months because I didn't find the music to be very inspiring.

STABLE AUDIO (STABILITY AI)

URL: stability.ai/stable-audio

Description: Stable Audio utilizes advanced audio diffusion models to generate custom-length music and sound effects from textual descriptions, catering to both amateur creators and professional musicians.

What's Unique about It: It offers high-quality tracks up to three minutes long and allows users to transform audio samples into a wide array of sounds using natural language prompts.

Challenges: At present, Stable Audio's music isn't as realistic as options like Suno or Udio.

SUNO (SUNO INC.)

URL: suno.ai

Description: Suno offers tools for AI-based music composition, helping users generate music tracks from various inputs. It was the first of its kind in this space.

What's Unique about It: It targets ease of use, with intuitive interfaces and quick generation processes, to democratize music creation.

Challenges: The voices and instrumentation sound synthetic from time to time, but they will continue to improve with every iteration.

UDIO (UDIO)

URL: udio.com

Description: Udio is a best-in-class AI music generator that enables users to create music quickly. The platform allows for the exploration and creation of various musical compositions, making it easy for users to generate and interact with their own creations and those of other users.

What's Unique about It: Udio stands out due to its user-friendly interface and the ability to instantly generate high-quality music, catering to both novices and seasoned musicians. Users can generate music with or without lyrics. Udio can write lyrics and does a great job of doing so. It also has excellent controls for shaping your songs with the ability to extend the music multiple times. Rumor has it that stems (individual instrument and vocal tracks) may come in the future.

Challenges: Udio does not appear to be censoring content in any way. Be aware that much of the music in the Discover section on the site is not safe for work.

CONCLUSION

I'm so excited about what's to come. We stand on the cusp of a new era in creative expression and communication. While AI video generation is still in its early stages, the rapid advancements we've witnessed in tools like Sora, Vidu, and others hint at a future where high-quality AI-generated video content is not only possible but increasingly accessible to creators at all levels.

The potential applications for this technology in the church are vast, from creating engaging sermon illustrations and promotional materials to developing immersive educational content and fostering new forms of digital ministry. However, as with any powerful tool, we must approach AI video with thoughtfulness, care, and a commitment to using it in ways that align with our values and mission.

While the future of AI in video and beyond remains unwritten, one thing is clear: as Christians, we are called to engage this new frontier with wisdom, creativity, and a steadfast commitment to using all the tools at our disposal to further God's kingdom and make Christ known. In the next chapter, we'll put many pieces together and cover ten different ways AI can be used in the church.

CLAUDE'S QUESTIONS FOR REFLECTION

1. How can we use AI-generated imagery in ways that enhance rather than replace human creativity and artistry?

2. What ethical considerations should guide our use of image generation tools, particularly around issues of bias, representation, and consent?

3. How might visuals created by AI deepen or distract from the worship experience and the communication of biblical truths?

PART IV
AI AND THE CHURCH

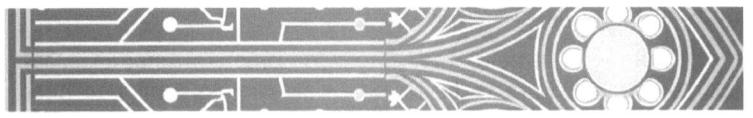

Chapter 10

TEN WAYS TO USE AI IN THE CHURCH

We've established the why and tackled some of the what. Now I'd like to focus on how to use AI in the church. There may be a little bit of what thrown in here too. I want to get you started with at least ten ways that you can start using AI in your church. Many of these come from personal experience, and some are more theoretical.

10. SERMON SERIES DESIGN AND BRANDING

One of my favorite ways to use AI is for sermon series development. It can help you brainstorm with your team about everything from scriptural foundations to follow-up calls to action. It shouldn't do all the work for you, but it can significantly enhance your creative process. Over the following few pages, I will let you peek over my shoulder as I work with AI to develop a series and the associated branding. This is a demo I designed for my training, and it'll help walk you through how to use ChatGPT for brainstorming and other tools to create the branding. I am not going to post the conversation in its entirety. You should also do more back-and-forths than I'm doing here.

A SAMPLE SERIES DESIGN

Jason:

Can you play the role of brainstorming partner for a sermon series design?

ChatGPT:

Absolutely, I'd be delighted to help you brainstorm for a sermon series design. To provide the best possible assistance, I'd need a bit more information:

1. What is the general theme or topic you're considering?
2. Who is the target audience?
3. How many sermons will be in the series?
4. Is there any specific scripture or religious text you want to focus on?
5. Do you have any particular goals for the series (e.g., spiritual growth, community outreach, theological understanding)?

Commentary

If ChatGPT does not ask you clarifying questions as it did here, ask it what it needs from you to be successful in your process. It will usually ask a few questions similar to these. For this example, I chose to answer three of those questions.

Jason:

1.) The life of Jesus, starting with his birth and ending with his death and resurrection. I want to focus on his miracles. 2.) People looking for the miracle in their lives. 3.) This will be a six-week series.

ChatGPT:

That's a wonderful theme for a sermon series. Here is a draft structure for your six-part series:

Week 1—"Birth of the Miracle": The series begins with a sermon on the miraculous birth of Jesus, signifying the entrance of the divine into the human world. This could inspire attendees to see miracles in beginnings and new opportunities in their own lives.

Week 2—"Miracle of Transformation: Water into Wine": This sermon could explore Jesus' first miracle, transforming water into wine at Cana. The transformation can serve as a metaphor for personal growth and change, encouraging attendees to seek and embrace their own transformations.

Week 3—"Miracle of Provision: Feeding the 5000": Discuss the miracle of Jesus feeding 5000 with five loaves and two fish, highlighting themes of divine provision and generosity. The message could inspire attendees to trust in God's provision and share generously with others.

Week 4—"Miracle of Healing: The Blind and the Lame": This week, you could delve into the numerous healing miracles performed by Jesus. This might encourage attendees to seek healing (emotional, spiritual, or physical) and believe in the possibility of recovery and renewal.

Week 5—"Miracle of Mastery Over Nature: Calming the Storm": Discuss Jesus' calming of the storm, symbolizing peace amidst life's chaos and control over intimidating circumstances. Encourage attendees to find peace in their own storms and believe in their ability to overcome challenges.

Week 6—"Miracle of Resurrection: Triumph Over Death": Conclude the series with the ultimate miracle of Jesus' death and resurrection, demonstrating the victory of life over death, hope over despair. This could inspire attendees to believe in the possibility of new life and redemption, even in the face of death or loss.

In each sermon, you could draw practical lessons from these miracles and inspire attendees to see potential miracles in their everyday lives. Consider including personal stories or testimonials to make these messages more relatable.

Commentary

I prepared the topic I covered beforehand, knowing what I wanted the series' focus to be. I'd already studied, prayed, and prepared for this conversation. I'm in the driver's seat here. Also, simply identifying these miracles in this order saves me a lot of time looking them up. Finally, while this order works fine for me, I can tell GPT to reorder it, throw some out, and find new ones, or I can start over completely.

Jason:

Can you provide the scripture references for each week in the series using the Common English Translation?

ChatGPT:

Of course! For your six-week series on the life of Jesus focusing on his miracles, I'll provide scripture references from the Common English Bible (CEB). Here's a breakdown:

Week 1—"Birth of the Miracle":

Scripture: Luke 2:1-20

This section describes the birth of Jesus, with Mary and Joseph in Bethlehem and the appearance of angels to the shepherds.

Week 2—"Miracle of Transformation: Water into Wine":

Scripture: John 2:1-11

This passage recounts the first miracle of Jesus where he turned water into wine at the wedding in Cana.

Week 3—"Miracle of Provision: Feeding the 5000":

Scripture: Matthew 14:13-21 (Parallel passages: Mark 6:30-44, Luke 9:10-17, and John 6:1-15)

These verses detail the feeding of the five thousand with five loaves of bread and two fish.

Week 4—"Miracle of Healing: The Blind and the Lame":

Scripture: Mark 10:46-52 (for the blind) and Matthew 9:1-8 (for the paralyzed).

Mark 10 describes the healing of Bartimaeus, a blind man, whereas Matthew 9 narrates the story of Jesus healing a paralyzed man.

Week 5—"Miracle of Mastery Over Nature: Calming the Storm":

Scripture: Mark 4:35-41 (Parallel passages: Matthew 8:23-27 and Luke 8:22-25)

This section captures the episode where Jesus calms the storm, showcasing his power over nature.

Week 6—"Miracle of Resurrection: Triumph Over Death":

Scripture: Luke 24:1-12 (Parallel passages: Matthew 28:1-10, Mark 16:1-8, and John 20:1-18)

This is the account of the resurrection of Jesus, where the tomb is found empty, and angels proclaim his resurrection.

These references can serve as your foundational texts for each week, which you can then expand upon or narrow down as needed for your series.

Commentary

Here's another example of time savings. I love that it also gave me a synopsis of each text.

Jason:

Summarize how each week relates to someone's life. Name a specific takeaway for each week and an application.

ChatGPT:

Absolutely, here are the specific takeaways and applications for each week:

Week 1—"Birth of the Miracle":

• Takeaway: Miracles often begin with humble and unexpected beginnings.

• Application: Encourage attendees to look for the miracles in their own beginnings, whether that's the start of a new job, relationship, or personal journey. Ask them to embrace these new starts with optimism, seeing them as opportunities for divine intervention.

Week 2—"Miracle of Transformation: Water into Wine":

• Takeaway: Transformation is a crucial aspect of miracles and often requires faith and patience.

• Application: Challenge attendees to identify areas in their lives where they desire transformation. Ask them to commit to a process of change, fueled by faith and patience, trusting in God's timing.

Week 3—"Miracle of Provision: Feeding the 5000":

• Takeaway: God is a provider and invites us to share generously with others.

• Application: Encourage attendees to trust in God's provision, especially in times of scarcity. Encourage acts of generosity in their daily lives, whether that's sharing time, resources, or kindness.

Week 4—"Miracle of Healing: The Blind and the Lame":

• Takeaway: Healing is possible in all areas of life and often begins with faith.

• Application: Invite attendees to seek healing in areas where they are hurting. This could mean seeking professional help, prayer, or opening up to loved ones. Remind them that faith is the first step toward healing.

Week 5—"Miracle of Mastery Over Nature: Calming the Storm":

• Takeaway: Peace is possible, even amidst life's storms, and often requires us to relinquish control.

• Application: Encourage attendees to identify the 'storms' in their lives and to surrender them to God. Ask them to practice peace, perhaps through prayer, meditation, or other spiritual disciplines, trusting that God has control over the chaos.

Week 6—"Miracle of Resurrection: Triumph Over Death":

• Takeaway: Hope and new life can emerge from even the most despairing circumstances.

• Application: Encourage attendees to identify areas in their lives where they feel 'dead' or hopeless. Remind them of the miracle of resurrection and inspire them to seek new life and hope in these areas, trusting in God's power to bring about resurrection.

Commentary

Reminder: You're the decider. You can use or reject this stuff, but I like that it's giving me ways to think about the purpose of the series.

Jason:

What are 5 potential titles for this series? I'd like for it to feel cinematic.

ChatGPT:

Absolutely, I understand that a compelling title can set the tone for the entire series. Here are five cinematic suggestions:

1. "Beyond Belief: The Miraculous Story of Jesus"
2. "Celestial Wonders: Jesus and His Miracles"
3. "Divine Impact: The Life and Miracles of Jesus"
4. "Supernatural Journey: The Saga of Jesus"
5. "The Ultimate Miracle: Jesus' Journey from Birth to Resurrection"

Each of these titles aims to convey the miraculous nature of Jesus' life and works, aligning with your cinematic theme.

Commentary

I skipped showing you the part where I rejected the first fifteen titles it gave me. None of them hit me. When this round came up, the first one hit my nostalgia bone. There was an old cheesy Petra album I wore out in high school with the same title, *Beyond Belief*. I didn't need to look any further.

Jason:

Help me write a 30-second movie trailer for this series. The script should be cinematic in tone. The video will incorporate a series of still images inspired by the miracles laid out in the series. As we see those scenes, we will hear the voice of a narrator.

Please describe each image and the accompanying voiceover for me. Remember to make it feel dramatic, like a movie trailer.

End the script with the title "Beyond Belief: The Miraculous Story of Jesus."

Do you understand?

ChatGPT:

Absolutely, I understand your requirements. Here's a dramatic, cinematic-style script for your 30-second movie trailer:

[Image 1]: A humble, starlit stable in Bethlehem.

Voiceover: "In a world where hope was born in the humblest of places . . ."

[Image 2]: A transformation, water pouring into a cup and coming out as wine.

Voiceover: " . . .a man emerged, turning the ordinary into the extraordinary."

[Image 3]: An overflowing basket of fish and loaves amidst a crowd of thousands.

Voiceover: "With a mere touch, scarcity became abundance . . ."

[Image 4]: A blind man, eyes opening wide in awe and disbelief.

Voiceover: " . . . the impossible became possible."

[Image 5]: A stormy sea becoming calm, the waves gently lapping against a boat.

Voiceover: "In the face of turmoil, he commanded peace . . ."

[Image 6]: A tomb with the stone rolled away, light emanating from within.

Voiceover: " . . . and in the shadow of death, he brought life."

[Image 7]: The title "Beyond Belief: The Miraculous Story of Jesus" fades in, glowing against a backdrop of the heavens.

Voiceover: "This is 'Beyond Belief: The Miraculous Story of Jesus'. Witness the miracles."

I hope this script helps create a dramatic and compelling trailer for your sermon series.

Commentary

This is a demo, so I went with it, but in a real-world scenario, I might go back and forth with ChatGPT for quite a while to tweak everything to dial it in perfectly. For demo purposes, this really captures the feel of what I was after. Next up, I asked for assistance with music selection. I spoke to United Methodists for this demo, so you'll see references to their hymnal. To keep things short, I will include only part of ChatGPT's response—the first two weeks—for the following output.

ChatGPT:

Certainly! Here are some hymn suggestions from the United Methodist Hymnal that can complement each week's theme in your sermon series. The selected hymns reflect the theological and emotional narrative of each sermon:

Week 1—"Birth of the Miracle":

Hymn: "O Little Town of Bethlehem" (UMH 230)

Synopsis: This hymn captures the quiet, miraculous wonder of Jesus' birth. Its lyrics focus on the humble beginnings of Jesus in Bethlehem, evoking a sense of awe and reverence appropriate for introducing the series.

Week 2 —"Miracle of Transformation: Water into Wine":

Hymn: "Come, Thou Fount of Every Blessing" (UMH 400)

Synopsis: The hymn speaks to the abundant blessings and the transformative power of God's grace, mirroring the theme of transformation seen in Jesus' first miracle.

Each hymn was chosen to resonate with the respective week's focus on the life and miracles of Jesus, designed to enhance the congregational worship experience and deepen the thematic connection of the sermons.

Commentary

I went on to ask the same thing for movie clips. It started with faith-based first-century "bathrobe" films like *Jesus of Nazareth*. I went back and asked for secular films. It provided one for every week in the series. I'm not including the whole list here, but I want to show you my exchange about the first clip.

ChatGPT:

Choosing secular movie clips that can metaphorically align with the themes of each week's sermon on the life and miracles of Jesus can be a creative way to engage your audience. Here are some suggestions:

Week 1—"Birth of the Miracle":

Movie Clip: "The Lion King" (1994)

- Scene: The presentation of Simba to the animal kingdom.

- Why It Fits: This scene, while secular, captures a sense of wonder, new beginnings, and the significance of birth in a grander scheme, paralleling the miraculous birth of Jesus.

Jason:

Can you provide timestamps for The Lion King for the scene you described?

ChatGPT:

For the 1994 animated version of "The Lion King," the scene where Simba is presented to the animal kingdom, often referred to as the "Circle of Life" scene, occurs at the very beginning of the film.

In most versions of the DVD or streaming formats, this scene starts approximately from the 0:00 mark and lasts until around the 3:45-4:00 mark. It includes the iconic moment where Rafiki lifts Simba up on Pride Rock for all the animals to see.

However, please note that the exact timestamps can vary slightly depending on the format of the movie (DVD, Blu-ray, digital streaming, etc.). It's always a good idea to preview the clip to ensure it aligns with the specific moment you intend to showcase.

Commentary

This is an unbelievable time savings! When I was on staff at Ginghamsburg United Methodist Church, we'd sometimes spend half a day looking for clips, and now AI can make the suggestion and even help you go right to the clip you're after.

That concludes my work with ChatGPT for this demo, but I want to highlight the incredible time savings. Looking up Scripture, finding all the miracles, scouring the hymnal, looking for movie clips, and more would take three-quarters of a day or more. Here, we knocked it out in mere moments.

What might we spend that time doing instead? Hospital visits to check out our congregants? Preparing a Bible study? Serving in a soup kitchen? Getting out into the community? Or (as one pastor recently said to me at a training) taking a nap! He exclaimed, "Can we just take a nap? Pastors are tired and overworked." Yes! You can take a nap. AI can free us up for relationship development, rest, and focus on other things.

Now let's look at how we take this brainstorming work and turn it into a bumper video. ChatGPT already helped write the script, and now we'll take the image ideas over into Midjourney to generate the images. (It's worth noting that I did create more robust prompts than the image descriptions here. The descriptions ChatGPT offered were just a starting point and not created for Midjourney.)

[**Image 1**] A humble, starlit stable in Bethlehem.

[**Image 2**] A transformation, water pouring into a cup and coming out as wine.

[**Image 3**] An overflowing basket of fish and loaves amidst a crowd of thousands.

[**Image 4**] A blind man, eyes opening wide in awe and disbelief.

[**Image 5**] A stormy sea becoming calm, the waves gently lapping against a boat.

[**Image 6**] A tomb with the stone rolled away, light emanating from within.

[**Image 7**] The title "Beyond Belief: The Miraculous Story of Jesus" fades in, glowing against a backdrop of the heavens.

From there, I took every image into Immersity AI, which I described in the last chapter. Immersity AI added depth to the images and allowed me to output videos in which the camera was perpetually pushing in on the images.

The next step was to create the voiceover. I went over to ElevenLabs, found a voice I liked, and then pasted in the script (developed by ChatGPT):

"In a world where hope was born in the humblest of places . . ."

". . . a man emerged, turning the ordinary into the extraordinary."

"With a mere touch, scarcity became abundance . . ."

". . . the impossible became possible."

"In the face of turmoil, he commanded peace . . ."

" . . . and in the shadow of death, he brought life."

"Beyond Belief: The Miraculous Story of Jesus. Witness the miracles."

I used the AI music resource Soundraw to generate a music track, and then I took everything into Adobe Premiere to assemble the edit. I added the text to the end of the video, and here is the final result: **bit.ly/BBelief-demo**

All told, that first version of the video probably took me about twenty hours from start to finish. That was actually my first time using these tools, so the time includes learning what each of the tools is, signing up for them, and learning them on the fly. Today, I could do something like that same piece in seven to ten hours. Considering it could be shown each week for six weeks, I'd call that a good day's work.

Because AI doesn't have to do it all for you but should do it with you, I poured another thirty hours into this piece and did my normal production process. I used Photoshop to make adjustments, such as placing the chalice in Jesus' hand to pour the water that becomes wine and adding the mud you see around the blind man's eyes. I also greatly enhanced the calming of the storm scene and redid the text with higher-end tools. You can see the fancy version of the video here: bit.ly/BBelief-Deluxe

As you embrace AI for developing your series, use it to research, to get unstuck, to help with creativity, and so on. Now you can even ask it to create an image for you, and you just might be able to prompt for a video. Whatever you do, do it; make sure you are the driver. Come prayed up. Study your Scripture, do some conceptual work first, then use the tool to help you get there.

9. SERMON PREPARATION ASSISTANCE

In addition to using AI for series development, tools like Claude, Chat-GPT, and Gemini can be used in sermon preparation. Or you might just use Magai, which has access to all those chatbots and more. Resist the temptation to treat AI like a glorified Google search engine. It's capable of so much more than that. Think of it more as a creative assistant.

I've pounded this into your head from the beginning, so you've undoubtedly gotten it by now, but AI shouldn't be writing your sermon for you. It has no soul and no relationship with God. You have both of those things; if you bring them to the conversation, God can move in mighty ways through this technology. Letting AI do too much will result in soulless sermons and other content.

Lean into being a cocreator with Christ, with AI as your tool in your toolbox. He will arrange the bits and bytes to make these algorithms produce transformational content. And it's just one tool amongst others. Your concordances, commentaries, Logos Bible software, and Google can all continue to be in the mix.

Come to your collaborative session with AI having already thought about where you want to lead your flock. Bring a point of view. Use AI to help you communicate that point of view in compelling ways. Use it to brainstorm metaphors and analogies. Gather additional relevant Scriptures, stories, and verbal and visual illustrations. Use it to illustrate your sermon points if that's your thing.

Don't farm out your exegetical work to AI. Something important happens when you toil in the fields, wrestling with Scripture. It's okay to use AI to assist you as you exegete Scripture. I realize that may sound contradictory, but there's a huge difference between letting AI think for you and you thinking for yourself, then using AI to go deeper.

Ask AI to argue the opposite point of view. Empower it to ask hard, clarifying questions. Have it summarize your ideas and see if they match your intentions. And make sure to double-check, confirm, and fact-check everything you receive from your chatbot. It can and will (sometimes) get it wrong.

Using AI with restraint will strengthen sermon content while allowing the pastor's unique perspective and guidance from the Holy Spirit to shape the final message.

8. LANGUAGE TRANSLATION ACCESSIBILITY AND INCLUSION

This aspect of AI stands out as one of my favorite applications of the technology. I attend Mosaic Church, located in Beavercreek, Ohio. This suburb of Dayton and its neighboring areas are home to a diverse community of immigrants who live, work, and worship here. Part of our DNA at Mosaic is to be a welcoming place for people of all cultural backgrounds. Our tagline is "Better Together," and we believe it.

Dayton is a sanctuary city, and we've had an influx of refugees and non–English speakers in our area at various points in time. Our church offers ESL (English as a second language) classes and has a Spanish-language service.

To live into our mission as a "Dynamic Mosaic of Jesus Followers," it is customary for our Sunday services to include prayers and Scriptures in multiple languages. For instance, a prayer may initially be recited in Japanese or a Scripture passage read in Mandarin, immediately followed by an English translation. This practice enriches our worship experience, reflecting the diverse fabric of all welcomed into our community.

When I shared an AI technology called HeyGen with my pastor and friend Rosario Picardo, he got very excited about its potential use at our church. If HeyGen sounds familiar, it should; I wrote about it in the last chapter. HeyGen has a feature that lets you upload a video clip in one language, analyze and clone the speaker's voice, and output it in another language. And it doesn't just overdub the voice; it moves the speaker's mouth to match the new language.

Rosario asked me, "Wouldn't it be cool to have this technology read the Scripture in another language in my voice, and then I follow it up with English?" This ritual in our church has always relied on multi-lingual volunteers to perform, but now—with the power of AI—those non–English speakers could hear the Scripture in Rosario's voice for the first time.

Now I think a disclaimer would be in order if we ever did this. We don't want to fool people or make them think Rosario suddenly speaks another language. I think he should simply say, "I wanted those of you who speak Spanish to hear this verse in your own language, and I thought it might be nice for you to hear it in my voice. Through the power of AI, hear these words." We could then play the video and follow up that video with his English reading.

This is just one way that we could use AI to bring more equity into a world that is very upper-middle-class English-speaking Caucasian-centric. We might consider using AI to deliver more diverse messages that aren't always exclusively English. AI-powered translation tools can help translate sermons or religious texts for multilingual congregations or missionaries, breaking language barriers. Churches can also use AI-powered tools for closed captioning to make services and resources more accessible to individuals with disabilities or language barriers.

I recently heard about a sign language technology that would use an AI avatar to sign in ASL in real-time for those who don't have an interpreter on-site. What an incredible gift that would be to people who are deaf or have difficulty hearing.

To see a quick demo I did using HeyGen, you can check out this link: **bit.ly/HeyGen-Demo**

7. BIBLE READING PLANS AND BIBLE STUDY

AI can also enhance discipleship within your church by aiding in Bible studies and personal-growth plans. Customizing Bible-reading plans for individuals or groups based on their preferences, past readings, and desired pace is a snap for AI. For instance, if an individual wants to explore themes of "hope" or "patience," chatbots can curate verses related to that theme over a set period. ChatGPT, paired with DALL-E, can even generate inspirational images to accompany the text.

Chatbots can also generate discussion questions, study guides, and other materials to support Bible studies and small groups. This saves time but also empowers lay leaders who may feel uncomfortable or lack the skill to create such materials.

Leveraging these tools to create tailored devotional content based on individual preferences, spiritual needs, and learning styles fosters a more engaging and meaningful faith journey. Of course, this still requires human oversight and customization in the end. Humans should always be driving the oversight of spiritual growth.

6. MUSIC AND WORSHIP

There are several ways to use AI to assist with music and worship, from managing the scheduling of musicians to play in your band or sing in your choir to keeping music charts cataloged and organized. Chatbots can assist in communication by helping craft emails to keep your team inspired or recruit new members.

Some musicians have reluctantly admitted to using chatbots to help generate ideas for songwriting, from song lyrics to song titles. Chatbots might also help craft some of the spoken words offered throughout worship before and after songs.

I talked with a worship director last week who told me he intends to use Udio to help him create new songs. These would likely be drafts, but it's conceivable that entire songs could be written with AI (preferably with humans writing the lyrics). Imagine a scenario where every series has its own theme song. AI can help you do that.

Generative music tools can create unique royalty-free soundtracks for worship services, prayer times, or personal reflection that won't trigger the Facebook or YouTube bots. Editors could use these tracks in videos and various promos.

We have to consider what lines we don't want to cross. AI music shouldn't replace human musicians or compete with our own agency in songwriting.

5. ATTENDANCE TRACKING AND ANALYSIS

ChatGPT allows you to upload your data to "chat with it." You can gain valuable insights about your attendance numbers and other relevant data to assist in predicting optimal dates, times, and resources for future events, ensuring maximum participation and efficient resource use.

For instance, ChatGPT might indicate that your best-attended Sunday is the third Sunday of the month. You may usually kick off a new series on the first Sunday, but the data insights might motivate you to consider launching a series on your best-attended week.

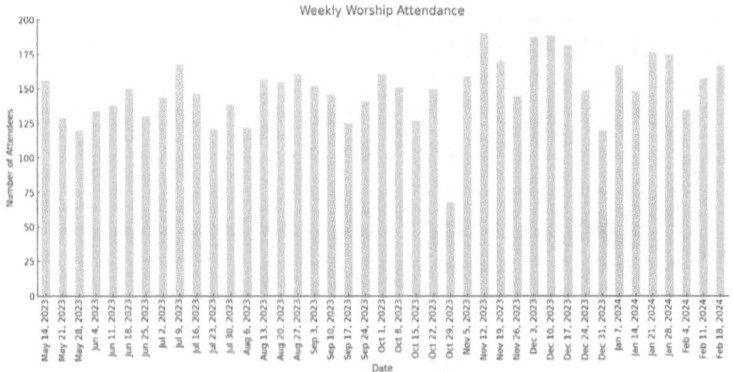

Be sure to look into proper privacy and security liabilities, especially if you're using this data on a public server like ChatGPT, Claude, or Gemini. Data exploitation becomes an even more significant concern when analyzing sensitive financial data.

4. COMMUNITY OUTREACH AND ENGAGEMENT

You can use AI to analyze community demographics, needs, and interests to inform outreach strategies and develop targeted content for social media and other platforms. If you can access MissionInsite or other demographic data, feed it into your favorite chatbot to see what you can learn about your community.

3. ARCHIVING AND DIGITAL PRESERVATION

Maintaining and honoring a church's history is a high priority for some faith communities. Keeping accurate records of historical events, previous pastors, members, and so on is easier than ever with AI. It can assist in digitizing, organizing, preserving, and restoring church records, sermons, hymns, and other valuable historical information. All of these things can be easily searchable and accessible for future generations through the power of AI.

One of my responsibilities in working with the California-Pacific Conference of the United Methodist Church is to craft a memorial video that honors the clergy and clergy spouses who have passed. Last year, for the first time, I could take the time to restore and improve the photos submitted because of the newest AI tools available. Otherwise I wouldn't have had the time or the budget to fix the dozens of photos I received, many of which were low quality.

2. AI-ASSISTED FUNDRAISING AND STEWARDSHIP

You could also leverage AI to analyze giving patterns, predict future financial needs, and develop personalized stewardship resources and communications to support the church's mission and vision. Relationship development for legacy and ongoing giving is so important. AI can help craft contextual and individualized emails to specific donors, finding just the right language to honor those relationships.

Capital and other giving campaigns can benefit from both text and image-generation tools. Well-designed media can be used to both build a strategy and communicate that strategy to your congregation.

If financial data is involved, privacy and security concerns must be considered. Investigate the risks involved in sharing this data outside of your local network.

1. ARTWORK, GRAPHIC DESIGN, AND COMMUNICATIONS

Using AI-powered tools like DALL-E, Midjourney, Leonardo, or Stable Diffusion to create unique and inspiring artwork for church buildings, prayer rooms, or meditation spaces can enhance the visual experience of sacred environments. What might you create to better tell your story, bring biblical stories and symbols to life, and make your sacred spaces inviting?

AI-powered design tools can also automatically generate graphic design templates for church events, sermons, social media, and more. The AI can create a visually appealing design when you input basic information like event date, theme, or Scripture reference.

You can use platforms like Ideogram, DALL-E, and others to draft logos, icons, and other assets for print pieces, sermon graphics, and internal and external communications. Using these tools will save you time and money, and as they continue to improve, (for some churches) they bring a significant aesthetic upgrade.

CONCLUSION

I hope these ten practical ways to integrate AI into our churches are helpful, but they only scratch the surface of what's possible. This technology offers a wealth of opportunities to enhance our effectiveness, creativity, and reach. AI tools can help us work smarter, communicate better, and extend our impact in new and exciting ways.

As we embrace these tools, let us remember that they are just that—tools. They are not a substitute for the wisdom, discernment, and personal touch that only human beings can bring to ministry. As we seek to harness the power of AI for the sake of the gospel, may we do so with prayerful consideration, biblical grounding, and a commitment to using these technologies in ways that honor God and serve others.

The goal is to use AI to enhance and extend human capabilities, not to replace the essential human elements of ministry. As you explore these applications, prioritize the principles of doing no harm, maintaining transparency, and relying on God's guidance in navigating the complex landscape of AI in ministry.

CLAUDE'S QUESTIONS FOR REFLECTION

1. Which of the ten use cases for AI in the church are you most interested in exploring further, and why?

2. How can we prioritize and sequence the implementation of AI tools in our specific ministry contexts?

3. What success metrics or evaluation processes should we use to assess the impact and effectiveness of our AI initiatives?

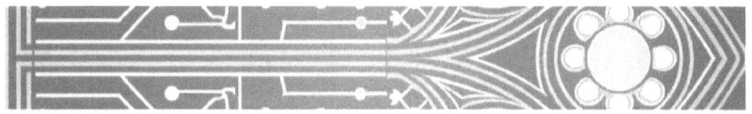

THE FUTURE OF AI

It's hard to believe so much has happened with AI over the last couple of years, and we're just getting started. It's hard even to imagine what might come next in the world of AI and how it might affect the church, but I wanted to share a little speculation with you based on what I'm seeing and hearing.

Before I do that, though, I want to address the thing that has weighed so heavily on me over the six months or so that it has taken me to complete this book. I knew that no matter what I wrote here, some portion of it would be out of date before the ink ever hit the press. I've scrapped sections and added things that extended my writing several times. It is impossible to keep up with the daily news on AI, but I wanted to give you a way to get updates on this technology beyond the printed page.

Visit **https://www.inviteresources.com/** for the latest information related to this book's content. Before it is published, I'll update it with any relevant changes organized by chapter. I intend to update it at least twice yearly, but I'll jump in and update it more frequently than that for big news. Be sure to check back every now and then to see what's changed.

I also offer a six-month AI cohort, where up to ten churches (per cohort) can engage in monthly calls breaking down the latest best practices, experience bonus teaching sessions with AI experts, and receive one-on-one coaching sessions for every participating church. If you'd like to learn more about this, follow this link to sign up for more information. I offer partial scholarships for those who want to participate but cannot afford the sticker price: **bit.ly/AI-Cohort**

I also participate in two Facebook AI communities that I'd recommend you join. They are:

> AI for Church Leaders and Pastors: www.facebook.com/
> groups/aiforchurchleaders
>
> AI for Churches: www.facebook.com/groups/aiforchurches

Now let's speculate about what's to come. I get several different AI emails daily that cover a range of things, from the latest news to ethics, technical information, and predictions for the future. Here are five things I believe will happen with AI in the future.

1. AI Agents Will Play a Major Role in Our Daily Lives

Autonomous (or semi-autonomous) AI agents will get to know us at a deep level. They will know our goals, aspirations, desires, likes, and dislikes. Unlike the LLMs we have at our disposal today, which require that we give them specific instructions, agents will anticipate our needs and act to help us in meaningful ways. We'll still call the shots but allow agents to participate in various aspects of our lives.

I can see a day coming when I tell an AI agent I've just booked a speaking engagement in a specific part of the country. It will then confirm the details, write my contract, and email it to my host. It will then look up flights (knowing my preferences for window seat, front of the plane, and what time of day I like to travel). From there, it'll confirm itineraries and book the flight. It will also know to book me a car and hotel and will make an itinerary that gives me suggestions of where I might want to dine or what I might see when I'm in the area.

Agents may replicate some of our AI tools too. They'll know how to prompt an LLM and an image generator to make your spouse a perfect custom birthday card. They'll even send it to your printer for you. You will, however, need to load the paper and fold it. Agents may eventually move with you from your home to your car, driving you to the restaurant where they already made your reservations and told you to have birthday cake on hand for the end of your meal.

Agents will be able to assist you in writing a program, and you'll never have to learn to code. You'll just describe what you want it to do, and it'll figure out how to make it a reality. That may involve telling a chatbot what to do.

Like KITT in *Knight Rider*, these agents will still need you to be their Michael Knight in the driver's seat. You'll still be leading the mission, but they'll be there to assist you in heroic ways that make the mission accomplishable.

Believe it or not, this isn't that far off. Agents are already here in rudimentary form. They're not at the AGI level, but agents can accomplish some of these tasks now through automation. In the next few years, they will become commonplace, and many of us will be using them. We'll wonder how we lived without them in the past.

2. AI Will Merge with VR to Create New Worlds

Just around the time COVID hit, affordable VR came on the scene. Meta released the Meta Quest 2 headset, and for the first time, VR was within the reach of a much more significant portion of the population. For a while, especially because of social distancing, the church began to experiment with these tools. It seemed like the next big thing, and then ChatGPT showed up.

While VR didn't disappear, its excitement shifted to generative AI. Programmers are still developing VR worlds, games, and experiences, but in news cycles, VR has kind of taken a back seat in recent years. It won't be long before AI and VR intersect in ways that enhance both technologies.

AI will soon be able to generate worlds just by describing them. People will be able to step into their creations, combining generative music, AI 3D modeling, voice simulation, and everything else needed to make an experience.

Chatbots will generate stories on the fly in VR worlds, and a "choose your own adventure" style movie will play out in nearly photorealistic forms. Can you imagine Sunday school with a virtual trip to first-century northern Israel to experience Jesus delivering the Sermon on the Mount amongst the crowd of onlookers? Just remember to prompt him to be Middle Eastern—not a blond mulleted dude from Middle America.

3. Generative AI Tools Will Become Multifaceted

In the future, AI apps will become more multipurpose. Rather than having to talk to a chatbot here, generate an image there, and create a voiceover over there—it'll all happen in one place. Perhaps companies will combine to offer multiple solutions like OpenAI, which offers ChatGPT, DALL-E, and Sora, or the various tools will expand to other areas.

Agents may be the bridge that combines all these things under one umbrella. I just hope they can figure out a way to make them more affordable. OpenAI's solution is attractive because it's currently one fee for text and image generation. (No word on what will happen with Sora.)

4. AI Will Be Embraced by Higher Education

There's a lot of resistance right now in higher education around AI. The use of ChatGPT is forbidden in some schools, while others are embracing strict ethical guidelines for its use in the classroom.

In the future, every educational institution will fully accept and utilize AI in the classroom. Professors and instructors will teach students how to use AI for critical thinking. Students will learn how to operate whatever new technologies develop, and instruction will take place with the assistance of AI. In the next five years, the educational system will look entirely different than it does today. AI will be tomorrow's "Google" in the classroom. In a world where the workforce collaborates with AI to augment their work, students will actually be required to do the same.

5. AI Will Be Regulated by the Government

Whether you love or hate the idea, the government will be more involved in AI, regulating and legislating it to safeguard our society. From copyright protections to banning certain uses (such as misleading use of cloned voices), the world will be different from the Wild West we live in today. This technology is so powerful that I'm for some degree of oversight and regulation. I just hope they don't go too far.

I recently learned of the Generative AI Copyright Disclosure Act. This federal bill mandates that AI companies disclose any copyrighted works used in training their models. The disclosure must be filed with the U.S. Copyright Office before the model is released, and similar disclosures are necessary for significant updates to existing models. The legislation aims to enhance transparency and ensure fair compensation for creators by setting clear guidelines for the use of copyrighted materials in AI technologies. Penalties for noncompliance are determined on a case-by-case basis.[29]

The White House has drafted a "Blueprint for an AI Bill of Rights" to protect US citizens from AI's potential harms. It has five principal areas of concern:

Safe and Effective Systems: You should be protected from unsafe or ineffective systems.

Algorithmic Discrimination Protections: You should not face discrimination by algorithms, and systems should be used and designed in an equitable way.

Data Privacy: You should be protected from abusive data practices via built-in protections, and you should have agency over how data about you is used.

Notice and Explanation: You should know that an automated system is being used and understand how and why it contributes to outcomes that impact you.

Human Alternatives: You should be able to opt out, where appropriate, and have access to a person who can quickly consider and remedy problems you encounter.[30]

---

29. Sarkis Yeretsian, "Generative AI Copyright Disclosure Act Introduced to Protect Creators," Lewis Brisbois Bisgaard & Smith, April 11, 2024, https://lewisbrisbois.com/newsroom/legal-alerts/generative-ai-copyright-disclosure-act-introduced-to-protect-creators.

30. Office of Science and Technology Policy, "Blueprint for an AI Bill of Rights," The White House, https://www.whitehouse.gov/ostp/ai-bill-of-rights/.

We'll see if either of these things becomes actual law, but I predict that the future of AI will be regulated, including what we can do, what can be copyrighted, and more.

CONCLUSION

As we look to the future of AI, it's clear that this technology will continue to advance and shape our world in profound ways. From the development of more sophisticated AI agents to the integration of AI with virtual reality and the ongoing evolution of AI tools, the possibilities are both exciting and daunting.

None of my predictions are earth-shattering or super out-of-the-box, but I think they're pretty safe bets. Time will tell. Some of these may come true even before the book is out, especially if AGI is achieved.

I encourage you to stay informed, be adaptable, and remain grounded in our faith, so that we can navigate the challenges and opportunities ahead. When we stay committed to that, we can harness the power of AI to advance God's kingdom and make a positive impact on the world.

In the next chapter, I want us to examine creating an AI policy for your church. I've drafted a robust policy that will help you consider everything you need to include in yours.

CLAUDE'S QUESTIONS FOR REFLECTION

1. How can we cultivate a posture of openness and adaptability to the continued rapid development of AI technologies?

2. What steps can we take now to prepare ourselves and our ministries for the future realities of AI?

3. How do we maintain our grounding in timeless Christian truths while also engaging proactively with the ever-shifting technological landscape?

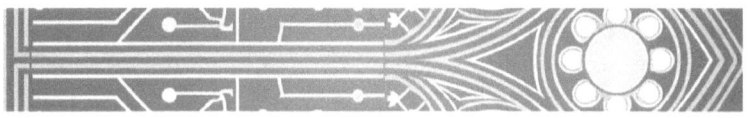

Chapter 12

DEVELOPING AN AI POLICY

To date, I've done over two dozen "Using AI Tools in the Church" trainings, and in nearly every single one of them, I've been asked if I have an AI policy to share. Using AI in the church is such new territory that very few such policies exist. While preparing to write this, I could only find a few examples.

This technology is becoming so integrated into the world we live in that it cannot be ignored. Every church should know where it stands with AI, and an AI policy will help you determine how you do and don't use it.

With the help of ChatGPT and Claude, I've put together a sample policy that you are free to use as much of or as little of as you'd like. I reviewed the entire book and extracted all the items I felt should be included in such a policy. I then created a bullet list with subpoints and asked both chatbots to organize my list into categories. From there, I asked the chatbots to include any other ideas not on my list but related to the policy. I added some of those suggestions and rejected others.

I made additional tweaks, reordered things, and put a few final touches on it. You'll see it on the following pages.

Let's be honest: most people never read the various policies we develop. It's like how most of us treat the manual or instructions that come with an item we purchase. You mostly ignore them until something isn't working right. In the same way, an AI policy may best serve to get you out of a jam when something goes awry.

Developing an AI policy forces you to think through as many of the issues related to this technology as possible so you can underpin your usage with purpose. It's also good to have answers worked out for when people ask you about various aspects of your AI usage.

I've used these phrases throughout the book, but my core principles around AI are these:

1. AI should be a "do it with you, not a do it for you."

2. Working with AI should be a conversation, not a query or command.

3. You have a soul. AI doesn't. If you don't bring your soul to the conversation, there is no soul in the conversation.

These core principles drove me to write this book and underpin everything I do with this technology. What are yours, and how can they be reflected in your AI policy?

What follows is a comprehensive and robust AI policy. For some of you, it'll perfectly fit your context. For others, it's overkill. Use the parts of it that pertain to your ministry and ignore the parts that don't. Think of it like a buffet! Load up the plate with the bits you like and leave the rest behind. You'll also find a TLDR (Too Long, Didn't Read) version of the policy that is just the basics.

SAMPLE AI POLICY

Introduction: Purpose of the AI Policy

This AI policy establishes guidelines and a framework for the responsible and ethical use of Artificial Intelligence (AI) at [Church Name]. The policy ensures that AI is employed in a manner that aligns with our core values, mission, and vision, maximizing its potential benefits while minimizing potential risks.

As AI technologies become increasingly integrated into various aspects of society and the lives of our congregation, we must proactively address AI's use and implications. We must also help our congregants navigate their faith in a world where AI is everywhere. This policy ensures that AI is utilized to enhance our ministry efforts, support our congregation, and uphold the church's biblical, ethical, and moral standards as well as any applicable denominational standards. We aim to create a balanced approach to AI usage that adheres to the principles of doing no harm, doing good, and remaining wholly reliant on God (not AI).

Defining AI

Artificial intelligence (AI) refers to computer systems that simulate human intelligence to perform various tasks. AI includes tools such as chatbots, image and video generators, voice and music generation, and more. While AI consists of a vast and sophisticated array of applications, it relies on human input, guidance, and discernment to function effectively and ethically. We see AI as a tool designed to complement and augment human capabilities rather than replace them entirely.

Core Values and AI Alignment

[Church Name] is committed to faithfully living out our core values of [Insert core values]. We will utilize AI when appropriate to responsibly assist in our work of executing these core values.

We are dedicated to a human-centric strategy where AI is guided by faithful Christian leaders who embody our core values. This human direction is paramount, from brainstorming in various ministry areas to utilization of AI in communications, ordering the life of the church, and faith formation.

We commit to valuing the Holy Spirit's work over AI's contributions. AI will never be allowed to become a proxy God but will be used to assist us in living out the Spirit's convictions as expressed in our core values.

We pledge to value human individuals above AI and will use AI to promote justice, equity, and dignity for all people according to our core values. [You might also consider adding in any denominational statements that apply, such as the World Methodist Social Affirmation (UMH 886).]

We are committed to continuously developing guidelines and principles that ensure AI is utilized consistently with the church's core values, prioritizing transparency, fairness, privacy, and the preservation of human agency and decision-making.

Our staff and leaders will adhere to these guidelines and be held accountable for the ways they use AI.

We pledge to use AI openly and transparently (including verbal or written attributions per the policy outlined in this document) within our church.

Range of AI Integration

We may use AI across church ministries in the following ways:

Creative Collaboration: AI may be used to enhance and augment various initiatives, but strictly as a creative collaborator. Our philosophy is that AI should be a "do it with you, not a do it for you."

Sermon/Series Development: AI tools may be used to stimulate ideation, assist in sermon research, and help organize thoughts and critical thinking. However, the pastor should never abdicate his or her unique perspective, prophetic authority, and spiritual discernment to AI-generated content. We emphasize the importance of personal reflection, prayer, and the guidance of the Holy Spirit in crafting the final message.

Content Creation Assistance: We may utilize AI to generate images and videos for sermon graphics, branding, and other promotional material. We may also generate text to draft and assist in developing blog posts, devotionals, and study materials, with human staff and volunteers refining, personalizing, and ensuring theological accuracy in the final content.

Communication Support: We may utilize AI to enhance church communications by generating social media post ideas, newsletter content, and email templates. Human staff will personalize and tailor messages to maintain an authentic connection with the congregation.

Administrative Efficiency: We may employ AI to streamline administrative tasks such as scheduling, data management, and workflow optimization, allowing staff to focus on relationship building, providing personal care to the congregation, and other essential ministry tasks.

Research Assistance: We may leverage AI to gather and analyze data on topics relevant to the church's mission and ministry, such as community needs assessments, scriptural analysis, and social trends, while ensuring human discernment in applying insights.

Volunteer Coordination: We may implement AI tools to help match volunteers with opportunities based on their skills, interests, and availability while emphasizing the importance of personal relationships and human touch in volunteer management.

Data Analysis and Decisions: We may employ AI to analyze church data such as attendance, giving, and engagement metrics to inform strategic decision-making. Human leaders will interpret insights and apply wisdom in ministry planning. We will ensure proper safeguards are in place to protect this data.

Accessibility Improvement: AI may be used to make church services and materials more accessible by providing real-time transcription, AI translation tools such as HeyGen and ElevenLabs, and closed captioning, enabling broader participation and inclusion.

WHY WE EMBRACE AI

Increased efficiency and productivity in administrative workflows
Enhanced personalization and engagement with congregants
Expanded ministry reach and impact through improved communication

Potential Drawbacks and Considerations

- Need for monitoring and mitigating potential biases in AI systems

- Importance of maintaining human touch in spiritual care and community building

- Ethical considerations related to privacy, transparency, and accountability

Scriptural Guidance

a. Foundational Scriptures:

[Insert your favorite texts (see chapter 5 or pick your own).]

b. Applying scriptural principles to AI use:

- We will bathe the process of using AI tools in prayer, taking a cautious, reverent approach.

- We seek God's wisdom and discernment in navigating AI's complexities and uncertainties.

- We strive to use AI in a manner that glorifies God and serves the well-being of the church and our community.

Alignment with Mission, Vision, and Values

a. Evaluating AI's impact on the church's mission and vision:

- We commit to regularly assessing how AI technologies support and enhance the church's purpose and goals.

- We pledge to prioritize AI initiatives that align with the church's strategic priorities.

b. Monitoring AI's influence on church culture and values:

- We will continuously evaluate the impact of AI on interpersonal relationships, communication, and community dynamics.

- We will adjust AI practices as needed to maintain alignment with the church's values and culture.

Ethical Considerations

a. Bias in AI-generated content:

- We are committed to using AI tools to represent the diversity of humanity (in its various forms) in the imagery and other media we generate with AI.

b. Prioritizing privacy and data security:

- We will maintain high privacy and data security standards when using AI tools, especially when handling sensitive personal information.

- We will adhere to established protocols and best practices for data protection.

c. Compliance with platform policies and legal standards:

- We require staff and volunteer team members to adhere to the terms of service policies of the AI platforms they use.

- We respect intellectual property rights and will use AI tools that are consistent with legal and ethical standards.

d. Regular review and adjustment of ethical guidelines:

- We commit to periodically reviewing and updating ethical guidelines to address emerging challenges and ensure ongoing alignment with our core values and societal norms (when those things don't conflict).

AI Tool Selection and Management

a. Specific AI platforms currently in use:

[Insert list of applications]

b. Evaluation and selection criteria for AI tools:

- Each of these applications is vetted to ensure it aligns with church values and ethical principles.

- The function of each of these tools has been matched with a specific ministry need.

- Applications that involve personal data have been evaluated for proper privacy and security protections.

c. Review and approval process for AI-generated content:

[Supervisor Name] is responsible for approving/disseminating AI-generated content.

AI Governance

a. Roles and responsibilities of staff members:

- [Name] has been designated as the overseer of AI usage to ensure compliance with the policy and address any concerns that may arise.

- Staff members, including ministry leaders, are responsible for using AI tools ethically and aligning with the church's values and mission.

b. Training and development:

- Staff members are encouraged to engage in continuous learning about AI tools. [Church Name] will provide the necessary training resources.

c. Accountability and oversight mechanisms:

- Clear reporting and escalation channels for AI-related concerns or policy violations have been established. See [Name] for more information.

Disclosure and Transparency

In our commitment to transparency and integrity, it is vital to discern when and how to give attribution for the use of artificial intelligence (AI) within our church's operations and ministries. While AI enhances our capabilities, it is essential to maintain trust and uphold ethical standards in its application.

See attribution guidelines below.

Attribution and Acknowledgment

a. Guidelines for using attribution with AI-assisted content:

- We've established the following threshold to determine when AI-generated content should include attribution:
- Attribution is required when . . . [Insert specific criteria]
- Attribution is not required when . . . [Insert specific criteria]
- If you're not sure whether to include attribution, see [Name of responsible party] for further guidance.

b. Specific circumstances and methods for acknowledgment:

- Verbally acknowledge AI assistance in live sermons or presentations where appropriate, according to the guidelines.
- Attribution should be included in written materials like bulletins, posts, or social media where appropriate, according to the guidelines.
- Provide links or references to specific AI tools or resources used, where appropriate, according to the guidelines.

Privacy and Security

a. Data protection protocols and best practices:

- Implement robust measures to protect congregant data in AI use

- Obtain explicit consent for personal data collection, use, and storage

- Ensure AI systems and databases are secure against unauthorized access

b. Regular updates and monitoring:

- Stay informed on the latest privacy regulations and security technologies.

- Conduct periodic risk assessments to identify vulnerabilities and improvements.

- Provide ongoing staff and volunteer training on best practices for privacy and security.

AI EXCLUSIONS AND LIMITATIONS

We acknowledge that AI does not have a soul or a relationship with the Holy Spirit and is incapable of empathy and spiritual guidance. We will not use AI in the following ways:

[Insert specific AI restrictions according to your convictions]

Regular AI Policy Review
a. Ongoing evaluation and updates:

- We commit to regularly schedule periodic AI policy reviews to assess this policy's relevance, effectiveness, and alignment with our mission, vision, and values. Those reviews shall happen [Insert specific interval].

- Our leadership board will be involved in the review and revision process.

- We will communicate policy updates and changes to all relevant parties in the following ways.

[Insert specifics]

b. Continuous improvement and adaptation:

- We will monitor AI practices' effectiveness and impact, identifying areas for improvement.
- We will actively seek feedback from staff, congregation, and leadership board to inform future adjustments.
- We will adapt our AI policy to address emerging challenges, new technological advancements, and best practices.

TLDR (TOO LONG, DIDN'T READ) VERSION:

AI Policy for [Church Name]

1. **Introduction and Purpose:** This policy provides guidelines for the responsible and ethical use of artificial intelligence (AI) at [Church Name], ensuring alignment with our core values, mission, and vision. As AI becomes increasingly integrated into society, we must proactively address its use and implications while helping our congregants navigate their faith in an AI-driven world.

2. **Defining AI:** AI refers to computer systems designed to simulate human intelligence, including tools such as chatbots, image and video generators, voice and music generation, and more. We value AI as a tool to complement and augment human capabilities rather than replace them entirely.

3. **Core Values and AI Alignment:** We are committed to a human-centric approach to AI, guided by Christian leaders and the Holy Spirit.

    AI will never become a proxy for God but will assist us in living out our core values.

    We pledge to value human individuals above AI and to use AI to promote justice, equity, and dignity.

    Our staff and leaders will adhere to guidelines and be held accountable for using AI.

4. **Range of AI Integration:** AI may be used in various minis-

tries, with heavy human oversight, including:
Creative collaboration and content creation
Sermon development and research assistance
Communication support and administrative efficiency
Volunteer coordination and data analysis
Accessibility improvement

5. **Benefits and Considerations:** We embrace AI for its potential to increase efficiency, personalization, and ministry impact.
   We acknowledge the need to mitigate biases, maintain human touch, and address ethical considerations.

6. **Scriptural Guidance:** Our use of AI is grounded in scriptural principles. We seek to glorify God and serve the well-being of the church and community. We will prayerfully navigate the complexities and uncertainties of AI.

7. **Alignment with Mission, Vision, and Values:** We will regularly evaluate AI's impact on our mission, vision, and values, making adjustments as needed to maintain alignment.

8. **Ethical Considerations:** We are committed to representing diversity, maintaining privacy and security, adhering to legal and ethical standards, and regularly reviewing our guidelines.
   Specific AI tools are vetted and matched to ministry needs, with a designated approval process for AI-generated content.

9. **AI Governance:** Staff are trained and held accountable for ethical AI use, with clear reporting channels for concerns or violations.
   We have guidelines for giving attribution and acknowledging AI use, ensuring transparency and integrity.

10. **AI Exclusions and Limitations:** AI will not be used in areas requiring empathy or spiritual guidance or where it may undermine human connection and leadership.

11. **Privacy and Security:** We will implement robust measures to protect congregant data, obtain consent for data collection and use, and ensure the security of AI systems and databases.

12. **Regular AI Policy Review:** This policy will be regularly

reviewed and updated to address emerging challenges and opportunities, with input from staff, congregation, and leadership.

By adhering to this policy, we aim to harness the power of AI in a manner that aligns with our values, enhances our ministry efforts, and supports our congregation in navigating their faith journey in an increasingly AI-driven world.

CLAUDE'S QUESTIONS FOR REFLECTION

1. What unique considerations or priorities should shape the AI policy for your specific church or ministry context?

2. How can we involve key stakeholders and diverse perspectives in the process of crafting an AI policy?

3. What mechanisms should we put in place to ensure regular review of, adaptation of, and accountability to our AI guidelines?

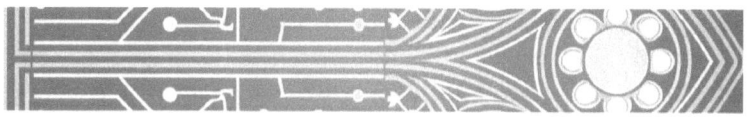

CONCLUSION

As we come to the end of this exploration of AI and its implications for the church, it's clear that we stand at a pivotal moment in history. The rapid advancement of artificial intelligence is not just a technological revolution; it's a paradigm shift that rivals the impact of Gutenberg's press and the church's embracing of electronic media in the 1980s and 1990s.

This moment in time challenges us to reimagine what it means to be the church in a world where machines can think, create, and engage in ways that were once the sole domain of human beings. It also forces us to consider how we might find new ways to reach and disciple people who must now navigate their faith in a world where AI is everywhere. Answers to every conceivable question are just a click or spoken query away. In a world where this is reality, why would a "seeker" need God?

Throughout this book, we've grappled with profound questions and possibilities raised by AI. We've traced its history, explored its concepts, and examined the ethical and theological foundations that must guide our engagement with this powerful technology. We've also traversed a path into practical applications of AI in ministry, from using chatbots and image generators to enhance our communication and creativity to harnessing the power of AI video and other cutting-edge tools.

At every turn, we've witnessed that AI is not just a tool for efficiency or innovation; it's a catalyst for reflection and transformation. It invites us to consider what it means to be created in the image of God, to steward the gifts of technology for the greater good, and to bear witness to the gospel in a world where the line between the human and the artificial is becoming increasingly blurred.

As we look to the future, it's clear that AI will only become more prevalent and more powerful. From the rise of AI agents that can anticipate our needs and shape our decisions to the integration of AI with virtual reality and the metaverse, the possibilities are both exhilarating and, let's be honest, just a little scary. As Christians, we cannot afford to sit on the sidelines or retreat into a posture of fear or resistance. The only way to guarantee a negative outcome at this time is to ignore AI. Instead, we are called to engage this new frontier with courage, wisdom, and discernment, always seeking to use AI in ways that align with our values and serve the mission of the church.

This engagement will require ongoing education, experimentation, and dialogue. It will demand that we cultivate a deep grounding in our faith and a commitment to the greater good. It will challenge us to be both innovative and discerning, embracing the opportunities presented by AI while also being clear-eyed about its limitations and potential pitfalls.

But if we approach this task with humility, curiosity, and a spirit of faithful stewardship, I believe that AI can be a powerful ally in our efforts to share the gospel of Jesus Christ, make disciples, and transform the world. It can help us communicate more effectively, bring more equity, serve more compassionately, and reach new audiences with the message of Christ's love. It can also deepen our own faith and spiritual growth as we use these tools to explore the mysteries of God and the wonders of creation in new ways.

So, friends, let us not shrink back from the challenges and opportunities before us. Let us instead embrace them with confidence, knowing that the same God who has guided the church through countless technological revolutions in the past is also with us now, leading us into a future that is bright with possibility.

As you go forth from these pages, I invite you to continue the conversation and the exploration. Engage with Claude's reflection questions in each chapter, even after you're done reading the book. Share your own experiences and insights with others in your church. If you're a pastor, talk with other pastors about what you're learning and where you have concerns. If you're not a pastor, talk with other colleagues to bounce ideas off of them. Most of all, keep seeking God's wisdom and guidance as you navigate the uncharted waters of AI and its implications for your life and ministry.

Together, let us dream big dreams and ask bold questions. Let us experiment and iterate, learning from our successes and failures alike. Let us be the church in a world where AI is not just a tool but a partner in our efforts to love God and neighbor, to seek justice and mercy, and to proclaim the good news of Jesus Christ to all people.

Above all, let us commit to a balanced approach to using these tools. They should never replace personal study, prayer, and collaboration work with others. Should we ever find ourselves living in a place where we can't function without these tools, may we quickly correct course. We must not only embrace but also exercise restraint. We cannot risk becoming overreliant on AI.

The future of AI is uncertain, but our calling is clear. May we rise to the challenge with grace, humility, and a fierce commitment to using all the tools at our disposal to further God's kingdom and make Christ known. And may we always remember that, no matter how advanced our technologies become, it is ultimately the power of the Holy Spirit that brings transformation, renewal, and abundant life.

So let us go forth with courage and hope, trusting in the God who holds the future and who calls us to be cocreators in the ongoing work inviting people into relationship with Jesus. The journey ahead may be uncharted, but with the Holy Spirit as our guide and AI as our ally, I believe that the best is yet to come.

CLAUDE'S QUESTIONS FOR REFLECTION

1. How will you balance the potential benefits of AI in ministry with the need to maintain authentic human connections and spiritual practices?

2. In what ways might AI challenge or enhance your understanding of what it means to be created in the image of God?

3. How can you effectively educate and guide your congregations in the responsible and ethical use of AI tools while still emphasizing the primacy of faith and the Holy Spirit's work?

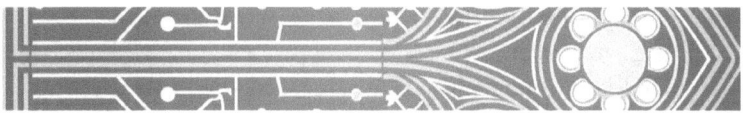

GLOSSARY

Here are many of the terms you've seen me use throughout the book. I've included additional terms that are related but not specifically mentioned. This glossary only scratches the surface of the many established and emerging terms used in the field of AI.

AI (Artificial Intelligence): The simulation of human intelligence in machines designed to think and act like humans.

Algorithm: A set of instructions or rules that a computer follows to solve a problem or complete a task.

API (Application Programming Interface): A set of protocols and tools for building software applications that specify how software components should interact.

Artifacts: Inconsistencies or errors in AI-generated content, such as distorted faces or misshapen objects.

Artificial General Intelligence (AGI): A theoretical form of AI that can understand, learn, and apply intelligence across a wide range of domains, similar to human cognitive abilities.

Artificial Super Intelligence (ASI): A hypothetical future form of AI that surpasses human intelligence in all aspects, including creativity, problem-solving, and emotional intelligence.

Aspect Ratio: The proportional relationship between an image's width and height.

Autonomous Vehicles: Vehicles capable of sensing their environment and operating without human involvement.

Autoregressive Models: A type of machine-learning model that predicts future values based on past observations. These models are commonly used in natural language processing for text generation and language-modeling tasks.

Berne Convention: An international agreement governing copyright, which mandates that countries recognize copyrights held by citizens of all participating countries.

Bias in AI: The inherent bias present in AI systems due to the data they are trained on or the humans who design them, leading to unfair or discriminatory outcomes.

Character and Style References: Tools in AI image generation that allow users to maintain consistent character appearances and artistic styles across multiple images.

Chatbots: Computer programs designed to simulate human conversation and interact with users through natural language.

Context Window: The amount of surrounding text or information an AI model considers when processing or generating language.

ControlNet: An extension for Stable Diffusion that allows users to generate images with specific pose, depth, and segmentation control.

Convolutional Neural Networks (CNNs): A type of deep learning algorithm commonly used for image and video recognition.

Deepfakes: Synthetic media in which a person's likeness is replaced with someone else's, sometimes used maliciously to spread misinformation or commit fraud.

Deep Learning Models: AI models that use multiple layers of artificial neural networks to learn and make decisions based on large amounts of data.

Deep Neural Networks (DNNs): Artificial neural networks with multiple hidden layers between the input and output layers, capable of learning complex patterns and representations.

Diffusion Models: A class of generative models that learn to reverse a gradual noising process, allowing for more stable and controllable image generation compared to generative adversarial networks.

Edge AI: AI algorithms and models that are processed locally on a device, rather than relying on cloud computing.

EULAs (End-User License Agreements): Contracts between a software developer or publisher and the end user, specifying the terms under which the user may use the software.

Face ID: A facial recognition system designed by Apple for user authentication on iPhone and iPad Pro devices.

Face Swap: A technique in AI image generation that allows users to replace a face in an image with another face.

Facial Recognition: A type of biometric technology that uses AI algorithms to identify or verify individuals based on their facial features.

Fair Use: A legal doctrine that allows limited use of copyrighted material without permission from the rights holder for purposes such as criticism, commentary, news reporting, teaching, scholarship, or research.

Generative Adversarial Networks (GANs): AI models consisting of two neural networks (a generator and a discriminator) that compete against each other to generate new synthetic data that closely resembles real-world data.

Generative AI: A subset of AI focused on creating new content, such as images, videos, music, or text, based on learned patterns and rules.

Gen ID: A unique identifier assigned to each image generated by DALL-E, used for reproducing the same image or variations of it.

GPT (Generative Pre-trained Transformer): A type of language model developed by OpenAI that can generate human-like text based on a given prompt.

Hallucinations: Inaccurate, inconsistent, or entirely fabricated information generated by AI models, particularly in the context of chatbots and language models.

Inpainting: A technique in AI image generation that allows users to edit or fill in specific regions of an image while maintaining coherence with the rest of the image.

Iterative Refinement: The process of repeatedly generating, evaluating, and adjusting AI outputs based on feedback and desired improvements.

Large Language Models (LLMs): AI models trained on vast amounts of text data, capable of understanding and generating human-like language across a wide range of tasks.

Machine Learning (ML): A subset of AI that focuses on the development of algorithms and models that enable computers to learn and improve from experience without being explicitly programmed.

Multimodal AI: AI systems that can process and understand multiple types of data, such as text, images, audio, and video, simultaneously.

Natural Language Processing (NLP): A branch of AI that focuses on enabling computers to understand, interpret, and generate human language.

Neural Network: A set of algorithms designed to recognize patterns in data, inspired by the way the human brain processes information.

Neural Style Transfer: A technique that uses deep learning to compose an image in the style of another image while preserving the content of the original image.

Open-Source: Software or technology whose source code is publicly available for anyone to use, modify, and distribute.

Outpainting: A technique in AI image generation that extends an image beyond its original borders while maintaining visual coherence.

Persona: An AI's simulated personality or character, designed to make interactions more engaging and natural.

Predictive Analytics: A branch of advanced analytics that uses data, statistical algorithms, and machine-learning techniques to identify the likelihood of future outcomes based on historical data.

Predictive Modeling: The process of using data and statistical algorithms to predict outcomes and future trends.

Prompts: Text-based instructions or descriptions provided by users to guide AI models in generating content such as images or text.

PyTorch: An open-source machine-learning library for the Python programming language, used for developing and training deep-learning models.

Recurrent Neural Network (RNN): A type of neural network that can process sequential data by maintaining an internal state or memory, making it well-suited for tasks like language modeling and speech recognition.

Reinforcement Learning: A type of machine learning in which an AI agent learns to make decisions by interacting with an environment and receiving rewards or punishments for its actions.

Remix: A feature in AI image generation that allows users to create variations of an existing image by adjusting prompts or parameters.

Scraping: The process of extracting data from websites or other sources using automated tools or scripts.

Seed Number: A numerical value used to initialize a random number generator, allowing for reproducible results in AI image generation.

Speech Recognition: The ability of a computer or software to identify and process spoken language, converting it into text or commands.

Strong AI: A theoretical form of AI that can match or exceed human intelligence across a wide range of domains and tasks.

TensorFlow: An open-source software library for machine learning and deep learning, developed by Google.

Tokens: The basic units of text that chatbots and AI language models process, which can be individual words, punctuation marks, or sections of words.

Transfer Learning: A machine-learning technique where knowledge gained from solving one problem is applied to a different but related problem, allowing for faster and more efficient learning.

Transformer-Based Models: AI models that utilize the transformer architecture, which is particularly well-suited for processing sequential data such as natural language.

Uncanny Valley: A phenomenon in which a computer-generated figure or humanoid robot bearing a near-identical resemblance to a human being arouses a sense of unease or revulsion in the person viewing it. This feeling of eeriness is often associated with subtle imperfections or inconsistencies in the artificial entity's appearance or behavior.

Variational Autoencoders (VAEs): A type of generative model that learns to encode input data into a lower-dimensional latent space and then decode it back into the original space, allowing for the generation of new data similar to the training examples.

Weak/Narrow AI: AI systems designed to handle specific tasks with limited capabilities and no ability to think or function outside their predefined scope.

Word Embedding: A technique in natural language processing in which words are mapped to vectors of real numbers, capturing the semantic relationships between words in a dense, low-dimensional space.

SCAN HERE to learn more about Invite Press, a premier publishing imprint created to invite people to a deeper faith and living relationship with Jesus Christ.

www.ingramcontent.com/pod-product-compliance
Lightning Source LLC
Chambersburg PA
CBHW021708120626
46545CB00004B/1461